ManhattanElitePrep

Admissions, Test Prep & Training

GMAT Verbal Workbook

- ✓ *Elite Strategy Guide*
- ✓ *Basic & Advanced Content*
- ✓ *Questions by Concept*
- ✓ *Section-by-Section Navigation*
- ✓ *Quick Answer Keys*
- ✓ *Comprehensive Solutions*

- ✓ *Complete & Challenging Training Sets*
- ✓ *Sentence Correction – 250 Questions*
- ✓ *Critical Reasoning – 60 Questions*
- ✓ *Reading Comprehension – 40 Passages*

www.ManhattanElitePrep.com

Copyright and Terms of Use

CopyRight and Trademark

All materials herein (including names, terms, trademarks, designs, images and graphics) are the property of Manhattan Elite Prep, except where otherwise noted. Except as permitted herein, no such material may be copied, reproduced, displayed or transmitted or otherwise used without the prior written permission of Manhattan Elite Prep. You are permitted to use material herein for your personal, non-commercial use, provided that you are not permitted to combine such material into a combination, collection or compilation of material. If you have any questions regarding the use of the material, please contact Manhattan Elite Prep at info@manhattaneliteprep.com

This material may make reference to countries and persons. The use of such references is for hypothetical and demonstrative purposes only.

Terms of Use

By using this material, you acknowledge and agree to the terms of use contained herein.

No Warranties

This material is provided without warranty, either express or implied, including the implied warranties of merchantability, of fitness for a particular purpose and non-infringement. Manhattan Elite Prep does not warrant or make any representations regarding the use, accuracy or results of the use of this material. This material may make reference to other source materials. Manhattan Elite Prep is not responsible in any respect for the content of other source materials, and disclaims all warranties and liabilities with respect to the other source materials.

Limitation on Liability

Manhattan Elite Prep shall not be responsible under any circumstances for any direct, indirect, special, punitive or consequential damages ('Damages') that may arise from the use of this material. In addition, Manhattan Elite Prep does not guarantee the accuracy or completeness of its course materials, which are provided 'as is' with no warranty, express or implied. Manhattan Elite Prep assumes no liability for any Damages from errors or omissions in the material, whether arising in contract, tort or otherwise.

GMAT is a registered trademark of the Graduate Management Admission Council.
GMAC does not endorse nor is it affiliated in any way with the owner of this product or any content herein.

Verbal Workbook:

10-Digit International Standard Book Number: 0-9824324-7-X
13-Digit International Standard Book Number: 978-0-9824324-7-1

Last Updated September 2012

About Manhattan Review, India

Manhattan Review, India is the exclusive Indian Partner of Manhattan Elite Prep, based in New York, USA. The US website of Manhattan Review, India is www.manhattaneliteprep.com and the India website is www.indiamr.com. Our India office locations can also be found at:
http://www.manhattaneliteprep.com/students-about-us-india-venues/

Manhattan Review, India originally started off as the exclusive Indian partner of Manhattan Review, USA. However when Manhattan Elite prep was launched to cater to the students who prefer a broader array of classroom and one-on-one training, by the same group of management, administrative team and teachers who used to be the backbone of Manhattan Review, we decided to continue to operate as Manhattan Review in India with our US Partner as Manhattan Elite Prep.

Over the years, Manhattan Review in India has delivered the results that have made our competitors envious. We are proud to have successfully completed 5 years of our operations in India and as we enter into the 6th year, the commitment to the student community, and the passion towards delivering quality instruction continue to drive us forward. We are the first test preparation company to have delivered a 780 on the GMAT in Hyderabad, India in the last 5 years. We are so far ahead of our competitors when we look at the number of top scores we have produced on the GMAT®, GRE®, and SAT, that when we look behind, we cannot identify the next best player.

We are pioneers in GRE® training as well. We are the first in India, to design and develop study material for the new GRE®. Our top score of 327 on the GRE® is a testimony of the quality of our material and training. Our R&D department spends more than 14,000 hours each year developing new material for GMAT®, GRE®, SAT, TOEFL®, IELTS and PTE to ensure that our students are given the most up to date and current study material. Our top score of 2280 on SAT, 116 on TOEFL® iBT® and 8.5 bands on IELTS are proof of our commitment to helping our students get top scores.

Anyone can help a student secure admission into a tier-3 business school. But only the best can help gain admission into the Ivy League business schools. We have helped our students gain admissions into Harvard business school and Wharton and we take pride in our success.

We wish you all the very best as you embark on your journey with us for your test preparation training. We hope to partner with you in fulfilling your dream of making it to a top business school. We are committed to your success and when coupled with your commitment, we can become a force that is unstoppable. We look forward to a fruitful and a successful journey with you. We look forward to hearing your feedback on how we are doing. You can send us an email at support@indiamr.com

Our contact information:

USA
Headquarters: 521 Fifth Ave, 17th Floor (enter on 43rd St.)
New York, NY 10175
+1 (888) 215-6269
+1 (646) 873-6656

India
Headquarters: 4th Floor, Sudheer Thapani Towers,
Suite # 402, Opp Telugu Academy,
Himayatnagar, Hyderabad – 500 029, AP.
Ph: 040 4241 7788

Branch offices:

Hyderabad:
Student Help line: 9177 500 100

Greenlands:
4th Floor, Afzia Towers, Opp. Life Style.
Ph: 040 4230 0748 / 4017 5497

Kukatpally:
MIG-II, 3rd Floor, Shreshta Complex,
Above Reebok Showroom, KPHB Colony, Road No1.
Ph: 040 401 000 12 / 13 / 14

Madhapur:
2nd Floor KSR Towers, Next to
Indian Oil Petrol Pump.
Ph: 040 4026 6531 / 4026 7652

Tarnaka:
Flat # 305, 3rd Floor, Kaveri Queens Plaza,
Opp. Aradhana Theatre.
Ph: 040 4011 8018 / 4011 8019

Dilsukhnagar:
D No. 16-11-767 to 770, 4th Floor,
Mathru Chaya Commercial Complex,
Near Moosarambagh X Roads.
Ph: 040 4006 3535 /4006 5353

Guntur:
Student Help line: 9247 000 711

Brodipet:
#4/13, Above Fast track show room.
Ph: 668 0722.

Bengaluru:
Student Help line: 9945 602 222

Jaya Nagar:
No.23, Vasavi Plaza, 11th Main Road,
4th Block.
Ph: 080-41210071/72

Contents

Chapter 1

Verbal Training Set I - Sentence Correction

1. A powder derived from the North American Echinacea flower, <u>which has been effective in preventing colds,</u> is grown by many small farmers out West.

    (A) A powder derived from the North American Echinacea flower, which has been effective in preventing colds,

    (B) A derivative, which has been effective in preventing colds, of the North American Echinacea flower

    (C) A North American Echinacea flower derivative, which has been effective in preventing colds

    (D) The North American Echinacea flower has a derivative which has been effective in preventing colds, that

    (E) The North American Echinacea flower, a derivative of which has been effective in preventing colds,

2. Trying to mimic some of the pitch variations of a dolphin chattering is <u>the same as attempting to sing like a sick parakeet when one is intoxicated</u>; the complete lack of harmony and apparent randomness of the noise means the human vocal chords are completely incapable of reproducing these sounds.

    (A) the same as attempting to sing like a sick parakeet when one is intoxicated

    (B) similar to an intoxicated person singing like a sick parakeet

    (C) like singing like a sick parakeet as an intoxicated person

    (D) the same as an intoxicated person singing like a sick parakeet

    (E) like the intoxicated person is singing like a sick parakeet

3. The possibility of an attack on Indian Point, a nuclear power plant, has caused local governmental officials to <u>plan evacuation routes, build shelters, and offering citizens potassium pills so there will be</u> fewer casualties in case of a leak.

    (A) plan evacuation routes, build shelters, and offering citizens potassium pills so there will be

    (B) plan evacuation routes, build shelters, and offer citizens potassium pills in order to have

    (C) planning evacuation routes, building shelters, and the offer of potassium pills to citizens so there will be

    (D) evacuation route planning, building shelters, and offering citizens potassium pills in order to have

    (E) a planning of evacuation routes, shelter building, and offering potassium pills to citizens to have

4. Although the sting of <u>Egyptian Scorpions are rarely dangerous, they cause red welts to appear, posing minor health risks to infants, who are particularly vulnerable to its</u> venom.

    (A) Egyptian Scorpions are rarely dangerous, they cause red welts to appear, posing minor health risks to infants, who are particularly vulnerable to its

    (B) Egyptian Scorpions are rarely dangerous, they cause red welts to appear and pose minor health risks to infants, who are particularly vulnerable to their

    (C) Egyptian Scorpions is rarely dangerous, it causes red welts to appear, posing minor health risks to infants, who are particularly vulnerable to their

    (D) Egyptian Scorpions is rarely dangerous, it causes red welts to appear and poses minor health risks to infants, who are particularly vulnerable to its

    (E) Egyptian Scorpions is rarely dangerous, they cause red welts to appear, posing the greatest danger to the infant, who are particularly vulnerable to its

5. The catastrophic San Francisco Earthquake at the turn of the century destroyed numerous buildings and <u>many were led to believe that the city had become</u> a permanent disaster zone.

   (A) many were led to believe that the city had become
   (B) many had been led to believing of the city as if it were
   (C) the belief this led to was that the city had become
   (D) led many to the belief of the city as if it were
   (E) led many to believe that the city had become

6. Besides offering such physiological rewards as toned muscles, <u>karate, if practiced regularly, can turn the body into a dangerous weapon</u> and produce numerous other benefits.

   (A) karate, if practiced regularly, can turn the body into a dangerous weapon
   (B) one can turn the body into a dangerous weapon through karate, if it is practiced regularly
   (C) the body can be turned into a dangerous weapon as a result of karate if practiced regularly
   (D) when karate is practiced regularly, the body can be turned into a dangerous weapon
   (E) when practiced regularly, the results of karate can be to turn the body into a dangerous weapon

7. The new government requires <u>employers to inform an employee of their</u> legal right to holidays and overtime pay.

   (A) employers to inform an employee of their
   (B) employers to inform employees that he has a
   (C) employers to inform employees that there is a
   (D) that employers inform an employee of their
   (E) that employers inform the employees that they have a

8. Riddled with bullets, shattered by bombs, and hidden in alleys, <u>the historic buildings in Lodz, Poland, were long ignored by tourists, traveling</u> instead to more well-known memorial museums.

   (A) the historic buildings in Lodz, Poland, were long ignored by tourists, traveling
   (B) the historic buildings in Lodz, Poland, were long ignored by tourists, who traveled
   (C) tourists long ignored the historic buildings in Lodz, Poland, traveling
   (D) tourists long ignored the historic buildings in Lodz, Poland and traveled
   (E) tourists long ignored the historic buildings in Lodz, Poland; they depended

9. <u>Rallies organized in conjunction with the dissemination of democratic principles which was once prohibited by Communist Chinese leaders, are</u> beginning to take shape at a grass roots level permitted by the new Chinese leadership.

   (A) Rallies organized in conjunction with the dissemination of democratic principles which was once prohibited by Communist Chinese leaders, are
   (B) Rallies organized in conjunction with the dissemination of democratic principles, a practice that Communist Chinese leaders once prohibited, is
   (C) Organizing rallies in conjunction with the dissemination of democratic principles, as once prohibited by Communist Chinese leaders, is
   (D) Communist Chinese leaders once prohibited organizing rallies in conjunction with the dissemination of democratic principles, but they are
   (E) Communist Chinese leaders once prohibited organizing rallies in conjunction with the dissemination of democratic principles, but such principles are

10. By the end of the nineteenth century, five of the Western European states had developed a railroad system, but <u>only one in the East</u>.

    (A)   only one in the East

    (B)   only one eastern state

    (C)   in the East there was only one state

    (D)   in the East only one state did

    (E)   only one in the East had

11. <u>Unlike in the other states in the tri-stat area, there are no gasoline taxes set by state or local authorities</u> in New Jersey.

    (A)   Unlike in the other states in the tri-state area, there are no gasoline taxes set by state or local authorities

    (B)   Unlike the other states in the tri-state area that have gasoline taxes set by state or local authorities, there are none

    (C)   Although state or local authorities usually set gasoline taxes in the tri-state area, no such one has been set

    (D)   Although state or local authorities usually set gasoline taxes in the tri-state area, no such tax has been set

    (E)   Although there are usually gasoline taxes set by state or local authorities in the tri-state area, no such taxes has been set

12. Historians and philosophers in the late nineteenth century both argued that Plato's work was perhaps the ultimate work of political philosophy, <u>that it was the one paradigm of political discourse that there was no possibility to supersede</u>.

    (A)   that it was the one paradigm of political discourse that there was no possibility to supersede

    (B)   the one paradigm of political discourse that could not be superseded

    (C)   for it was the one paradigm of political discourse, and that it was impossible to supersede

    (D)   a paradigm of political discourse that there was no possibility to supersede

    (E)   as being the one paradigm that could not be superseded in political discourse

13. Although the initial setup of generators and a power grid by Edison and JP Morgan was rather costly, <u>the electrification of lighting in lower Manhattan doubled work efficiency when the energy costs were cut in half</u>.

    (A)   the electrification of lighting in lower Manhattan doubled work efficiency when the energy costs were cut in half

    (B)   the electrification of lighting in lower Manhattan doubled work efficiency while cutting energy costs in half

    (C)   the electrification of lighting in lower Manhattan doubled work efficiency while as costs were cut to half

    (D)   lighting electrification in lower Manhattan doubled work efficiency while energy costs were cut in half

    (E)   lighting electrification in lower Manhattan doubled work efficiency while costs were cut to half

14. Because the economic cycle in the United States changes little during its twenty year interval <u>between recessing</u>, it is fairly easy for analysts to predict analogous trends in the stock market.

    (A)   between recessing

    (B)   of recessing

    (C)   between its recessions

    (D)   of its recessions

    (E)   as it recesses

15. After the attack on the World Trade Center, the President ordered intelligence agencies <u>should prepare lists of who were America's most wanted terrorists</u>.

    (A) should prepare lists of who were America's most wanted terrorists

    (B) would do the preparation of lists of America's most wanted terrorists

    (C) preparing lists of most wanted terrorists in America

    (D) the preparing of a list of the most wanted terrorists in America

    (E) to prepare lists of the most wanted terrorists in America

16. The exhibit, created by painstaking craftsmanship in the jungles of Burma, consisted of hundreds of paintings, <u>each painting a tiny etched landscape inside its</u> own ceramic work of pottery.

    (A) each painting a tiny etched landscape inside its

    (B) all the paintings a tiny etched landscape inside their

    (C) all the paintings a tiny etched landscape inside its

    (D) every painting a tiny etched landscape inside their

    (E) each painting a tiny etched landscape inside their

17. More than one hundred years ago, students of ornithology reported that hummingbirds can hover <u>as insects flitting gracefully from one flower to another</u>.

    (A) as insects flitting gracefully from one flower to another

    (B) like insects flitting gracefully from one flower to another

    (C) as insects do that flit gracefully from one flower to others

    (D) like insects do that flit gracefully from one flower to others

    (E) as do insects that flit gracefully from one flower to some other one

18. In an effort to shorten the time span and cut the costs needed to grow full size beef stock, many ranchers substitute cornmeal and ground bones <u>for their cattle's regular diet, branded by them</u> to become generic-grade beef.

    (A) for their cattle's regular diet, branded by them

    (B) for the regular diet of their cattle which have been branded

    (C) for the regular diet of their cattle, having been branded

    (D) in place of their cattle's regular diet, for those of them branded

    (E) in place of the regular diet of their cattle to have been branded by them

19. New high-combustion models of engines show the potential of being able to produce high horsepower and performance without the costly <u>requirements of maintenance and consuming of special racing fuel by earlier high horsepower models</u>.

    (A) requirements of maintenance and consuming of special racing fuel by earlier high horsepower models

    (B) requirements by earlier high horsepower models of consuming of special racing fuel and maintenance

    (C) requirements for consuming of special racing fuel and maintenance of earlier high horsepower models

    (D) consumption of special racing fuel and maintenance that was required by earlier high horsepower models

    (E) maintenance and consumption of special racing fuel that were required by earlier high horsepower models

20. Forced to cut back their stock, automobile dealers in the area have cut prices; their pick-up trucks <u>have been priced to sell, and they are</u>.

    (A)   have been priced to sell, and they are

    (B)   are priced to sell, and they have

    (C)   are priced to sell, and they do

    (D)   are being priced to sell, and have

    (E)   had been priced to sell, and they have

21. In the most bizarre court case this month, the judge ruled <u>that two ping-pon ball manufacturers owed restitution to four national ping-pon teams for the illegal weighting of</u> the ping-pong balls in an effort to fix the tournament.

    (A)   that two ping-pong ball manufacturers owed restitution to four national ping-pong teams for the illegal weighting of

    (B)   that two ping-pong ball manufacturers owed restitution to four national ping-pong teams because of their illegal weighting of

    (C)   that two ping-pong ball manufacturers owe restitution to four national ping-pong teams for their illegal weighting of

    (D)   on two ping-pong ball manufacturers that owed restitution to four national ping-pong teams because they illegally weighted

    (E)   on the restitution that two ping-pong ball manufacturers owed to four national ping-pong teams for the illegal weighting of

22. The electronics manufacturer announced that while earnings grew by 5% in the last quarter, revenue decreased whereas <u>it might have been expected for it to rise</u>.

    (A)   it might have been expected for it to rise

    (B)   it might have been expected to rise

    (C)   it might have been expected that it should rise

    (D)   its rise might have been expected

    (E)   there might have been an expectation it would rise

23. The Chinese army consists of several million young men, about <u>equivalent to the enrollment of</u> colleges in India.

    (A)   equivalent to the enrollment of

    (B)   the equivalent of those enrolled in

    (C)   equal to those who are enrolled in

    (D)   as many as the enrollment of

    (E)   as many as are enrolled in

24. In the United States, a larger percentage of the defense budget is spent on development of an anti-missil shield than is spent on nuclear missile technology in the People's Democratic Republic of North Korea.

    (A) In the United States, a larger percentage of the defense budget is spent on development of an anti-missile shield than is spent on nuclear missile technology in the People's Democratic Republic of North Korea.

    (B) In the United States they spend a larger percentage of the defense budget on development of an anti-missile shield than the People's Democratic Republic of North Korea does on nuclear missile technology.

    (C) A larger percentage of the United States' defense budget is spent on development of an anti-missile shield than the People's Democratic Republic of North Korea spends on nuclear missile technology.

    (D) The United States spends a larger percentage of its defense budget developing its anti-missile shield than the People's Democratic Republic of North Korea spending on nuclear missile technology.

    (E) The United States spends a larger percentage of its defense budget on developing its anti-missile shield than the People's Democratic Republic of North Korea does on nuclear missile technology.

25. Statisticians from the Department of Motor Vehicles have calculated that one human being should be struck every three minutes by a vehicle, while each minute two animals can be expected to die from such collisions.

    (A) one human being should be struck every three minutes by a vehicle

    (B) a human being should be struck by a vehicle once in every three minutes

    (C) a vehicle will strike one human being once in every three minutes

    (D) every three minutes a human being will be struck by a vehicle

    (E) every three minutes a human being should be struck by a vehicle

26. Acme, the family oriented entertainment company, has moved away from traditional family programming and now draws on the production both of adult entertainers who work for magazines and of those in the movie industry.

    (A) now draws on the production both of adult entertainers who work for magazines and of those

    (B) now draws on the works of adult entertainers, both those who work for magazines and those who work

    (C) it draws on the works of adult entertainers now, both those working for magazines and who work

    (D) draws now on the works both of adult entertainers working for magazines and who are working

    (E) draws on the works now of both adult entertainers working for magazines and those

27. Although coffee is not usually considered a drug, it is so addictive that it has become a critical part of breakfast for many people.

    (A) it is so addictive that it has become a critical

    (B) it is of such addiction, it has become a critical

    (C) so addicting is it as to become a critical

    (D) such is its addiction, it becomes a critical

    (E) there is so much addiction that it has become a critical

28. The survey showed that children are much more psychologically stable when raised in a family with two parents than in a family where one parent only cares for the child.

    (A) a family where one parent only

    (B) of a family where only one parent

    (C) that for families in which only one parent

    (D) a family in which only one parent

    (E) those of families in which one parent only

29. The CEO has proposed a new policy requiring that employees should retain all pensions indefinitely or be allowed to cash them in at retirement.

   (A) that employees should retain all pensions

   (B) that all pensions be retained by employees

   (C) the retaining by employees of all pensions

   (D) employee's retention of all pensions

   (E) employees to retain all pensions

30. The recently discovered notes of the writer suddenly revealed that this most timid and shy of women was an intellectual giant guided in both emotional and spiritual activities by a sharp sense of moral courage.

   (A) that this most timid and shy of women was an intellectual giant guided in both emotional and

   (B) that this most timid and shy of women was an intellectual giant also guided both in emotional as well as

   (C) this most timid and shy of women was an intellectual giant and that she was guided in both emotional and

   (D) this most timid and shy of women was an intellectual giant and that she was guided in both emotional as well as

   (E) this most timid and shy of women to have been an intellectual giant and that she guided herself in both emotional as well as

31. Declining values for bonds, the financial vehicles against which investors hedge to get through the bear market, is going to force currency trading to increase.

   (A) the financial vehicles against which investors hedge to get through the bear market, is

   (B) which investors use as financial vehicles to hedge against to get through the bear market, is

   (C) the financial vehicle which is hedged against by investors to get through the bear market is

   (D) which investors use as financial vehicles to hedge against to get through the bear market, are

   (E) the financial vehicles against which investors hedge to get through the bear market, are

32. Except for internal networks involve identical operating systems, whose identification protocol is the same, all legacy multi-system networks need software emulators to communicate.

   (A) Except for internal networks involve identical operating systems, whose identification protocol is the same

   (B) As well as internal networks involving identical operating systems with the same identification protocol

   (C) Unless internal networks involve identical operating systems, which have the same identification protocol

   (D) In addition to an internal network between identical operating systems with the same identification protocol

   (E) Together with internal networks between identical operating systems, whose identification protocol is the same

33. In one of the most surprising victories in WWI, the newly formed Russian communist state was routed by the Polish General, Jozef Pilsudski, demanding that it should push back its borders east of Vilnius.

   (A) demanding that it should

   (B) demanding it to

   (C) and their demand to

   (D) who demanded that it

   (E) who demanded them to

34. Recently discovered gravitational lensing around certain proximate stars strongly suggests that the nine planets of our solar system are a common phenomenon in the universe <u>rather than developing incidentally from</u> a unique galactic phenomenon several billion years ago.

   (A) rather than developing incidentally from

   (B) rather than a type that developed incidentally from

   (C) rather than a type whose development was incidental of

   (D) instead of developing incidentally from

   (E) instead of a development that was incidental of

35. The Great Wall Space Agency's recent attempts to launch a man into space, a major goal of their space program for the past few years, <u>has not substantially decreased the gaps existing</u> between the technology rich and technology poor cities around the space center.

   (A) has not substantially decreased the gaps existing

   (B) has not been substantial in decreasing the gap that exists

   (C) has not made a substantial decrease in the gap that exists

   (D) have not substantially decreased the gap that exists

   (E) have not been substantial in a decrease of the gap that exists

36. Most MBA programs now <u>mandate that potential applicants be finished</u> with an undergraduate degree before applying.

   (A) mandate that potential applicants be finished

   (B) mandate potential applicants to be finished

   (C) mandate that potential applicants will be finished

   (D) have a mandate for a potential applicant finishing

   (E) have a mandate to finish potential applicants

37. The manager of the plastic fork factory tried to convince the unruly factory workers <u>they should join forces to optimize production on the belt rather than attempting to be contrary</u>.

   (A) they should join forces to optimize production on the belt rather than attempting to be contrary

   (B) that they should join forces to optimize production on the belt rather than attempt to be contrary

   (C) about joining forces to optimize production on the belt instead of attempting to be contrary

   (D) for the joining of forces to optimize production on the belt rather than attempt to be contrary

   (E) to join forces to optimize production on the belt rather than attempting to be contrary

38. <u>Although he is as brilliant as, if not more brilliant than, many of his fellow students, he is very lazy and his thesis will be unfinished.</u>

   (A) Although he is as brilliant as, if not more brilliant than, many of his fellow students, he is very lazy and his thesis will be unfinished.

   (B) Although he is as brilliant as, if not more brilliant than, many of his fellow students, he is very lazy with his thesis remaining unfinished.

   (C) Although he is as brilliant as, if not more brilliant than, many of his fellow students, he is very lazy and will not finish his thesis.

   (D) Despite his being brilliant as, if not more brilliant than his fellow students, he is very lazy and will not finish his thesis.

   (E) Being as brilliant as, or more brilliant than, many of his fellow students, he is very lazy and his thesis will be unfinished.

39. Doctors are loath to prescribe powerful painkillers because <u>their abuse as addictive drugs is</u> a danger for many patients.

    (A)   their abuse as addictive drugs is

    (B)   as addictive drugs, their abuse is

    (C)   the abuse of such addictive drugs is

    (D)   the abuse of such addictive drugs are

    (E)   the abuse of them as addictive drugs is

40. The beginning of the show always brought in lots of money, yet the average singer ended the show <u>with a decrease in what their tip may be.</u>

    (A)   with a decrease in what their tip may be

    (B)   with what was a decrease in what their tips were able to be

    (C)   having decreased that which their tips might be

    (D)   decreasing in their tips

    (E)   with a decrease in tips

41. Because memory weakens with age, for the experiment to be valid, it is important that a group <u>to be tested for drug induced memory loss be compared with</u> a control group.

    (A)   to be tested for drug induced memory loss be compared with

    (B)   being tested for memory loss induced by drugs are compared with

    (C)   being tested for drug induced memory loss should be compared to

    (D)   being tested for drug induced memory loss are to be compared to

    (E)   that is to be tested for drug induced memory loss are to be comparable with

42. As the journalist left to interview the convicted murderer, she was advised <u>of the man's short temper, told she should not anger him, and was</u> given a tape recorder.

    (A)   of the man's short temper, told she should not anger him, and was

    (B)   of the man's short temper, told she should not anger him, and

    (C)   of the man's short temper and that she should not anger him and

    (D)   that the man had a short temper, should not anger him, and was

    (E)   that the man had a short temper, that she should not anger him, and was

43. <u>The average individual's cost of going into space is estimated at a fraction of the price per economy ticket of transatlantic airplane travel by the end of the 21st century.</u>

    (A)   The average individual's cost of going into space is estimated at a fraction of the price per economy ticket of transatlantic airplane travel by the end of the 21st century.

    (B)   The average individual's cost by the end of the 21st century of going into space is estimated at a fraction of the price per economy ticket of transatlantic airplane travel.

    (C)   By the end of the 21st century, the average individual's cost of going into space is estimated at a fraction of the price per economy ticket of transatlantic airplane travel.

    (D)   To go into space, the cost to the average individual is estimated at a fraction of the price per economy ticket of transatlantic airplane travel by the end of the 21st century.

    (E)   It is estimated that by the end of the 21st century the cost to the average individual of going into space will be a fraction of the current price per economy ticket of transatlantic airplane travel.

44. Praise for Johnny Starstruck and his entourage <u>are common, although statistics show Americans still associate his name with</u> the ritualistic murders.

    (A)   are common, although statistics show Americans still associate his name with

    (B)   are common, although statistics shows Americans still associate his name with

    (C)   are common, although statistics shows Americans still associate his name to

    (D)   is common, although statistics show Americans still associate his name with

    (E)   is common, although statistics shows Americans still associate his name to

45. If seriously mentally ill people do not receive medication, they can grow unable to support themselves, become irrational, <u>and perhaps even threatening</u> the safety of themselves or others.

    (A)   and perhaps even threatening

    (B)   and may even threaten

    (C)   and even a possible threat to

    (D)   as well as possibly threatening

    (E)   as well as a possible threat to

46. When Henry dreams about his late wife, <u>he sees her as she was during</u> her youth.

    (A)   he sees her as she was during

    (B)   he sees her as she had been during

    (C)   he sees her as if during

    (D)   she appears to him as she did in

    (E)   she appears to him as though in

47. <u>Unlike that of</u> the colonies of Portugal, France, and Germany, those of England are still affected by the former imperial power in modern days.

    (A)   Unlike that of

    (B)   Unlike those of

    (C)   Unlike

    (D)   In contrast to that of

    (E)   Dissimilar to

48. America's nuclear arsenal has expanded, <u>but China's and Pakistan's too.</u>

    (A)   but China's and Pakistan's too

    (B)   and also China's and Pakistan's

    (C)   but so have China's and Pakistan's

    (D)   and so also China's and Pakistan's

    (E)   but so did China's and Pakistan's

49. The average American may not think of sexual harassment to be a widespread issue, but 75 percent of all women report experiencing it in the workplace.

    (A) The average American may not think of sexual harassment to be

    (B) The average American may not think of sexual harassment being

    (C) An average American may not think of sexual harassment being

    (D) The average American may not think of sexual harassment as

    (E) Sexual harassment may not be thought of by the average American as

50. Seven out of ten households in the United States own two or more televisions.

    (A) Seven out of ten households in the United States own two or more televisions.

    (B) Out of every ten, seven households in the United States owns two or more televisions.

    (C) Two or more televisions are owned by seven out of every ten households in the United States.

    (D) In the United States, seven out of every ten households owns two or more televisions.

    (E) Out of every ten households in the United States, two or more televisions are owned by seven.

51. Many are confused that the Atkins Diet, which permits such seeming less healthy foods as bacon, forbids bread.

    (A) which permits such seeming less healthy foods as

    (B) which permits such seemingly less healthy foods as

    (C) which is permitting such seeming less healthy foods like

    (D) permitting such foods that seem less healthy, for example

    (E) permitting such seeming less healthy foods like

52. The UN arms inspectors are reviewing Iraq's arsenal of weapons for the determination of whether they are meeting the requirements set by the Security Council.

    (A) for the determination of whether they are meeting the requirements set by the Security Council

    (B) for the determining of whether or not it meets the requirements set by the Security Council

    (C) for the determining of whether the requirements set by the Security Council are being met or not

    (D) determining whether the requirements set by the Security Council are being met

    (E) to determine whether the requirements set by the Security Council are being met

53. A survey of men from ages 18 to 30 revealed homosexual experiences in 30 percent of them and they ranged from an isolated incident to a permanent lifestyle.

    (A) homosexual experiences in 30 percent of them and they ranged

    (B) experiences in 30 percent were homosexual and ranging

    (C) the ranging of homosexual experiences in 30 percent of them to be

    (D) that 30 percent had had homosexual experiences ranging

    (E) that 30 percent of them had had experiences that were homosexual; the range was

54. George Brown <u>lost more than 180 pounds since having</u> an operation truncating his stomach three years ago.

    (A)   lost more than 180 pounds since having

    (B)   lost more than 180 pounds since having had

    (C)   has lost more than 180 pounds since

    (D)   has lost more than 180 pounds after

    (E)   has lost more than 180 pounds subsequently to

55. At school, Miruko is antisocial and sullen, but <u>in her home</u> she is a bubbly, even-tempered child.

    (A)   in her home

    (B)   in her home, in which

    (C)   it is in her home in which

    (D)   in her home where

    (E)   it is in her home and

56. A high school student fanatically devoted to modern art, <u>Fanny has toured five museums, perhaps most remarkably the enormous Museum of Modern Art.</u>

    (A)   Fanny has toured five museums, perhaps most remarkably the enormous Museum of Modern Art

    (B)   perhaps the most remarkable of the five museums toured by Fanny was the enormous Museum of Modern Art

    (C)   of the five museums toured by Fanny, perhaps the most remarkable was the enormous Museum of Modern Art

    (D)   five museums were toured by Fanny, of which the enormous Museum of Modern Art is perhaps the most remarkable

    (E)   the enormous Museum of Modern Art is perhaps the most remarkable of the five museums toured by Fanny

57. When the chorus divides the women into sopranos and altos, it will be able to sing songs many times more complicated <u>compared to those that can be sung</u> as it is now.

    (A)   compared to those that can be sung

    (B)   compared to those it can sing

    (C)   than that can be sung

    (D)   than those that can be sung

    (E)   than those singing

58. Angel food cake, a cholesterol-free cake, solves the problem of <u>how to bake a cake for a health-consciou family</u>.

    (A)   how to bake a cake for a health-conscious family

    (B)   having a health-conscious family for which to bake a cake

    (C)   how can one bake a cake for a health-conscious family

    (D)   how one could feed a health-conscious family a cake

    (E)   having a health-conscious cake to bake for a family

59. The local orchestra, which used to perform everything from <u>Bach and Handel to Bartok, appears to have</u> reduced its repertoire to only baroque music.

   (A) Bach and Handel to Bartok, appears to have

   (B) Bach, Handel, and Bartok, appears having

   (C) Bach, Handel, and Bartok, appears that it has

   (D) Bach and Handel to Bartok, appears that it has

   (E) Bach and Handel as well as Bartok, appears to have

60. Experts believe that senior citizens with higher than average cholesterol <u>and their families develop a predisposition to cardio-vascular disease</u> are more likely to die at an age below that of their life expectancy.

   (A) and their families develop a predisposition to cardiovascular disease

   (B) whose families have a predisposition to cardiovascular disease

   (C) and a predisposition to cardiovascular disease runs in the family

   (D) whose families have a predisposition to cardiovascular disease running in them

   (E) with a predisposition to cardiovascular disease running in their family

61. Sometimes, it seems like Mary does things only <u>to make it more inconvenient for her husband to have</u> a good time when he's out with his friends.

   (A) to make it more inconvenient for her husband to have

   (B) to make more inconvenient for her husband the having of

   (C) making it more inconvenient for her husband so he can have

   (D) that her husband more inconveniently can have

   (E) for her husband to more inconveniently

62. <u>His love of basketball, long legs, and athletic talent makes</u> him well suited for a place on the high school basketball team.

   (A) His love of basketball, long legs, and athletic talent makes

   (B) Long legs, his love of basketball, and athletic talent makes

   (C) Athletic talent, long legs, and his love of basketball makes

   (D) Long legs, athletic talent, and his love of basketball make

   (E) His love of basketball, as well as long legs and athletic talent, make

63. Stanford University gave the Musician of the Year Award to Joan White, <u>one of only eight musicians who had performed in the end-of-the-year revue</u>.

   (A) one of only eight musicians who had performed in the end-of-the-year revue

   (B) one of eight of the only musicians who have performed in the end-of-the-year revue

   (C) one of the only eight musicians who performs in the end-of-the-year revue

   (D) only one of eight musicians to perform in the end-of-the-year revue

   (E) only one of the eight end-of-the-year musicians who performs in the revue

64. As the United States Census showed, <u>college graduates are five times more likely to own houses as</u> to own apartments.

   (A) college graduates are five times more likely to own houses as

   (B) college graduates are five times as likely to own houses as it is for them

   (C) college graduates are five times more likely to own houses than

   (D) it is five times more likely for college graduates to own houses than they are

   (E) it is five times as likely that college graduates will own houses as they are

65. Hospitals are increasing the hours of doctors, <u>significantly affecting the frequency of surgical errors, which already are a cost to hospitals of</u> millions of dollars in malpractice lawsuits.

   (A) significantly affecting the frequency of surgical errors, which already are a cost to hospitals of

   (B) significantly affecting the frequency of surgical errors, which already cost hospitals

   (C) significantly affecting the frequency of surgical errors, already with hospital costs of

   (D) significant in affecting the frequency of surgical errors, and already costs hospitals

   (E) significant in affecting the frequency of surgical errors and already costs hospitals

66. The pharmaceutical company hired a consultant to supervise a division <u>studying lower salaries as to their effects on employees' morale</u>.

   (A) studying lower salaries as to their effects on employees' morale

   (B) studying the effects of lower salaries on employees' morale

   (C) for studying what are the effects in employees' morale that lower salaries would cause

   (D) studying the effects of employees' morale on lower salaries

   (E) studying what the effects lower salaries would have on employees' morale

67. Marian Corey has developed a chest cold <u>that, with persistent coughing, could gravely strain</u> the five-octave voice that earned her fame.

   (A) that, with persistent coughing, could gravely strain

   (B) that, because of persistent coughing, could be a grave strain for

   (C) with persistent coughing, and it could gravely strain

   (D) with persistent coughing and could be a grave strain for

   (E) with persistent coughing and could gravely strain

68. During gladiator matches, the unfair match-up between a prisoner with a short sword and ten soldiers with horses and whips can drive the prisoner to a state of manic frenzy, <u>like a rampaging bull whose rage increases when its hide is pierced with swords</u>.

   (A) like a rampaging bull whose rage increases when its hide is pierced with swords

   (B) like the increased rage of a rampaging bull when its hide is pierced with swords

   (C) like a rampaging bull that increases rage while rampaging with its hide pierced with swords

   (D) just as a rampaging bull that increases rage by piercing its hide with swords

   (E) just as a rampaging bull's rage increases when it is pierced with swords

69. Eye movement occurs <u>more rapidly during dreams than when waking</u>.

    (A)   more rapidly during dreams than when waking

    (B)   when dreaming more rapidly than waking hours

    (C)   more rapidly during dreaming than waking

    (D)   more rapidly during dreams than during the period of time when a person is awake

    (E)   more rapidly when dreaming than when waking

70. The Jukes family lost all of their money gambling, and <u>they were forced to move to a suburb bordering the city from their apartment</u>.

    (A)   they were forced to move to a suburb bordering the city from their apartment

    (B)   they had been forced to move from their apartment to a suburb that bordered the city

    (C)   they were forced to move from their apartment to a suburb bordering the city

    (D)   they having been forced to, moved from their apartment to a suburb that bordered the city

    (E)   they withdrew, because they were forced to, from their apartment to a suburb bordering the city

71. Parents' disagreements on how to discipline their child, <u>has made problems for teachers as they are teaching such</u> spoiled students.

    (A)   has made problems for teachers as they are teaching such

    (B)   has made problems for teachers teaching such

    (C)   has made problems for teachers as they are teaching

    (D)   have made it problematic for teachers to teach such

    (E)   have made it problematic for teachers as they are teaching such

72. Despite her recent promise not to talk about her divorce with the media, she decided to <u>do so at the press conference because she thought that many women, likely most, would appreciate</u> her message of empowerment.

    (A)   do so at the press conference because she thought that many women, likely most, would appreciate

    (B)   talk at the press conference since she thought that many women, likely most, would have appreciated

    (C)   so talk at the press conference due to her thinking that many women, even most, would likely appreciate

    (D)   do so at the press conference because she thought that many women, if not most, would appreciate

    (E)   do so at the press conference since she thought many women, and even most, would likely appreciate

73. Students of violin can distinguish a good tone quality from a bad one long before <u>the identification that</u> a given instrument is out of tune.

    (A)   the identification that

    (B)   they can identify that

    (C)   they would identify

    (D)   they could have the identification of

    (E)   having the identification of

74. <u>Like their sister schools in England, the American School of Ethical Culture has always</u> embraced the philosophy of nonviolence.

    (A)   Like their sister schools in England, the American School of Ethical Culture has always

    (B)   Like that of their sister schools in England, the American School of Ethical Culture has always

    (C)   Like its sister schools in England the American School of Ethical Culture always have

    (D)   Like that of its sister schools in England, the American School of Ethical Culture always has

    (E)   Like its sister schools in England, the American School of Ethical Culture has always

75. The leader of the physics seminar was prepared to start discussions herself, <u>for not everyone in attendance was knowledgeable</u> that the material being discussed involved new theories of quantum mechanics unknown to many in the profession.

    (A)   for not everyone in attendance was knowledgeable

    (B)   for everyone in attendance did not know

    (C)   with everyone in attendance not knowing

    (D)   with everyone attending not knowledgeable

    (E)   for not everyone attending knew

76. Isabelle so loved her dead husband that when forced to sell his collection of Genghis Khan's diaries to raise money, <u>she first made copies of more than fifty.</u>

    (A)   she first made copies of more than fifty

    (B)   first she made more than fifty copies

    (C)   more than fifty copies first were made

    (D)   copies of more than fifty were made

    (E)   she copies more than fifty of them beforehand

77. <u>Using the methods employed by Soviet agents, a new form of torture has been developed by Chinese generals to</u> aid in extracting information from unwilling captives.

    (A)   Using the methods employed by Soviet agents, a new form of torture has been developed by Chinese generals to

    (B)   Using the methods employed by Soviet agents, a new form of torture that was developed by Chinese generals will

    (C)   Using the methods of Soviet agents, Chinese generals have developed a new form of torture to

    (D)   Employing the methods of Soviet agents there has been a development by Chinese generals of a new form of torture that will

    (E)   Employing the methods of Soviet agents, a new form of torture that was developed by Chinese generals will

78. Most people think that women have achieved equality with men, but sociologists know <u>that statistics for both post-graduat education and median income indicate as drastic of</u> a gap as there was ten years ago.

    (A)   that statistics for both post-graduate education and median income indicate as drastic of

    (B)   that statistics for both post-graduate education and median income indicate as drastic

    (C)   that both the post-graduate education and median income statistics indicate as drastic of

    (D)   of both post-graduate education and median income statistics that indicate as drastic of

    (E)   of statistics for both post-graduate education and median income indicating as drastic of

79.   Al Gore was vice-president of the United States, <u>while earlier his father has been</u> a senator.

    (A)   while earlier his father has been

    (B)   where his father earlier is

    (C)   just as earlier his father had been

    (D)   as his earlier father has been

    (E)   his father earlier being

80.   Two disabled children, one with crutches and <u>the other one with a wheelchair, enters</u> the class on Monday.

    (A)   the other one with a wheelchair, enters

    (B)   the other one a wheelchair, enter

    (C)   the other with a wheelchair, enters

    (D)   the other with a wheelchair, enter

    (E)   one with a wheelchair, enters

81.   In Pomona College, a rule has been passed that <u>permits students to cook and serve their food, as well as to buy it</u>.

    (A)   permits students to cook and serve their food, as well as to buy it

    (B)   permits students to cook, serve, and to buy their food

    (C)   permits students to cook, to serve, and buy food

    (D)   will permit the student to cook, serve, as well as to buy food

    (E)   will permit food to be cooked, served, as well as bought by students

82.   <u>Some of them burned out eons ago, the night sky is spotted with thousands of stars.</u>

    (A)   Some of them burned out eons ago, the night sky is spotted with thousands of stars.

    (B)   Burned out eons ago, the night sky is spotted with many thousands of stars.

    (C)   Thousands of stars, some of them burned out eons ago, are spotting the night sky.

    (D)   The night sky is spotted with thousands of stars, some of which are burnt out eons ago.

    (E)   The night sky is spotted with thousands of stars, some of them burned out eons ago.

83.   The humidity, air pollution, and noise have <u>affected the children of Maria less drastically than those of</u> her neighbor.

    (A)   affected the children of Maria less drastically than those of

    (B)   affected the children of Maria less drastically than

    (C)   affected the children of Maria less dramatically than they have

    (D)   dramatically affected the children of Maria less than

    (E)   dramatically affected the children of Maria and

84.   <u>Content though she seems, the unhappiness of the housewife</u> is evident to those who know her well.

    (A)   Content though she seems, the unhappiness of the housewife

    (B)   Even though she seems content, the unhappiness of the housewife

    (C)   Though content, the housewife's unhappiness

    (D)   Though the housewife seems content, her unhappiness

    (E)   The unhappiness of the housewife who seems content

85. Language immersion experiences are valuable because they can quickly teach students <u>who may be unlikely to learn the language in other settings or months of regular teaching</u>.

 - (A) who may be unlikely to learn the language in other settings or months of regular teaching
 - (B) whose learning the language is unlikely in other settings or months of regular teaching
 - (C) who might not learn the language in other settings or during months of regular teaching
 - (D) who may not learn the language under other settings or months of regular teaching
 - (E) unlikely not to learn the language during months of regular teaching or in other settings

86. <u>During the late 1960's and the 1970's, funding for space missions fell by nearly seventy percent from its peak in 1968 down to its nadir in 1977.</u>

 - (A) During the late 1960's and the 1970's, funding for space missions fell by nearly seventy percent from its peak in 1968 down to its nadir in 1977
 - (B) During the late 1960's and the 1970's, funding for space missions fell by nearly seventy percent from its peak in 1968 to its nadir in 1977
 - (C) At the time of the late 1960's and the 1970's funding for space missions fell by almost seventy percent from its 1968 peak down to its 1977 nadir
 - (D) At the time of the late 1960's and the 1970's, funding for space missions fell from its peak in 1968, by nearly seventy percent, to its nadir in 1977
 - (E) During the late 1960's and the 1970's, funding for space missions fell from its peak in 1968 to its nadir in 1977 by nearly seventy percent

87. In his speech last night, the Mayor acknowledged Citizens for Communities, a grassroots organization that has <u>been active in drawing residents of impoverished neighborhoods together</u>.

 - (A) been active in drawing residents of impoverished neighborhoods together
 - (B) been active as a drawing together of residents of impoverished neighborhoods
 - (C) been active to draw together residents of neighborhoods that are impoverished
 - (D) become active to drawing together residents of impoverished neighborhoods
 - (E) become active to draw together neighborhoods that are impoverished

88. The actors in *The Mystery of Edwin Drood* have become known as <u>a prime example of the interaction between performers with</u> the audience.

 - (A) a prime example of the interaction between performers with
 - (B) a prime example of the interaction of performers and
 - (C) being prime examples of the interaction between performers with
 - (D) prime examples of the interaction between performers with
 - (E) prime examples of the interaction between performers and

89. The pharmaceutical company must report to the FDA the number of casualties <u>suffered by its test subjects and that the statistics be released</u> to the public.

 - (A) suffered by its test subjects and that the statistics be released
 - (B) that its test subjects suffered and that the statistics be released
 - (C) that was suffered by its test subjects with the statistics being released
 - (D) suffered by its test subjects and release the statistics
 - (E) suffered by its test subjects and released the statistics

90. The PTA decided that <u>just as alcohol is discussed in health class to protect those who might actually abuse it</u>, other drugs should also be covered to prevent students from falling prey to addiction.

   (A)   just as alcohol is discussed in health class to protect those who might actually abuse it

   (B)   like alcohol, which is discussed in health class to protect those who might abuse it

   (C)   similar to alcohol, which is discussed in health class in order to protect those who might actually abuse it

   (D)   while, to protect those who might actually abuse it, alcohol is discussed in health class

   (E)   similar to the discussion of alcohol in health class in order to protect those who might actually abuse it

91. The child psychologist suggests that the formation of social groups of young children, like <u>the adults who raised them</u>, is based on common interests and hobbies.

   (A)   the adults who raised them

   (B)   that of the adults who raised them

   (C)   that among the adults who raised them

   (D)   they that raised the adults

   (E)   the formation of social groups of the adults who raised them

92. The <u>shipping of raw materials being improved has become an economical</u> factor in the transformation of Japan into a world-wide economic power.

   (A)   The shipping of raw materials being improved has become an economical

   (B)   The improved shipping of raw materials has become an economical

   (C)   That the shipping of raw materials is improved has become an economical

   (D)   The shipping of raw materials being improved has become an economic

   (E)   The improvement in shipping of raw materials has become an economic

93. Ms. Kardon spent three years studying the puffin in order to learn more about <u>their social organization, mating rituals, and foods that they prefer</u>.

   (A)   their social organization, mating rituals, and foods that they prefer

   (B)   their social organization, mating rituals, and their preferred foods

   (C)   its social organization, mating rituals, and preferred foods

   (D)   its social organization, mating rituals, and about preferred foods

   (E)   social organization, mating rituals, and foods that are preferred

94. Contrary to popular opinion, it may be that <u>increasing fatal automobile accidents as a result of producing</u> faster cars would be beneficial to society at large.

   (A)   increasing fatal automobile accidents as a result of producing

   (B)   increased fatal automobile accidents resulting from the production of

   (C)   increasing fatal accidents in automobiles resulting from the production of

   (D)   fatal automobile accidents that had increased from producing

   (E)   fatal automobile accidents that increased from producing

95. Factories can mass-produce beautiful glass vessels <u>that are valued almost as much as that of the old-fashione glass-blower that remain</u>.

    (A) that are valued almost as much as that of the old-fashioned glass-blowers that remain

    (B) of a value that is almost as much as that of the old-fashioned glass-blowers that remain

    (C) almost as much in value as those of the remaining old-fashioned glass-blowers

    (D) almost as much in value as that of the remaining old-fashioned glass-blowers

    (E) valued almost as much as those of the remaining old-fashioned glass-blowers

96. Because her parents will no longer support her, Julie <u>either now or after she graduates from college will be forced to enter the job market</u>.

    (A) either now or after she graduates from college will be forced to enter the job market

    (B) will either be forced to enter the job market after she graduates from college or is now

    (C) will be forced to enter the job market either soon or after she graduates from college

    (D) either will be now forced to enter the job market or will be after she graduates from college

    (E) is either now or will be after she graduates from college forced to enter the job market

97. <u>Unlike that of the French, who linger when they eat</u> meals, Americans are so enamored of eating quickly that they have a type of meal called 'fast food'.

    (A) Unlike that of the French, who linger when they eat

    (B) Unlike the French, who linger when they eat

    (C) Unlike the French, lingering when eating

    (D) Dissimilar to the French, lingering during

    (E) Lacking similarity to the French, who linger during

98. The field of <u>mathematics, which in recent years was</u> neglected by elementary school teachers, who prefer topics that can be easily illustrated by hands-on activities.

    (A) mathematics, which in recent years was

    (B) mathematics that was to be

    (C) mathematics, one which has, in recent years, been

    (D) mathematics is one that in recent years has been

    (E) mathematics, in recent years, is one that was

99. The incidence of rape in rural areas is <u>equally high or more so than in urban areas</u>.

    (A) equally high or more so than in urban areas

    (B) equal to or higher than in urban areas

    (C) as high as in urban areas or more

    (D) equal to, if not more, than in urban areas

    (E) as high as it is in urban areas, if not higher

100. Sociologists have discovered that caregivers subconsciously enjoy the chance to nurse someone; <u>the workers are, in fact, disappointed when patients recover</u>.

   (A)   the workers are, in fact, disappointed when patients recover

   (B)   and the workers are, in fact, disappointed when patients recovered

   (C)   the workers are, in fact, disappointed when patients recovered

   (D)   in fact, they are disappointed when patients recovered

   (E)   the workers are disappointed at the recovery of patients, in fact

101. The president's ill-advised economic policies affected <u>the employed and the jobless alike; vast quantities of people were precariously balanced</u> on the edge of poverty.

   (A)   the employed and the jobless alike; vast quantities of people were precariously balanced

   (B)   both the employed and the jobless alike; large amounts of people precariously balanced themselves

   (C)   the employed and the jobless alike; great numbers of people were precariously balanced

   (D)   both the employed and the jobless alike; vast amounts of people precariously balanced themselves

   (E)   both the employed and the jobless; great quantities of people were precariously balanced

102. The pieces performed in their latest concert show <u>the chamber musicians have combined styles of music from the Middle East to that</u> of Russia.

   (A)   the chamber musicians have combined styles of music from the Middle East to that

   (B)   that the chamber musicians have combined styles of music from the Middle East to that

   (C)   the chamber musicians have combined styles of music from the Middle East to that

   (D)   that the chamber musicians have combined styles of music from the Middle East with those

   (E)   that chamber musicians have combined styles of music from Egypt and those

103. Fencing is a tantalizing sport, unappreciated at best, <u>where two opponents fight a pitched and lightning fast battle with</u> electrically connected swords and metal vests.

   (A)   where two opponents fight a pitched and lightning fast battle with

   (B)   when two opponents fight a pitched and lightning fast battle having

   (C)   which two opponents have pitched and in lightning fast battle fighting with

   (D)   having two opponents who fight a pitched and lightning fast battle that has

   (E)   in which two opponents fight a pitched and lightning fast battle with

104. Scientists have determined that the inner ear assists in awareness of body orientation, since people with disorders of the inner ear <u>were found to have increased difficulties</u> in maintaining balance.

   (A)   were found to have increased difficulties

   (B)   have been found to have increased difficulty

   (C)   were found to have increasing difficulty

   (D)   had been found to have increased difficulties

   (E)   have been found to have increasing difficulties

105. The city of Montreal spends a large portion of its annual budget on the construction of tourist attractions such as amusement parks, <u>even if it is by no means certain that the construction of tourist attractions increases</u> revenue from tourism.

- **(A)** even if it is by no means certain that the construction of tourist attractions increases
- **(B)** even if the city is by no means certain that the construction of tourist attractions will increase
- **(C)** even if there is no certainty that the construction of tourist attractions increases
- **(D)** even though the city is by no means certain that the construction of tourist attractions increases
- **(E)** though there is no certainty as to the construction of tourist attractions increasing

106. Certain painkilling drugs such as Oxycotin have recently been shown to be addictive to patients, <u>which may limit their potential to reduce</u> pain.

- **(A)** which may limit their potential to reduce
- **(B)** which may limit their potential for reducing
- **(C)** which may limit such drugs' potential to reduce
- **(D)** an effect that may limit their potential to reduce
- **(E)** an effect that may limit the potential of such drugs to reduce

107. Many fear the epidemic of obesity in America; the amount of food consumed per person in America is <u>as much as thrice that consumed in Japan</u>.

- **(A)** as much as thrice that consumed in Japan
- **(B)** as much as thrice that of Japan's consumption
- **(C)** up to three times of Japan's consumption
- **(D)** up to three times what Japanese consumed
- **(E)** up to triple the amount the Japanese consumed

108. Books to be added to the high school curriculum should be educational <u>and should have no profanity in them or be lewd</u>.

- **(A)** and should have no profanity in them or be lewd
- **(B)** and should not have profanity in them or not be lewd
- **(C)** and contain no profanity or lewdness
- **(D)** without containing profanity nor be lewd
- **(E)** without having any profanity or no lewdness in them

109. Some civil libertarians <u>insist that the best way to insure freedom of religion for all citizens is to reduce</u> the prominence of the Judeo-Christian god in politics.

- **(A)** insist that the best way to insure freedom of religion for all citizens is to reduce
- **(B)** have insisted the best way freedom of religion can be insured for all citizens is reducing
- **(C)** insist the best way to insure freedom of religion for all citizens is the reduction of
- **(D)** are insistent that the best way freedom of religion can be insured for all citizens is the reduction of
- **(E)** insist that the best way for the insurance of freedom of religion for all citizens is to reduce

110. Unchallenged as a result of having 16th century European firearms, <u>Native Americans viewed the white man with suspicion, for they</u> feared the thunder sticks of death that were pointed at them.

   (A)   Native Americans viewed the white man with suspicion, for they

   (B)   Native Americans were suspicious of the white man, and they

   (C)   the white man was viewed with suspicion by Native Americans, who

   (D)   the white man was suspicious to Native Americans, and it was

   (E)   the white man was viewed with suspicion by Native Americans, it being

111. When he could no longer play violin himself, Howard taught, <u>imparted his knowledge to students to encourage</u> them to be as successful as he once was.

   (A)   imparted his knowledge to students to encourage

   (B)   and he imparted his knowledge to students and encouraged

   (C)   and imparting his knowledge to students encouraged

   (D)   imparting his knowledge to students and encouraged

   (E)   imparting his knowledge to students and encouraging

112. Annabelle's pack-a-day smoking habit <u>has done seriously and potentially fatal damage to</u> her lungs.

   (A)   has done seriously and potentially fatal damage to

   (B)   did damage that is seriously and potentially fatal

   (C)   damaged, serious and potentially fatally

   (D)   has done serious and potentially fatal damage to

   (E)   did damage, serious and potentially fatal

113. <u>When deer damage plants, it</u> can be prevented if human hair is spread around the garden.

   (A)   When deer damage plants, it

   (B)   The damage to plants caused by deer

   (C)   The fact that deer cause damage to plants

   (D)   When deer cause plant damage, it

   (E)   Deer damage plants, which

114. Upset by the litter around her neighborhood, <u>the idea of after-schoo cleanups were substitutes for detention by Jane.</u>

   (A)   the idea of after-school cleanups were substitutes for detention by Jane

   (B)   after-school cleanups were ideas for substitution for detention suggested by Jane

   (C)   Jane suggested the after-school cleanup as a substitute for detention

   (D)   Jane suggested that detention be substituted as after-school cleanups

   (E)   the after-school cleanup was suggested to be a substitute for detention by Jane

115. Because of persuasive arguments made by both lawyers, juries often have difficulty distinguishing <u>the innocent from</u> the guilty; DNA testing helps prevent innocent people from being convicted.

    (A)   the innocent from

    (B)   the innocent and

    (C)   the innocent or

    (D)   for the innocent or

    (E)   among the innocent or

116. Research has found that <u>a child born into a family whose members have schizophrenia will most likely themselves develop schizophrenia</u> in their adolescence.

    (A)   a child born into a family whose members have schizophrenia will most likely themselves develop schizophrenia

    (B)   children born into families whose members have schizophrenia will most likely themselves develop schizophrenia

    (C)   a child born into a family the members of which have schizophrenia will most likely themselves develop schizophrenia

    (D)   in those families where members have schizophrenia, children will most likely develop schizophrenia themselves

    (E)   children born into families where there is schizophrenia will themselves most likely develop schizophrenia

117. <u>No less an expert than</u> John H. McWhorter has claimed that African-American children do poorly in schools because of implicit social pressure to fail academically.

    (A)   No less an expert than

    (B)   Not less an expert

    (C)   Not less expert

    (D)   Not less an expert than

    (E)   An expert not less than

118. Many police officers arrest African-Americans <u>not from their significance as perpetrators of suburban crime</u> but because they are members of an ethnic minority.

    (A)   not from their significance as perpetrators of suburban crime

    (B)   although they are not a significant perpetrators of suburban crime

    (C)   not in that they are significant as suburban perpetrators of crime

    (D)   not because they are significant perpetrators of suburban crime

    (E)   not because being significant perpetrators of crime in suburban areas

119. Punk teenagers infuriate adults as much by wearing provocative clothing <u>than by their disregard for authority</u>.

    (A)   than by their disregard for authority

    (B)   rather than by their disregard for authority

    (C)   than by disregarding authority

    (D)   as by their disregard for authority

    (E)   as by disregarding authority

120. After Georgio's Café got a favorable review in a travel guidebook, the number of tourists eating there <u>were in excess of the number of local customers</u> going regularly.

   (A) were in excess of the number of local customers

   (B) had an excess over the local customers who were

   (C) exceeded the local customers who were

   (D) numbered more than the local customers

   (E) exceeded the number of local customers

121. <u>Wretched and increasing mendicants are requesting money on the streets, money that seems</u> to be hard to come by in the deteriorating economy.

   (A) Wretched and increasing prevalent mendicants are requesting money on the streets, money that seems

   (B) Wretched and increasing prevalent mendicants request money on the streets, money seeming

   (C) On the streets wretched and increasingly prevalent mendicants are requesting money that seems

   (D) Wretchedly and increasingly prevalent mendicants request money on the streets seeming

   (E) Wretchedly and increasingly prevalent mendicants are requesting money on the streets that seems

122. <u>Though without understanding a word of what is being said, savvy communicators</u> can follow a conversation in a foreign language by interpreting tone of voice and body language.

   (A) Though without understanding a word of what is being said, savvy communicators

   (B) Without understanding a word of what is being said, savvy communicators

   (C) Even though the person has not understood a word of what is being said, a savvy communicator

   (D) Even when the person has not understood a word that is being said, savvy communicators

   (E) In spite of not understanding a word of what is being said, a savvy communicator

123. <u>The new Xerox machine does more than simply copying</u> documents; it can resize, lighten, and collate.

   (A) The new Xerox machine does more than simply copying

   (B) The new Xerox machine's functions are more than a simple copying of

   (C) The new Xerox machine has done more than a simple copying of

   (D) The new Xerox machine's functions have done more than copy simply

   (E) The new Xerox machine does more than simply copy

124. Because both parents worked full-time, they had a nanny who not only watched the children <u>and also cleaned the house should it be</u> messy.

   (A) and also cleaned the house should it be

   (B) but also did the cleaning of the house if it were

   (C) and the house was cleaned if it were

   (D) but also cleaned the house if it was

   (E) and cleans the house if it were

125. Surprisingly obedient, the <u>Smiths have a cat that follows</u> simple instructions like 'come' or 'sit', words to which usually only dogs respond.

    (A)   Smiths have a cat that follows

    (B)   Smiths of their cat follows

    (C)   cat belonging to the Smiths follows

    (D)   cat belonging to the Smiths has followed

    (E)   cat belonging to the Smiths, following

126. Actors on Broadway have the difficult task <u>of being singers who must also perform as dancers.</u>

    (A)   of being singers who must also perform as dancers

    (B)   of singers who must also perform like dancer

    (C)   that they are singers who must perform like dancer

    (D)   that, as a singer, they must also perform as a dancer

    (E)   to be a singer that must also perform as a dancer

127. Regardless of the amount of dairy food they consume in adulthood, people who consumed little dairy food in childhood <u>seem to be prone to bone fractures</u>, a disadvantage that suggests a need for higher calcium consumption in childhood.

    (A)   seem to be prone to bone fractures

    (B)   seemingly are prone to bone fractures and have

    (C)   seem to be prone to bone fractures and have

    (D)   seemingly are prone to bone fractures and to have

    (E)   are, it seems, prone to bone fractures, and they have

128. The defending attorney weakened the prosecution's arguments so much that, at the end of the trial, the jury <u>doubted that the victim had even existed.</u>

    (A)   doubted that the victim had even existed

    (B)   doubts that the victim has even existed

    (C)   was in doubt as to the existence of the victim

    (D)   was doubtful concerning the victim's existence

    (E)   had doubts about the victim's even existing

129. If the draft is not re-instated, <u>less people will join the army in the coming 10 years than</u> did in any other 10-year period in our nation's history.

    (A)   less people will join the army in the coming 10 years than

    (B)   less people will be joining the army in the coming 10 years as

    (C)   fewer people will join the army in the coming 10 years as

    (D)   fewer people will be joining the army in the coming 10 years as

    (E)   fewer people will join the army in the coming 10 years than

130. Germany's most infamous leader, Hitler's policies were responsible for the slaughter of 6 million Jews.

   (A) Germany's most infamous leader, Hitler's policies were responsible for

   (B) Germany's most infamous leader, the policies of Hitler caused

   (C) More infamous than other leaders of Germany, the policies of Hitler were responsible for

   (D) Germany's most infamous leader, Hitler caused

   (E) Hitler, Germany's most infamous leader, had policies that caused

131. No school policies forbid a teacher from scolding a student or to call the student's parents based only on another child's accusations.

   (A) a teacher from scolding a student or to call

   (B) a teacher to scold a student or call

   (C) that teachers scold a student or call

   (D) the scolding by a teacher of a student or calling of

   (E) scolding by teachers of a student or calling of

132. The miners were reluctant to embrace the company's new unionization policy because they thought it was merely meant to be a publicity stunt with no commitment to contract negotiation and eventually salary increases.

   (A) stunt with no commitment to contract negotiation and eventually salary increases

   (B) stunt, having no commitment to contract negotiation and eventually salary increases

   (C) stunt and did not reflect a commitment to contract negotiation and eventual salary increases

   (D) stunt, reflecting a commitment to contract negotiation and eventual salary increases

   (E) stunt, not one that reflected that contract negotiation and eventual salary increases was a commitment

133. Many companies pay almost twice as much to men, if the effect of faster promotions, more bonuses, and better benefits are regarded as salary, than to women, who earn 77 cents for every dollar their male counterparts earn in base salary

   (A) are regarded as salary, than

   (B) are regarded as salary, as

   (C) is regarded as salary, than it pays

   (D) is regarded as salary, as is paid

   (E) is regarded as salary, as they pay

134. The Planned Parenthood representative suggested that all sexually active teenagers be protected from STDs as thoroughly as possible and also encouraged all parents who have post-pubescen children to talk to their children about birth control.

   (A) be protected from STDs as thoroughly as possible and also encouraged all parents who have post-pubescent children

   (B) should be protected from STDs as thoroughly as possible and also encourages all parents that have post-pubescent children

   (C) are protected from STDs as thoroughly as possible and also encourages those parents who are having post-pubescent children

   (D) be protected from STDs as thoroughly as possible and also encouraged parents with post-pubescent children

   (E) should be protected from STDs as thoroughly as possible and also has encouraged all those parents with a post-pubescent child

135. SAS is a database-forming programming language, <u>a means to organize, in order to analyze, the huge amount</u> of seemingly unrelated facts on a topic.

- **(A)** a means to organize, in order to analyze, the huge amount
- **(B)** a means to organize, in order to analyze, the huge number
- **(C)** the means of organizing for analyzing the huge number
- **(D)** the means that organizes, in order to analyze, the huge amount
- **(E)** the means for organizing in order to analyze the huge amount

136. Unlike Christians, Jews only see Jesus as a prophet; they do not think of him as the Messiah, <u>nor do they view him</u> as the son of God.

- **(A)** nor do they view him
- **(B)** but they do not view him
- **(C)** neither do they view him
- **(D)** and they neither view him
- **(E)** while viewing him neither

137. Partial-birth abortion, a procedure <u>used in the third trimester of pregnancy involving the partial delivery and the euthanasia of a fetus, is now the subject of controversy because it involves</u> killing a fetus that could live outside the mother.

- **(A)** used in the third trimester of pregnancy involving the partial delivery and the euthanasia of a fetus, is now the subject of controversy because it involves
- **(B)** used in the third trimester of pregnancy involving the partial delivery and the euthanasia of a fetus, is now the subject of controversy because of involving
- **(C)** used in the third trimester of pregnancy, involves the partial delivery and the euthanasia of a fetus and is now the subject of controversy because it involves
- **(D)** in the third trimester of pregnancy that involves the partial delivery and the euthanasia of a fetus, is now the subject of controversy because it involves
- **(E)** in the third trimester of pregnancy involving the partial delivery and the euthanasia of a fetus, which is now the subject of controversy, involves

138. <u>Where once housewives had submitted to the authority of their husbands by agreeing</u> with them on every political issue, after many men supported America's decision not to sign an international treaty on the rights of women, many housewives decided to form their own political ideas.

- **(A)** Where once housewives had submitted to the authority of their husbands by agreeing
- **(B)** Where once housewives submitted to their husbands' authority for the agreement of
- **(C)** While once housewives had submitted to the authority of their husbands by agreement
- **(D)** While once housewives submitted to their husbands' authority by agreeing
- **(E)** While once housewives had submitted to the authority of their husbands by their agreeing

139. To end violent tendencies in young children, mothers want peaceful conflict resolution, readily available counseling, and decreasing the prominence of television shows that contain abundant and often casual violence.

    (A) decreasing the prominence of television shows that contain abundant and often casual violence

    (B) decreasing the prominence of television shows containing often casual but abundant violence

    (C) a decrease of the prominence of television shows, containing as they do often casual violence in abundance

    (D) a decreased prominence of the abundant and often casual violence contained in television shows

    (E) a decreased prominence of television shows that contain abundant but often casual violence

140. It may be many years before politicians again attempt to revive the draft, a program known to be unpopular with voters.

    (A) again attempt to revive the draft, a program known to be

    (B) attempt to revive the draft again, a program known for being

    (C) will attempt to revive the draft again, a program known as being

    (D) attempt to revive the draft again, a program that is known to be

    (E) will again attempt to revive the draft, a program known as being

141. Over the last ten years, the population of deer in America increased dramatically over the past decade, while the number of drivers who report car accidents with deer on highways is more than four times what it was.

    (A) increased dramatically over the past decade, while the number of drivers who report car accidents with deer on highways is more than four times what it was

    (B) increased dramatically, while the number of drivers reporting car accidents with deer on highways is more than quadruple what it was at that time

    (C) has increased dramatically, while the number of drivers reporting car accidents with deer on highways has more than quadrupled

    (D) has increased dramatically over the past decade, while the number of drivers reporting car accidents with deer on highways is more than four times what it was at that time

    (E) has increased dramatically over the past decade, while the number of drivers who are reporting car accidents with deer on highways are more than quadruple what they once were

142. The organs of pigs genetically modified by human stem-cells are now viewed as forms of health insurance and as resources a human is able to use to take care of one's later illnesses.

    (A) a human is able to use to take care of one's

    (B) that a human is able to use to take care of oneself in

    (C) a human is able to use to take care of oneself in

    (D) humans are able to use to take care of them in

    (E) humans are able to use to take care of themselves in

143. The mayor regretted that Hurricane Bradley had affected the metropolitan area so much more dramatically than meteorologists had expected may occur.

    (A) had expected may occur

    (B) had expected

    (C) expected the occurrence of

    (D) expected may occur

    (E) expected

144. The intense humidity emphasized the fact <u>it was, which the records show</u>, the hottest day Ottawa had ever had.

    (A)   it was, which the records show,

    (B)   it was, and it is the records that show it,

    (C)   of it being, as the records show,

    (D)   that the day was, as the records show,

    (E)   shown in the records, that it was

145. Animal Rescue is a non-profit organization that tries <u>to find lost pets and that returns them</u> to their owners.

    (A)   to find lost pets and that returns them

    (B)   to find lost pets and return them

    (C)   to find lost pets for return

    (D)   at finding lost pets so as to return them

    (E)   finding lost pets and that returns them

146. National Bank of Canada's employee insurance coverage <u>is little improved from how it was</u> in the past ten years.

    (A)   is little improved from how it was

    (B)   is a little improved from how it was

    (C)   has improved little

    (D)   has improved little from how it has been

    (E)   is little improved from the way it was

147. Not since Communist China crushed the democratic demonstrations at Tianenmen Square <u>has a country so brutally denied the right of its citizens that they could speak freely</u>.

    (A)   has a country so brutally denied the right of its citizens that they could speak freely

    (B)   did a country so brutally deny the right of its citizens that they could speak freely

    (C)   has a country so brutally denied the right of its citizens to speak freely

    (D)   did a country so brutally deny the right of its citizens to speak freely

    (E)   has a country so brutally denied whether its citizens had the right that they could be speaking freely

148. In recent years, despite the ethnocentrism of Western cultures, Eastern customs <u>are understood</u> in the international community.

    (A)   are understood

    (B)   are becoming better understood

    (C)   which have gained understanding,

    (D)   have become understood

    (E)   have since become understood

149.   Lately, union leaders have been divided in arguments <u>over if the union should fight for increased benefits or raised safety awareness</u>.

    (A)   over if the union should fight for increased benefits or raised safety awareness

    (B)   over whether the union should fight for increased benefits or raised safety awareness

    (C)   about the union fighting for increased benefits or raised safety awareness

    (D)   about if increased benefits should come from the union or raised safety awareness

    (E)   concerning the union and its fighting for increased benefits or raised safety awareness

150.   Montreal, <u>where the tourist industry is larger than any other Canadian city</u>, has neighborhoods entirely composed of souvenir shops and cafes.

    (A)   where the tourist industry is larger than any other Canadian city

    (B)   which has a tourist industry larger than that of other Canadian cities

    (C)   which had a tourist industry larger than any other Canadian city

    (D)   whose tourist industry is larger than any other Canadian city

    (E)   whose tourist industry is larger than that of any other Canadian city

151.   With a salary <u>of less than fifteen thousand dollars a year and fewer</u> sources of alternate income than before, Mrs. Greenman is in financial difficulty.

    (A)   of less than fifteen thousand dollars a year and fewer

    (B)   lower than fifteen thousand dollars and less

    (C)   lesser than fifteen thousand dollars and fewer

    (D)   fewer than fifteen thousand dollars and less

    (E)   of fewer than fifteen thousand dollars and of fewer

152.   The Johnson family is to be pitied for, first of all, becoming ineligible for welfare, and <u>secondarily, for their failure to</u> find a well-priced apartment.

    (A)   secondarily, for their failure to

    (B)   secondly, for their failure to

    (C)   secondly, that they failed and did not

    (D)   second, that they failed to

    (E)   second, failing to

153.   <u>Notice of the upcoming execution being given to convicted murderers two days before executing</u> them is the standard practice in certain police states in Asia.

    (A)   Notice of the upcoming execution being given to convicted murderers two days before executing

    (B)   Giving notice of the upcoming execution to convicted murderers two days before executing

    (C)   Notice of the upcoming execution to give to convicted murderers two days before executing

    (D)   Giving notice of the upcoming execution two days before executing

    (E)   To give notice of the upcoming execution two days before having to execute

154. <u>More than ever, Manolo Blahniks are expected to be sold this season</u>, due to their mention on the popular television show *Sex and the City*.

    (A)   More than ever, Manolo Blahniks are expected to be sold this season

    (B)   It is expected that more Manolo Blahniks than ever will be sold this season than previously and that is

    (C)   The Manolo Blahniks expected to be sold this season is more than ever

    (D)   The amount of Manolo Blahniks that will be sold this season is expected to be greater than ever

    (E)   A great increase in the number of Manolo Blahniks expected to be sold this season is

155. Distressed by the nutritional content of the junk food sold in the school cafeteria, <u>the possibility of removing vending machines was discussed by the PTA at its monthly meeting</u>.

    (A)   the possibility of removing vending machines was discussed by the PTA at its monthly meeting

    (B)   the removal of vending machines was discussed as a possibility by the PTA at its monthly meeting

    (C)   removed vending machines was discussed by the PTA at its monthly meeting as a possibility

    (D)   the PTA discussed at its monthly meeting the possibility of vending machines being removed

    (E)   the PTA, at its monthly meeting, discussed the possibility of removing vending machines

156. Robert Wood Johnson University requires <u>that a professor with classes of more than 60 students schedule smaller extra-hel sessions for their students before or after the standard classes</u>.

    (A)   that a professor with classes of more than 60 students schedule smaller extra-help sessions for their students before or after the standard classes

    (B)   a professor with classes of more than 60 students schedule smaller extra-help sessions for their students before or after the standard classes

    (C)   that professors with classes of more than 60 students schedule smaller extra-help sessions for their students before or after the standard classes

    (D)   a professor with classes of more than 60 students to schedule smaller extra-help sessions for their students before the standard classes or after

    (E)   a professor with classes of more than 60 students schedule smaller extra-help sessions for his students, before or after the standard classes

157. <u>Just as the Russian communists of the early 20th century believed that they were overcoming the tyranny of the czars, so too</u> did the Chinese communists believe they were avoiding the misrule of the Guomindang.

    (A)   Just as the Russian communists of the early 20th century believed that they were overcoming the tyranny of the czars, so too

    (B)   The Russian communists of the early 20th century believed that they were overcoming the tyranny of the czars, and in a similar way

    (C)   Like the case of the Russian communists of the early 20th century who believed that they were overcoming the tyranny of the czars, so too

    (D)   As in the belief that they were overcoming the tyranny of the czars held by the Russian communists of the early 20th century

    (E)   Similar to the Russian communists which believed in the early 20th century that they were overcoming the tyranny of the czars

158. Jewish immigrants from Poland, <u>Schwartz's Deli was opened by Eli and Rivka Schwartz in 1843 after unsuccessfully at-tempting to find office work</u>.

    (A)   Schwartz's Deli was opened by Eli and Rivka Schwartz in 1843 after unsuccessfully attempting to find office work

    (B)   Eli and Rivka Schwartz opened Schwartz's Deli in 1843, after unsuccessfully attempting to find office work

    (C)   after unsuccessfully attempting to find office work, Schwartz's Deli was opened by Eli and Rivka Schwartz in 1843

    (D)   Schwartz's Deli was opened in 1843 by Eli and Rivka Schwartz after unsuccessfully attempting to find office work

    (E)   Eli and Rivka Schwartz opened after unsuccessfully attempting to find office work Schwartz's Deli in 1843

159. After firing Danny, his boss discovered that not only had he skimmed money from the cash register <u>he in addition sexually harassed a female coworker</u>.

    (A)   he in addition sexually harassed a female coworker

    (B)   he had sexually harassed a female coworker in addition

    (C)   but also he had sexually harassed a female coworker

    (D)   he had also sexually harassed a female coworker

    (E)   but his female coworker was sexually harassed as well

160. An attempt <u>to elect a woman as President of the United States, begun fifteen years ago</u>, has had no success despite the willingness of the Democratic Party to back a female candidate.

    (A)   to elect a woman as President of the United States, begun fifteen years ago

    (B)   begun fifteen years ago, to elect a woman as President of the United States

    (C)   begun for electing a woman as President of the United States fifteen years ago

    (D)   at electing a woman as President of the United States, begun fifteen years ago

    (E)   that has begun fifteen years ago to elect a woman as President of the United States

161. After a murderer has been convicted, it is the judge who decides <u>whether his crime calls for executing him or imprisoning him</u> for life.

    (A)   whether his crime calls for executing him or imprisoning him

    (B)   if there is a crime that calls for an execution or an imprisonment of him

    (C)   whether or not his crime calls for the execution or, imprisonment of him

    (D)   if there is a crime that calls for executing him or his imprisonment

    (E)   if his crime would call for him being censured or that he be imprisoned

162. Because Albert is the most experienced <u>and he is therefore the best ballet dancer in the company, he is being increasingly viewed</u> by the director as the best candidate for the role of the Nutcracker.

    (A)   and he is therefore the best ballet dancer in the company, he is being increasingly viewed

    (B)   he is therefore the best of ballet dancers, and it has increased the view

    (C)   and therefore the best ballet dancer, he is being increasingly viewed

    (D)   and therefore he is the best of ballet dancers, there is an increasing view

    (E)   therefore being the best of ballet dancers, it is increasingly viewed

163. The political and social forces that may facilitate a dictator's rise to power include sudden crashes in the economy, discrimination and other methods of finding scapegoats, <u>inciting the masses to rebellion, and their protesting that the current government may still be inadequate.</u>

   (A) inciting the masses to rebellion, and their protesting that the current government may still be inadequate
   (B) inciting the masses to rebellion, and a protest that the current government may still be inadequate.
   (C) an incitement of the masses to rebellion, and a protesting that the current government may still be inadequate.
   (D) an incitement of the masses to rebellion, and a protest of the still inadequate current government
   (E) an incitement of the masses to rebellion, and a protest that the current government may still be inadequate.

164. Like the play that came before it, <u>Shakespeare's Othello is the inspiration for the new play.</u>

   (A) Shakespeare's Othello is the inspiration for the new play
   (B) the inspiration for the new play is Shakespeare's Othello
   (C) Shakespeare's Othello is the new play's inspiration
   (D) the new play has been inspired by Shakespeare's Othello
   (E) the new play has an inspiration of Shakespeare's Othello

165. <u>To compare the thunderous brilliance of Beethoven with the bubble-gu pop tunes of Britney Spears is to compare the value of diamonds with that of plastic baubles.</u>

   (A) To compare the thunderous brilliance of Beethoven with the bubble-gum pop tunes of Britney Spears is to compare the value of diamonds with that of plastic baubles.
   (B) To compare the thunderous brilliance of Beethoven with the bubble-gum pop tunes of Britney Spears is comparing the value of diamonds with that of plastic baubles.
   (C) Comparing the thunderous brilliance of Beethoven with the bubble-gum pop tunes of Britney Spears is to compare the value of diamonds with plastic baubles.
   (D) Comparing the thunderous brilliance of Beethoven with the bubble-gum pop tunes of Britney Spears is like comparing the value of diamonds with plastic baubles.
   (E) To compare the thunderous brilliance of Beethoven with the bubble-gum pop tunes of Britney Spears is to compare diamonds' value with plastic baubles' value.

166. When we visited the hospital, the doctors told us <u>that using a walker was much easier for Grandmother</u> than to try to walk on her own.

   (A) that using a walker was much easier for Grandmother
   (B) that for Grandmother, it was much easier to use a walker
   (C) that for Grandmother, a walker was much easier to use
   (D) for Grandmother, using a walker was much easier
   (E) for Grandmother, a walker was much easier than

167. The steps of the ceramic process in which the students will be involved <u>is in the molding and smoothing of the shape, and in the decoration</u> of the finished item.

   (A) is in the molding and smoothing of the shape, and in the decoration
   (B) is the molding and smoothing of the shape, and also the decorating
   (C) are the molding, smoothing of the shape, and in the decorating
   (D) are the molding and smoothing of the shape, and the decoration
   (E) is in the molding and smoothing of the shape, and the decorating

168. Since the President was caught having an affair, nearly ten thousand men have been sued for divorce, <u>which is more than had been sued</u> in the past five years combined.

    (A)   which is more than had been sued

    (B)   more than had been sued

    (C)   more than they had sued

    (D)   more than had experienced suits

    (E)   which is more than had experienced suits

169. Despite the doctor's urgings that she consider surgery, Marilyn decided not to go to the hospital because <u>she believed that herbal remedies would prove not only economical but</u> ultimately effective in curing her malady.

    (A)   she believed that herbal remedies would prove not only economical but

    (B)   herbal remedies will prove both economical and also

    (C)   she believed herbal remedies would prove themselves to be both economical and

    (D)   she believed herbal remedies would prove to be both economical and

    (E)   herbal remedies will prove her belief that they are both economical and

170. The pharmaceutical company should add many new strains of the disease to Prevnar, <u>making the vaccine much more effective than ten years ago</u>.

    (A)   making the vaccine much more effective than ten years ago

    (B)   and make the vaccine much more effective than ten years ago

    (C)   making the vaccine much more effective than it was ten years ago

    (D)   to make the vaccine much more effective than ten years ago

    (E)   in making the vaccine much more effective than it was ten years ago

171. <u>The disciplinary decisions teachers make are less strict for girls than they are for boys because they usually cause less trouble and are more repentant.</u>

    (A)   The disciplinary decisions teachers make are less strict for girls than they are for boys because they usually cause less trouble and are more repentant.

    (B)   Because they usually cause less trouble and are more repentant, the disciplinary decisions teachers make are less strict for girls than the disciplinary decisions are for boys.

    (C)   The disciplinary decisions teachers make are less strict for girls than boys because they usually cause less trouble and are more repentant.

    (D)   Because girls usually cause less trouble and are more repentant than boys, the disciplinary decisions that teachers make for girls are less strict than boys.

    (E)   The disciplinary decisions teachers make are less strict for girls than they are for boys because girls are usually less troublesome and more repentant than boys are.

172. In the cities, teenagers get more independence than <u>most suburbs</u>.

    (A)   most suburbs

    (B)   most suburbs do

    (C)   most suburbs are

    (D)   they are in most suburbs

    (E)   they do in most suburbs

173. Once near-slums with cheap rent, neighborhoods in the South Bronx have <u>been increasingly gentrified</u> in recent decades as urban renewal drives away the poor.

    (A) been increasingly gentrified

    (B) been increasing gentrification

    (C) been of increased gentrification

    (D) gentrified, increasingly,

    (E) increased gentrification

174. Not until Hammurabi's Code was enacted, <u>had a government granted the right to its citizens that they could be aware</u> of their laws.

    (A) had a government granted the right to its citizens that they could be aware

    (B) did a government grant the right to its citizens that they could be aware

    (C) had the government granted the right to its citizens for the awareness

    (D) did a government grant the right to its citizens to be aware

    (E) had the government granted that its citizens had a right that they could be aware

175. Police are mystified by the serial murderer and have no explanation as to why he attacks some of the prostitutes with whom he has contact <u>when he spares</u> most others.

    (A) when he spares

    (B) where he spares

    (C) where sparing

    (D) when sparing

    (E) while sparing

176. At the press conference, the President's spokesman <u>has announced that the government plans</u> to build up a reserve of the smallpox vaccine in case of a biological attack.

    (A) has announced that the government plans

    (B) announced that the government plans

    (C) has announced that the government will plan

    (D) announced that the government has a plan

    (E) has announced that the government planned

177. <u>Thought to emanate from a tiny gland on the underside of their bodies, ants leave behind pheromone trails that can be used</u> as signals or messages for other ants.

    (A) Thought to emanate from a tiny gland on the underside of their bodies, ants leave behind pheromone trails that can be used

    (B) Ants leave behind pheromone trails that are thought to emanate from a tiny gland on the underside of their bodies, and they can use this

    (C) Thought to emanate from a tiny gland on the underside of ants' bodies, pheromone trails left behind can be used

    (D) Emanating it is thought from a tiny gland on the underside of their bodies, ants leave behind pheromone trails they can use

    (E) Emanating, it is thought, from a tiny gland on the underside of their bodies, pheromone trails are left behind by ants that can be used

178. Although the public is accustomed to tax adjustments that benefit only the rich, economic experts were delighted to discover that both <u>rich and the poor people</u> would benefit from the President's tax plan.

    (A)   rich and the poor people

    (B)   rich people and the poor

    (C)   the rich and the poor people

    (D)   rich people and poor people

    (E)   people who are rich and those who are poor

179. When buying electronics, <u>one should request a guarantee for one's merchandise</u>; the guarantee may be necessary if your new purchase breaks and you wish to have it replaced.

    (A)   one should request a guarantee for one's merchandise

    (B)   you should request a guarantee for your merchandise

    (C)   a guarantee for your merchandise is what one should request

    (D)   a guarantee for one's merchandise is what should be requested

    (E)   a guarantee for your merchandise is what should be requested

180. <u>At the suggestion of</u> his guidance counselor, Brad applied to two Ivy League colleges and to the schools he knew would accept him.

    (A)   At the suggestion of

    (B)   When he was suggested by

    (C)   A suggestion coming from

    (D)   A suggestion that came from

    (E)   After having a suggestion from

181. The twelve hour documentary on the Civil War revealed many interesting quirks <u>that illustrates</u> how complex and peculiar the war that pitched brother against brother really was.

    (A)   that illustrates

    (B)   which illustrates

    (C)   that illustrate

    (D)   and illustrate

    (E)   who illustrate

182. <u>He was an orphan, and Kyle</u> founded the largest orphanage in China.

    (A)   He was an orphan, and Kyle

    (B)   An orphan, Kyle

    (C)   Orphan that he was, Kyle

    (D)   Kyle has been an orphan and he

    (E)   Being an orphan, Kyle

183. Many historians <u>regard the time of the Heian court as</u> the greatest period in Japanese history.

  (A) regard the time of the Heian court as

  (B) regard the time of the Heian court to be

  (C) regard the time of the Heian court to have been

  (D) consider that the time of the Heian court is

  (E) consider the time of the Heian court as

184. As concerned citizens continue to investigate the activities of the CIA, <u>their surprising similarity to Russia's infamous KGB has become</u> impossible to ignore.

  (A) their surprising similarity to Russia's infamous KGB has become

  (B) the surprise of their similarity to Russia's infamous KGB has become

  (C) the surprising similarity between them and Russia's infamous KGB has become

  (D) the surprising similarity between the CIA and Russia's infamous KGB becomes

  (E) the surprising similarity of the CIA with Russia's infamous KGB becomes

185. Henry never showed effort, and his essays were always pedestrian; since his latest paper is nearly flawless, the <u>obvious conclusion seems to be one of a more advanced student researching and writing at least part of Henry's impressive essay</u>.

  (A) obvious conclusion seems to be one of a more advanced student researching and writing at least part of Henry's impressive essay

  (B) conclusion of a more advanced student researching and writing at least part of Henry's impressive essay seems obvious

  (C) conclusion seems obvious that at least part of Henry's impressive essay was researched and written by a more advanced student

  (D) conclusion of at least part of Henry's impressive essay having been researched and written by a more advanced student seems obvious

  (E) seemingly obvious conclusion is that a more advanced student would have researched and written at least part of Henry's impressive essay

186. To the distress of fans of musical theater, the producers are closing *Meet Pauline*, the first Broadway musical <u>that had been written by a large group of composers and</u> the inspiration for a plethora of similar works that crowded Broadway for years after.

  (A) that had been written by a large group of composers and

  (B) written by a large group of composers and which was

  (C) to be written by a large group of composers and which was

  (D) written by a large group of composers and

  (E) to have been written by a large group of composers and was

187. <u>Based on the customs of countries such as</u> Mexico and an analysis of ancient records, historians have inferred that the Aztecs fed prisoners sumptuous meals before using the prisoners as human sacrifices.

  (A) Based on the customs of countries such as

  (B) On the basis of the customs of countries such as

  (C) Based on the customs of countries like

  (D) On the basis of the customs of countries, like those of

  (E) Based on such customs as those of countries like

188. Golf games often turn out to be more tiring than <u>they originally seemed</u>.

    (A) they originally seemed

    (B) they originally seem to

    (C) they seemingly would tire originally

    (D) it would have seemed originally

    (E) it originally seemed they would

189. Unlike conservatives who wish to substitute abstinence training <u>to full sex education, Mr. Jackson stresses how necessary it is to teach</u> teenagers how to make adult decisions.

    (A) to full sex education, Mr. Jackson stresses how necessary it is to teach

    (B) for full sex education, Mr. Jackson stresses the necessity of teaching

    (C) to full sex education, Mr. Jackson stresses that is necessary to teach

    (D) for full sex education, Mr. Jackson's stress is that it is necessary to teach

    (E) to full sex education, Mr. Jackson's stress is on the necessity of teaching

190. Those watching the libel suit might <u>speculate if the company, swift to take offense might have been</u> as responsible for the perceived slander as the newspaper was.

    (A) speculate if the company, swift to take offense might have been

    (B) speculate if the company, swift to take offense had been

    (C) speculate if, in its swiftness to take offense the company was

    (D) wonder as to whether, in its swiftness to take offense, the company was

    (E) wonder whether the company, swift to take offense, was

191. <u>Added to the increase in monthly wages discussed last spring, the dining hall employees are currently seeking improved insurance coverage.</u>

    (A) Added to the increase in monthly wages discussed last spring, the dining hall employees are currently seeking improved insurance coverage.

    (B) Added to the increase in monthly wages which had been discussed last spring, the employees of the dining hall are currently seeking an improved insurance coverage.

    (C) The dining hall employees are currently seeking improved insurance coverage added to the increase in monthly wages that were discussed last spring.

    (D) In addition to the increase in monthly wages that were discussed last spring, the dining hall employees are currently seeking improved insurance coverage.

    (E) In addition to the increase in monthly wages discussed last spring, the employees of the dining hall are currently seeking improved insurance coverage.

192. Ripe peaches are marked not so much by their color <u>but instead</u> by their firmness and fullness of aroma.

    (A) but instead

    (B) rather than

    (C) than

    (D) as

    (E) so much as

193. Ten percent of Clarkstown South High School students go on to Ivy League colleges, compared with from Clarkstown North High School it is five percent and Nyack High School, Pomona High School, and Ramapo High School it is two percent.

    (A) Ten percent of Clarkstown South High School students go on to Ivy League colleges, compared with from Clarkstown North High School it is five percent and Nyack High School, Pomona High School, and Ramapo High School it is two percent.

    (B) Ten percent of Clarkstown South High School students go on to Ivy League colleges; from Clarkstown North High School it is five percent and from Nyack High School, Pomona High School, and Ramapo High School it is two percent.

    (C) From Clarkstown South High School, ten percent of students go on to Ivy League colleges, compared with five percent from Clarkstown North High School and two percent from Nyack High School, Pomona High School, and Ramapo High School.

    (D) The percentage of students from Clarkstown South High School who go on to Ivy League colleges is ten, compared with Clarkstown North High School's ten, Nyack High School's two, Pomona High School's two, and Ramapo High School's two.

    (E) The percentage of Clarkstown South High School students going on to Ivy League colleges is ten, that from Clarkstown North High School is five, and that from Nyack High School, Pomona High School, and Ramapo High School is two.

194. The sharp contrast in sales of sports memorabilia seen in sports in which most of the participants are male and such sales in sports in which most of the participants are female have demonstrated that women's sports are still lacking dedicated fans.

    (A) seen in sports in which most of the participants are male and such sales in sports in which most of the participants are female have

    (B) seen in sports in which most of the participants are predominately male over those that are predominately female have

    (C) that favors sports in which most of the participants are male over sports in which most of the participants are female have

    (D) that favors sports in which most of the participants are male over sports in which most of the participants are female has

    (E) seen is sports in which most of the participants are male and such sales in sports in which most of the participants are female has

195. The National Organization for Women has insisted that discrimination against women is still rampant in modern society and that unanimous opposition to prejudice is necessary for improving any aspects of the situation.

    (A) that unanimous opposition to prejudice is necessary for improving any aspects of the situation

    (B) that unanimous opposition to prejudice is necessary if any aspects of the situation are to be improved

    (C) that unanimous opposition to prejudice is necessary to improve any aspects of the situation

    (D) unanimous opposition to prejudice is necessary in improving any aspects of the situation

    (E) the prejudice needs to be unanimously opposed so that any aspects of the situation is improved

196. According to the editor of *Elle* magazine, wearing the same clothes as are worn on undersized models will lead to a fashion failure for the plus-siz woman, who should shop at stores such as Lane Bryant that have clothing that will flatter her shape.

    (A) wearing the same clothes as are worn on undersized models will lead to a fashion failure for the plus-size woman, who

    (B) it will lead to a fashion failure for the plus-size woman to wear the same clothes as on the undersized models; they

    (C) fashion failure will result from wearing the same clothes as undersized models to the plus-size woman, who

    (D) fashion failure for the plus-size woman will result from wearing the same clothes as on the undersized models; they

    (E) the plus-size woman wearing the same clothes as are worn on undersized models will lead to fashion failure; they

197. The nutritionist defined an obese individual <u>as one handicapped by a severe excess of weight with difficulty refraining from</u> <u>eating</u>.

   (A)   as one handicapped by a severe excess of weight with difficulty refraining from eating

   (B)   to be one that is handicapped by an excess of weight with difficulty refraining from eating

   (C)   as one that is handicapped by an excess of weight and that has difficulty refraining from eating

   (D)   to have difficulty refraining from eating and being handicapped by a severe excess of weight

   (E)   as having difficulty refraining from eating and handicapped by a severe excess of weight

198. The Constitution of the United States protects more rights <u>for its citizens than does the constitution of any other country</u>, but there are many areas in which it could provide more freedom.

   (A)   for its citizens than does the constitution of any other country

   (B)   to its citizens as the constitution of any other country

   (C)   for its citizens as the constitution of any other country

   (D)   to its citizens as the constitution of any other country

   (E)   for its citizens than the constitution of any other country

199. Answering machines and microwaves are to the modern age <u>just like butler and cook was</u> to the Victorian era.

   (A)   just like butler and cook was

   (B)   as have been a butler and cook

   (C)   what butlers and cooks were

   (D)   what butlers and cooks are

   (E)   just the same as butlers and cooks had been

200. Teachers want students to be as well behaved as possible <u>for the reason that misbehavior on the part of students affect</u> the learning experience of the entire class.

   (A)   for the reason that misbehavior on the part of students affect

   (B)   for the reason because misbehavior on the part of students affects

   (C)   in that misbehavior on the part of students affect

   (D)   because misbehavior on the part of students affects

   (E)   because misbehavior on the parts of students affects

201. After the Communist Revolution in China, the Communist Party <u>embodied the dominant ideology of the Chinese, replacing</u> <u>older ideologies</u> and political systems.

   (A)   embodied the dominant ideology of the Chinese, replacing older ideologies

   (B)   embodied the dominant ideology of the Chinese, replacing ideologies that were older

   (C)   embodies the dominant ideology of the Chinese and it replaced older ideologies

   (D)   embodies the dominant ideology of the Chinese and it replaced ideologies that were older

   (E)   embodies the dominant ideology of the Chinese, having replaced ideologies that were older

202. New spray cans, which do not pollute <u>in the way aerosol cans do, hopefully will reduce</u> levels of pollution.

   (A)   in the way aerosol cans do, hopefully will reduce

   (B)   in the way aerosol cans do, will, it is hoped, reduce

   (C)   like aerosol cans, hopefully will reduce

   (D)   like aerosol cans, would reduce, hopefully

   (E)   such as aerosol cans do, will, it is hoped, reduce

203. With a total population of <u>less than five thousand and fewer</u> well-trained soldiers than ever before, the army base is still unprepared for a real war.

   (A)   less than five thousand and fewer

   (B)   lower than five thousand and less

   (C)   lesser than five thousand and fewer

   (D)   fewer than five thousand and less

   (E)   fewer than five thousand and of fewer

204. During the Stock Market crash in 1929 the run on the banks resulted in thousands of Americans losing hard earned savings <u>on which these depositors can</u> no longer rely.

   (A)   on which these depositors can

   (B)   on which these depositors could

   (C)   that these depositors can

   (D)   because these depositors can

   (E)   for which these depositors could

205. <u>If a song is played on the radio often, a practice favored by popular radio stations,</u> it increases the chance that the singer will become famous.

   (A)   If a song is played on the radio often, a practice favored by popular radio stations, it

   (B)   If a song is played on the radio often, and favored by popular radio stations, it

   (C)   A practice favored by popular radio stations, a song played on the radio often,

   (D)   A song played on the radio often, a practice favored by popular radio stations,

   (E)   The playing of a song on the radio often, and a practice favored by popular radio stations,

206. Most Americans surveyed think that international environmental treaties are useless now but <u>that they will, or could,</u> be useful in the future.

   (A)   that they will, or could,

   (B)   that they would, or could

   (C)   they will be or could,

   (D)   think that they will be or could

   (E)   think the treaties will be or could

207. Marine biologists believe that the sperm whale's head, from which hunters <u>are thought to have first extracted</u> oil, serves as an acoustic resonator for whale songs.

    (A)   are thought to have first extracted

    (B)   were thought first to extract

    (C)   were thought at first to extract

    (D)   are thought of as first extracting

    (E)   were thought to first extract

208. Contrary to popular opinion, the war on terrorism is <u>leading neither to better times for investing, more of a relaxed sense of national security, or</u> actually destroying the terrorists.

    (A)   leading neither to better times for investing, more of a relaxed sense of national security, or

    (B)   leading neither to better times for investing nor a more relaxed sense of national security, or

    (C)   not leading to either better times for investing nor to more of a relaxed sense of national security, and neither is it

    (D)   not leading to better times for investing, more of a relaxed sense of national security, and it is not

    (E)   not leading to better times for investing or to a more relaxed sense of national security, nor is it

209. Already controversial figures in the media, the Raelians advocate <u>that humans be cloned, a practice that, to the Raelians, reflects the origin of human life as coming from cloning practices used by aliens thousands of years ago.</u>

    (A)   that humans be cloned, a practice that, to the Raelians, reflects the origin of human life as coming from cloning practices used by aliens thousands of years ago.

    (B)   that humans practice cloning reflecting the origin of human life as coming from cloning practices used by aliens thousands of years ago.

    (C)   humans be cloned which was a practice which reflect the origin of human life as coming from cloning practices used by aliens thousands of years ago.

    (D)   cloning of humans be practiced to reflect the origin of human life as coming from cloning practices used by aliens thousands of years ago.

    (E)   humans return to the practice of cloning to reflect the origin of human life as coming from cloning practices used by aliens thousands of years ago.

210. If additional sources of deuterium are found, <u>it will expand the amount that can be used as heavy water for nuclear reactors and reduce the cost of energy,</u> even if the sources are not immediately mined.

    (A)   it will expand the amount that can be used as heavy water for nuclear reactors and reduce the cost of energy

    (B)   that amount that is able to used as heavy water for nuclear reactors will expand and the cost of energy will be reduced

    (C)   it will cause an increase in the amount that is able to be used as heavy water for nuclear reactors and a reduction in the cost of energy

    (D)   the amount that can be used as heavy water for nuclear reactors will increase and the cost of energy will drop

    (E)   it will increase the amount of deuterium that can be used as heavy water for nuclear reactors and cause a drop in the cost of energy

211. Astronomical occurrences can be viewed in a religious light; <u>many people are known to rekindle their faith after the observation of a meteor shower</u>.

   (A) many people are known to rekindle their faith after the observation of a meteor shower

   (B) many people are known to have rekindled their faith once a meteor shower has been observed

   (C) there are many known people who have rekindled their faith once a meteor shower has been observed

   (D) after a meteor shower is observed, there are many known people who have rekindled their faith

   (E) rekindling their faith is known for many people after a meteor shower is observed

212. Following the inordinate number of post-surgery complications, medical investigators and insurance fraud agents concluded that many medical personnel work an excessive amount of <u>overtime that has the potential of causing</u> errors in decision-making.

   (A) overtime that has the potential of causing

   (B) overtime that has the potential to cause

   (C) overtime that potentially can cause

   (D) overtime, a practice that has the potential for causing

   (E) overtime, a practice that can, potentially, cause

213. Some analysts of the latest technological advances argue that technology moves forward not so much <u>because of great sparks of ideas but because of</u> smaller contributions, such as improved practices, better laboratories and more knowledgeable designers.

   (A) because of great sparks of ideas but because of

   (B) because of great sparks of ideas as the results of

   (C) because of great sparks of ideas as because of

   (D) through great sparks of ideas but through

   (E) through great sparks of ideas but results from

214. Conquistadors began the destruction of South American cities, <u>which was characterized by ornate gold decorations, large populations</u>, and wonderful natural beauties .

   (A) which was characterized by ornate gold decorations, large populations

   (B) which was characterized by ornate gold decorations and large populations

   (C) which were characterized by ornate gold decorations, large populations

   (D) being characterized by ornate gold decorations and large populations

   (E) characterized by ornate gold decorations, large populations

215. <u>Although somewhat damaged, the librarians were able to read</u> the cover of the aging tome.

   (A) Although somewhat damaged, the librarians were able to read

   (B) Although somewhat damaged, the librarians had read

   (C) Although it had been somewhat damaged, the librarians were able to read

   (D) Somewhat damaged though it had been, the librarians had been able to read

   (E) Damaged somewhat, the librarians were able to read

216. At the end of the Second World War, the United States allocated huge sums of money to cover the <u>costs of reconstruction that it expected to undertake in Europe as a result of negotiations</u> with European governments.

    (A) costs of reconstruction that it expected to undertake in Europe as a result of negotiations

    (B) costly reconstruction it expected to undertake in Europe as a result from negotiations

    (C) costing reconstructions expected to be undertaken in Europe as a result of negotiating

    (D) negotiated costs in reconstruction it expected to undertake in Europe

    (E) costs expected to be undertaken in reconstruction in Europe from negotiating

217. <u>For all her asserted scorn of such books,</u> Jeanette had a bookcase full of romance novels.

    (A) For all her asserted scorn of such books,

    (B) Having always asserted scorn for such books,

    (C) All such books were, she asserted, scorned, and

    (D) Asserting that all such books were scorned,

    (E) In spite of assertions of scorning all such activities,

218. The <u>immolated monk, thought by some detectives to have occurred</u> around midnight, was a crucial factor in igniting the riots which ensued.

    (A) The immolated monk, thought by some detectives to have occurred

    (B) The immolated monk, which some detectives have thought to occur

    (C) Immolating the monk, occurred by some detectives at

    (D) The immolation of the monk, thought by some detectives to have occurred

    (E) The immolated monk, thought by some detectives to have been

219. By stealing atomic bomb secrets the Rosenbergs readily demonstrated their desire <u>to be in sympathy with</u> the communist regime.

    (A) to be in sympathy with

    (B) to sympathize with

    (C) for sympathizing with

    (D) that they should, sympathize with

    (E) that they should have sympathy for

220. Standardized test scores of minorities are <u>well below that of white students in spite of economic differences that are shrinking</u> between the races.

    (A) well below that of white students in spite of economic differences that are shrinking

    (B) much below that of white students' despite economic differences shrinking

    (C) much below white students in spite of shrinking economic differences

    (D) well below those of white students in spite of shrinking economic differences

    (E) below white students' despite their economic differences that are shrinking

221. The victories of the Canadian hockey teams were marked not so much by their brute effort <u>as it was by</u> their strategic planning.

- **(A)** as it was by
- **(B)** and also by
- **(C)** as by
- **(D)** and equally by
- **(E)** as there was

222. Plutonium and U235 result from the nuclear interchange of energies between U238 <u>with neutrons to produce extreme radiation and high temperatures.</u>

- **(A)** with neutrons to produce extreme radiation and high temperatures
- **(B)** with neutrons producing extreme radiation and high temperatures
- **(C)** and neutrons which has produced extreme radiation and high temperatures
- **(D)** and neutrons which have produced extreme radiation and high temperatures
- **(E)** and neutrons and are associated with extreme radiation and high temperatures produced by the interchange

223. It is common in Helen Hayes Theater, as <u>in almost every local theater, the opinion of administrators has played at least as large a part in deciding what to perform as has</u> the desires of the public.

- **(A)** in almost every local theater, the opinion of administrators has played at least as large a part in deciding what to perform as has
- **(B)** in almost every local theater, that the opinion of administrators has played at least as large a part in deciding what to perform as has
- **(C)** it is in almost every local theater, that the opinion of administrators has played at least as large a part in deciding what to perform as have
- **(D)** is in almost every local theater, that the opinion of administrators have played at least as large a part in deciding what to perform as have
- **(E)** it is in almost every local theater, the opinion of administrators has played at least as large a part in deciding what to perform as has

224. In disagreeing with the findings of the Warren Commission, the American public must take care to to avoid moving the target of criticism from <u>government agencies collaborating in a coup d'etat to collaborating to overthrow foreign governments.</u>

- **(A)** government agencies collaborating in a coup d'etat to collaborating to overthrow foreign governments
- **(B)** government agencies collaborating in a coup d'etat to foreign governments being overthrown with collaboration
- **(C)** the collaboration of government agencies in a coup d'etat to the collaboration of the agencies in overthrowing foreign governments
- **(D)** collaboration of government agencies by coup d'etat with foreign governments, that are overthrown
- **(E)** a coup d'etat that government agencies collaborate in to collaboration that overthrows foreign governments

225. Despite Britain's obvious interest in using oil to power the Royal Navy, the creation of a national oil company lagged behind the Dutch and the Americans and <u>developed only after when oil well construction was supported by foreign speculators.</u>

- **(A)** developed only after when oil well construction was supported by foreign speculators
- **(B)** developed only after foreign speculators supported oil well construction
- **(C)** developed only after foreign speculators' support of oil well construction by foreign speculators
- **(D)** develops only at the time after the supporting of oil well construction by foreign speculators
- **(E)** developed only after there being foreign speculators' support of oil well construction

226. The chemicals that enter your body by smoking cigarettes not only gather in your lungs, thereby reducing the amount of air that you can absorb, <u>and also damage or destroy</u> sensitive tissue in your trachea and mouth.

    (A)   and also damage or destroy

    (B)   as well as damaging or destroying

    (C)   but they also cause damage or destroy

    (D)   but also damage or destroy

    (E)   but also causing damage or destroying

227. There has been a drastic <u>decrease in crime caused by increasing the surveillance by undercover detectives against</u> drug dealers.

    (A)   decrease in crime caused by increasing the surveillance by undercover detectives against

    (B)   decrease in crime because of increased surveillance by undercover detectives of

    (C)   decreasing in crime because of increasing surveillance by undercover detectives to

    (D)   crime decrease caused by increasing surveillance by undercover detectives against

    (E)   crime decrease because of increased surveillance by undercover detectives to

228. Because many different cultures have different cultural norms, misunderstandings <u>among different cultures are far greater as that among individuals from</u> the same culture: slurping one's soup, in Japan a gesture of appreciation for the cook, is unforgivably rude in America.

    (A)   among different cultures are far greater as that among individuals from

    (B)   among different cultures are far greater than that among individuals from

    (C)   among different cultures are far greater than those among individuals of

    (D)   between different cultures are far more than that between individuals of

    (E)   between different cultures are greater by far than is that between individuals from

229. At a time when many English farmers had been virtually bankrupted by certain epidemics they were further required <u>to have destroyed animals with mad cow disease or foot and mouth disease</u>.

    (A)   to have destroyed animals with mad cow disease or foot and mouth disease

    (B)   to have had destroyed animals with mad cow disease or foot and mouth disease

    (C)   either to have had destroyed animals with mad cow disease or foot and mouth disease

    (D)   to destroy animals with either mad cow disease or foot and mouth disease

    (E)   either to destroy animals with mad cow disease or foot and mouth disease

230. Producers of Broadway shows have never before been able to stage <u>so extravagant productions of the kind they do today</u>.

    (A)   so extravagant productions of the kind they do today

    (B)   so extravagant productions as they are today

    (C)   such extravagant productions as they do today

    (D)   such extravagant productions of the kind today's have

    (E)   so extravagant a production of the kind they can today

231. When it becomes more frequent to have parents who both earn substantial incomes, paying for children's college tuition will become easier.

   (A) it becomes more frequent to have parents who both earn substantial incomes

   (B) it becomes more frequent to have parents both earning substantial incomes

   (C) it becomes more common that both parents should be earning substantial incomes

   (D) it becomes more common for both parents to earn substantial incomes

   (E) couples in which both of the parents earning substantial incomes become more common

232. Like the wines from Germany, also an area with a temperate climate, wineries in upstate New York create rich, full-bodie wines.

   (A) Like the wines from Germany, also an area with a temperate climate, wineries in upstate New York create rich, full-bodied wines.

   (B) Wineries in upstate New York create rich, full-bodied wines similar to the wines from Germany, which, like upstate New York, is an area with a temperate climate.

   (C) Wineries in upstate New York create rich, full-bodied wines similar to Germany's, which, like upstate New York, is an area with a temperate climate.

   (D) Like Germany's wines, wineries in upstate New York, also an area with a temperate climate, create rich, full-bodied wines.

   (E) Similar to those from Germany, wineries in upstate New York, also an area with a temperate climate, create rich, full-bodied wines.

233. Since 1990 there are three times as many cases of West Nile virus diagnosed, and there has been no progress in the search for a vaccine.

   (A) Since 1990 there are three times as many cases of West Nile virus diagnosed

   (B) The diagnosis of cases of West Nile virus was only one-third in 1990

   (C) The diagnosis of cases of West Nile virus has increased three times from 1990 on

   (D) Tripling since 1990, there are now three times as many cases of West Nile virus diagnosed

   (E) The number of diagnoses of West Nile virus has tripled since 1990

234. Many people discover a need for glasses in middle age, a consequence of sitting too close to the television screen for long periods of time.

   (A) a consequence of sitting too close to the television screen for long periods of time

   (B) a consequence from sitting for long periods of time too near to the television screen

   (C) a consequence which resulted from sitting too close to the television screen for long periods of time

   (D) damaged from sitting too near to the television screen for long periods of time

   (E) damaged because they sat too close to the television screen for long periods of time

235. The teacher lost control of her classroom as a result of poor discipline, a dull curriculum, as well as the destructive effects of student misbehavior that is persistent.

   (A) as well as the destructive effects of student misbehavior that is persistent

   (B) and the destructive effect of student misbehavior that is persistent

   (C) but persistent student misbehavior has had a destructive effect too

   (D) and the destructive effects of persistent student misbehavior

   (E) as well as the destructive effects of student misbehavior that persists

236. Touching on subjects like greed and corruption in corporate America and delivering a scathing condemnation of contemporary capitalism, <u>the novel will depict</u> one blue-collar man's attempts to succeed in the business world.

   (A)   the novel will depict

   (B)   the novel shall depict

   (C)   there will be a novel depicting

   (D)   it is a novel that depicts

   (E)   it will be a novel that depicts

237. During the internet boom in the 1990's, even a relatively small move in the tech market fooled many <u>investors having bought on rumor; they had to sell, and</u> the dumping of stock quickly revealed how over-valued many of the companies were.

   (A)   investors having bought on rumor; they had to sell, and

   (B)   investors who had bought on rumor; having had to sell,

   (C)   investors who had bought on rumor; they had to sell, and

   (D)   investors, those who had bought on rumor; these investors had to sell, and

   (E)   investors, who, having bought on rumor and having to sell,

238. The ways children adapt to new situations tell psychologists more about <u>how they absorb information than</u> the children's I.Q.s.

   (A)   how they absorb information than

   (B)   how one absorbs information than

   (C)   how children absorb information than do

   (D)   absorbing information than

   (E)   their information absorption than do

239. Although the new laws to protect children will be expensive to enforce, Senator Bailey believes that the laws are still practical, <u>on the basis that child abductions should be prevented</u>.

   (A)   on the basis that child abductions should be prevented

   (B)   on the grounds of preventing child abductions alone

   (C)   solely in that child abductions should be prevented

   (D)   while the abductions of children should be prevented

   (E)   if only because abductions of children should be prevented

240. In a recent survey, *Physical Fitness Weekly* found that people exercising daily consider themselves <u>no healthier than do people exercising</u> three to five times a week.

   (A)   no healthier than do people exercising

   (B)   not any healthier than do people exercising

   (C)   not any healthier than do people who exercise

   (D)   no healthier than are people who are exercising

   (E)   not as healthy as are people who exercise

241. <u>It may someday be feasible to try to retrieve organisms from tiny undersea vents</u>, but at the present time submersibles require such thick walls to withstand the high pressure that it is impossible.

   (A) It may someday be feasible to try to retrieve organisms from tiny undersea vents

   (B) Someday, it may be feasible to try and retrieve organisms from tiny undersea vents

   (C) Trying to retrieve organisms out of tiny undersea vents may someday be feasible

   (D) To try for the retrieval of organisms out of tiny undersea vents may someday be feasible

   (E) Retrieving organisms out of tiny undersea vents may be feasible to try someday

242. The great directors that create cult favorites are similar to <u>the world-clas conductors directing</u> orchestras; both are critical in molding the talents of many individuals into a cohesive and beautiful form.

   (A) the world-class conductors directing

   (B) the world-class conductor which directs

   (C) world-class conductors who direct

   (D) ones to direct the world-class conductors

   (E) ones used in directing the world-class conductors

243. The weather predictions delivered on television are usually reliable, but winds, <u>storms that could not be foreseen, and ocean currents often cause much more extreme weather conditions than they had</u> expected.

   (A) storms that could not be foreseen, and ocean currents often cause much more extreme weather conditions than they had

   (B) storms that cannot be foreseen, and ocean currents often cause much more extreme weather conditions than

   (C) unforeseeable storms, and ocean currents are the cause of much more extreme weather conditions than they had

   (D) storms that are not foreseeable, and ocean currents often cause much more extreme weather conditions than they had

   (E) unforeseeable storms, and ocean currents often cause much more extreme weather conditions than they had

244. <u>To witness</u> the atrocious conditions suffered by abandoned children in Chinese orphanages is to see the inhumanity of the Communist government's one-child policy.

   (A) To witness

   (B) Witnessing

   (C) Having witnessed

   (D) Once one witnesses

   (E) To have witnessed

245. A male musician can find a career as a solo performer, an orchestra member, or a music teacher after he graduates from college with a degree in music, depending on his talent.

- **(A)** A male musician can find a career as a solo performer, an orchestra member, or a music teacher after he graduates from college with a degree in music, depending on his talent.
- **(B)** After graduating from college with a degree in music, depending on his talent, a male musician can find a career as a solo performer, an orchestra member, or a music teacher.
- **(C)** After graduating from college with a degree in music, a male musician's talent will determine if he can find a career as a solo performer, an orchestra member, or a music teacher.
- **(D)** Talent determines whether a male musician, after graduating from college with a degree in music, can find a career as a solo performer, an orchestra member, or a music teacher.
- **(E)** The talent of a male musician, after graduating from college with a degree in music, will determine whether he can find a career as a solo performer, an orchestra member, or a music teacher.

246. Poor reading skills among students of inner-city schools have not resulted from failures in teaching but insufficiently supportive home environments.

- **(A)** not resulted from failures in teaching but
- **(B)** resulted not from failures in teaching but from
- **(C)** resulted from failures not in teaching but
- **(D)** resulted from failures not in teaching but have stemmed from
- **(E)** resulted not from failures in teaching but have stemmed from

247. The unsupervised party seeming to be innocuous teenage fun, Judith Larkin, mother of two well-behaved daughters, thought nothing of allowing her children to attend it after the prom.

- **(A)** The unsupervised party seeming to be
- **(B)** As the unsupervised party was
- **(C)** In that the unsupervised party seemed
- **(D)** Since the unsupervised party was
- **(E)** Because the unsupervised party seemed to be

248. Since her husband began playing violin, Molly has become much more expert in distinguishing a tuned instrument and an out of tune one, a Stradivarius and a student rental.

- **(A)** much more expert in distinguishing a tuned instrument and an out of tune one, a Stradivarius and
- **(B)** far more expert in distinguishing a tuned instrument from an out of tune one, a Stradivarius from
- **(C)** much more expert when it comes to distinguishing a tuned instrument and an out of tune one, a Stradivarius from
- **(D)** far more expert in distinguishing a tuned instrument and an out of tune one, a Stradivarius and
- **(E)** far more the expert when it comes to distinguishing between a tuned instrument, an out of tune one, a Stradivarius, and

249. Although the music superstar agreed to a new contract, <u>she says that it must be posted on her public website so that both her new listeners and her old fans will know what is</u> going on behind the scenes.

    (A)   she says that it must be posted on her public website so that both her new listeners and her old fans will know what is

    (B)   she says it had to be posted on her public website so that both her new listeners and her old fans knows what is

    (C)   sshe says that they would have to post the contract on her public website so that her new listeners and her old fans knew what was

    (D)   she says that the contract would have to be posted on her public website so that both her new listeners and her old fans would know what was

    (E)   saying that the contract had to be posted on her public website so that both new listeners and old fans would know what had been

250. With just a few quick slashes of the sword, <u>her opponents were defeated by the fencer, capitalizing on their slowness.</u>

    (A)   her opponents were defeated by the fencer, capitalizing on their slowness

    (B)   the fencer defeated her opponents, capitalizing on their slowness

    (C)   the fencer capitalized on the slowness of her opponents, defeating them

    (D)   the fencer defeated her opponents and also capitalized on their slowness

    (E)   her opponents and their slowness were defeated by the fencer

Chapter 2

Verbal Training Set II - Critical Reasoning

1. Bio-chemists at Perck Pharma Corporation have discovered a new type of allergy. Their research confirms that it is not just caused by pollen of a certain flower, as it was thought. In addition, the flower has to be pollinated by a certain kind of bee to cause the allergy.

    Which of the following would most likely support the data's implication?

    (A)   In the absence of the bee, the pollen does not cause allergic reactions.

    (B)   The bee has been shown to be a critical element in the reproduction of the particular flower.

    (C)   Many cases of the allergy have been observed only in the presence of the bee.

    (D)   In cases in which the allergy does not develop, the flower will grow without the presence of the bee.

    (E)   The onset of the allergy is usually caused by the flower even if the pollen is not present.

    The next two questions are based on the following:

2. Investing in fishing-boats could be very profitable at this time. A survey made by 'Hook, Line & Sinker' magazine shows that 75 percent of the magazine's readers want to buy a new fishing-boat during the summer. However, fishing-boat manufacturers can only produce enough boats to satisfy 30% of total potential buyers.

    Which of the following, if true, reveals a weakness in the evidence cited above?

    (A)   The fishing-boat industry is a highly labor-intensive business.

    (B)   Fishing-boats are not evenly distributed across the country.

    (C)   The number of fishermen who buy fishing-boats has been growing each year for the past six years.

    (D)   Readers of 'Hook, Line & Sinker' magazine are more likely than other consumers to want a fishing-boat.

    (E)   'Hook, Line & Sinker' magazine includes both articles about fishing and articles about building fishing-boats.

3. Which of the following, if true, would undermine the soundness of the investment advice in the paragraph above?

    (A)   Fishing-boats cost too much for the average fisherman.

    (B)   Approximately a quarter of all fishermen do not use fishing-boats.

    (C)   Approximately a quarter of all fishermen buy fishing-boats that can accommodate 2-3 fishermen.

    (D)   Only half of all fishermen use a fishing-boat.

    (E)   Only half of those who say they want to buy a fishing-boat actually end up buying one.

4. A study made by a psychologist shows that spending too much time in front of a computer causes insomnia. Two groups of adults took part in this study. During the study the first group spent 3 hours or less per day working on a computer; the second group spent 6 hours or more working on a computer. A greater proportion of the second group had trouble falling asleep during the period of the study than members from the first group.

    Which of the following, if true of the adults in the study, most challenges the psychologist's conclusion?

    (A)   Some adults who spent more than 6 hours per day working on a computer had fewer problems falling asleep than others in the same group.

    (B)   Some adults who spent 3 hours per day working on a computer did not have problems falling asleep.

    (C)   Some adults voluntarily stopped spending too much time in front of a computer after the study.

    (D)   Some adults spent time working on the computer without any breaks, while others took frequent breaks.

    (E)   Many of the adults in the second group had problems falling asleep before the study began.

5. Although we manufacture one hundred types of mobile phones, we currently limit our stock to only the ten best-selling models. Our plan is to increase the number of mobile phones we sell by expanding our stock to contain the twelve most popular types.

    Which of the following, if true, points out a major weakness in the plan above?

    (A) The capabilities of the four most popular mobile phones are approximately equivalent, with no model having consistent superiority in all respects.

    (B) The nine most popular types of mobile phones account for almost all mobile phones sold.

    (C) As the users of mobile phones have become more sophisticated, they are more willing to buy less well-known models.

    (D) Less popular types of mobile phones often provide less profit to the retailer because prices must be discounted to attract customers.

    (E) The leading type of mobile phone has been losing market position to less popular types that offer similar capabilities for less money.

6. In a certain socialist country, party members earn twice as much as non-party members do. But party members happen to work in the businesses that generally have higher wages. Non-party members who also work in these particular businesses earn about as much as party members. Therefore, higher incomes do not necessarily result from the connection with the party.

    Which of the following, if true, most seriously weakens the argument above?

    (A) Besides wage increases, party members also receive other benefits.

    (B) Some of the most highly paid business people in that country are capitalist executives in special economic zones and are not party members.

    (C) Wages in many industries vary from one part of the country to another, whether or not workers are in the party.

    (D) Non-party members in a given industry often receive higher wage as a result of the lobbying done by party members, which in turn increases the wage for the entire industry.

    (E) Becoming a member of the party within a given industry or business often encourages others to follow suit.

7. The Hale Burton Oil Pipeline Construction Corporation has had a bad quarter. Rather than lay off workers to cut costs, however, it will simply defer salaries for 30 days and hold them in a mutual fund to pick up interest to cover expenses. By doing this the company and its employees will avoid the negative consequences often associated with earning shortfalls.

    Which of the following, if true, is the best criticism of the corporation's plan?

    (A) Employees will not be able to control which mutual funds the salaries will be diverted into.

    (B) The corporation cannot save money by cutting staff because it is already understaffed.

    (C) Some employees will need to borrow money to hold them over until the 30 days are up and they will consequently have 30 days of interest on these loans.

    (D) Some employees will not be affected by the rollover because they have savings.

    (E) The corporation's budget was cut by 15% last year.

8. Countries that legalized the drug X twenty years ago, because a significant percentage of the population had been using X on a daily basis without any apparent harm to the community at large, reset the benchmark for what is appropriate and proper behavior among their citizens. Since X's legalization, there has been an increase in manic depression, suicide and certain kinds of cancer. In order for Andovia, a country that has not yet legalized X, to avoid the development of such undesirable tendencies and prevent the social problems stemming from broad usage of drug X, it should close its borders and not issue visas to any tourists from countries where drug X is legal.

Which of the following, if true, most seriously weakens the argument above?

(A) Drug X emits a faint smell that makes it very difficult for trained canines to identify at border control points.

(B) The detrimental side effects of drug X only become visible after several years of usage.

(C) Andovia is surrounded on three sides by water, but has an excellent naval border police force.

(D) Drug X resembles several other designer drugs currently on the market.

(E) Drug X is very easy to extract chemically from certain consumer products and is taken in droplet size doses that can easily be camouflaged as items such as hairspray or nail polish remover.

9. The Flerenchian government decided to limit the import of chocolate from the four countries which export the greatest amount of chocolate to Flerenchia. An analyst hired by the government maintains that in the near future this will cause a large increase in domestic sales of chocolate produced in Flerenchia.

Which of the following, if true, would most likely render this prediction inaccurate?

(A) A new tax bill that would discourage foreign investment in the chocolate industry is being debated by the Flerenchian government.

(B) Flerenchian companies' orders for milk chocolates, which account for 60 percent of sales by chocolate companies, rose faster than for other types of chocolates during the past year.

(C) Worldwide orders for chocolate made in Flerenchia dropped by more than 15 percent during the past year.

(D) Substantial inventories of foreign-made chocolate were stockpiled in Flerenchia during the past year.

(E) Companies in the chocolate industries of many countries showed a significantly increased demand for chocolate during the past year.

10. A private bus company wanted to increase profits. For twenty years it worked to make its buses more economical and faster by reducing the number of bus stops. Although the company was in some measure successful, the economy grew worse, and the industry almost went bankrupt. Assumptions and realities were vastly different. The real problem came not from passengers who wanted faster transport but from the number of passengers who stopped using the bus service because of the limited number of bus stops.

Which of the actions below would most likely lead to a solution to the problem faced by the bus company, as it is analyzed above?

(A) Providing buses with engines that run on a cheaper type of fuel than that traditionally used.

(B) Providing double-decker buses that will stop at as many more bus stops as possible.

(C) Providing buses that have more seating room than any other existing bus.

(D) Implementing a system to ensure that buses are loaded to capacity.

(E) Implementing a market plan that focuses on routes that are known to be less used by other bus companies.

11. According to a recent report on higher education in the United States, the fifteen universities with the highest annual tuition fees also gave out the largest financial aid awards to incoming students with outstanding achievements. Because of a belief in equal opportunity, these universities are able to redistribute resources from those who can give them to those who deserve them by virtue of merits.

Which of the following can be correctly inferred from the statement above?

(A) Following a belief in equal opportunity is a good way to mask charging higher tuition fees.

(B) It is possible for a university that believes in equal opportunity to put different financial demands on different students.

(C) A university that offers large financial aid awards must do so because it believes in equal opportunity.

(D) Universities that have high tuition fees tend to give out little financial aid.

(E) Universities that have large endowments tend to give out lots of financial aid.

12. An independent analyst asserts that the new Pokia digital camera for mobile phones is more precise, of higher quality and costs less than any of the popular competing models. As a result, Pokia will become the more desirable, low-priced alternative to currently existing models of digital cameras.

Which of the following, if true, would most challenge the argument above?

(A) Many retailers already carry one or more low-priced digital cameras and are disinclined to carry another.

(B) Several lower-priced models of digital cameras will soon be introduced by other mobile phone manufacturers.

(C) The Pokia Corporation's digital camera can be used in conjunction with higher-priced mobile phones manufactured by other companies.

(D) Most of the individuals and companies that would be expected to make up the potential market for the Pokia digital camera have already fulfilled their digital camera needs.

(E) The independent analyst whose views were incorporated in the statement above has used measures of quality that are not universally accepted by the consumer public.

13. Which of the following best completes the passage below?

Since an experienced, top-rated race car driver is now constantly losing a race he once won before he acquired a certain race car, he plans to junk the race car he is currently using and replace it with a better model. The improved and new race car model is more likely to improve the race car driver's performance than any other factor because

(A) the driver may have new personal problems that have nothing to do with his car's performance

(B) races tend to emphasize quality of the car over quality of the driver

(C) decisions to switch race cars should be based on that particular model's success rate

(D) the driver may not necessarily have been able to overcome other obstacles during recent races

(E) improved race cars are very expensive and difficult for many teams to afford

The following two questions are based on the following text:

Southern Haul Cargo Railway owns all of the railroad tracks in the city of Woe-be-gone, Idaho. Because of Woe-be-gone's sudden population explosion, Southern Haul Cargo is planning to make a Metropolitan Rail & Subway system using its pre-existing tracks. The city council has concluded, however, that if the cargo railway were to offer subway transport, the transport system would have an unfair advantage over the city's existing bus routes, because Southern Haul Cargo's subway system could be subsidized by the profits of their monopoly on cargo transport.

14. Which of the following, if true, would ease the city's fear of unfair competition?

   (A) In order to use existing tracks for a passenger transport system, the cargo railway would need to modernize tracks and build stations, a process so expensive it would virtually wipe out all the profit from their monopoly for the foreseeable future.

   (B) If the cargo railway were to offer subway transport within a particular area, it would have a monopoly within that area.

   (C) The cost of transport by railway-tracks, whether provided by trains or subway, rises only marginally as more passengers use this form of transport.

   (D) Bus transport is available for the same subway routes and costs much less. However, it is much slower.

   (E) Subway transport will never be able to compete with automobile transport, especially as more people have cars now than ever before.

15. Based on the information given above, which of the following questions can be answered?

   (A) Is a cargo railway as efficient as a subway in providing transport by rail?

   (B) If the cargo railway were allowed to provide bus transport, would it want to do so?

   (C) Does the city believe that Southern Haul Cargo Railway makes a profit on cargo transport?

   (D) Is the cargo railway forbidden to offer bus transport?

   (E) Is it expected that the cargo railway will have a long-term monopoly on commuter traffic?

16. In 1999, America Mart, which previously only sold through retail outlets, began selling on the internet while keeping its retail stores open. Total sales increased in 1999, but profits were less than in 1998.

Which of the following, if true, contributes most to explaining why America Mart's profits were more in 1998 than in 1999?

   (A) There was a two percent increase in sales tax in 1999 that consumers had to pay on all retail purchases.

   (B) A greater number of promotions for their internet site were made available to previous customers than to people who had never shopped at America Mart before.

   (C) In 1999, America Mart's wholesale purchase costs increased by a smaller amount than the selling price of goods on their internet site.

   (D) Customers who had never previously purchased products from America Mart purchased, on average, fewer products in 1999 than previous customers did.

   (E) The increase in costs due to setting up the web site in 1999 was greater than the increase in revenue from sales in 1999.

17. In the Piedmont Elementary School for Gifted Children, Jonathan is better than 75% of the students in his physics class. Homer is in the top ten. Alexander is not in the top 10%, but he is better than 33% of all the students in the class. Aristotle is better than 90% of the students.

If the information above is true, which of the following must also be true?

   (A)   Jonathan is better than Homer.

   (B)   Homer is better than Aristotle.

   (C)   Aristotle is better than Alexander.

   (D)   Jonathan is better than Aristotle.

   (E)   Alexander is better than Jonathan.

The following two questions are based on the following text:

Automobile manufacturers defend their substitution of steel frames in cars with cheaper plastic components by claiming that consumer demand is ruled by a desire for light cars with crumple zones rather than as a result of corporate profit motives. However, if this trend were true, then carbon reinforced tubing, which is lighter than steel and stronger, would be available as an option. It is not.

18. Which of the following, if true, best explains how the automobile manufacturers' claim about consumer desire for lighter and stronger materials could be true and maintain the exclusion of carbon tubing from the market?

   (A)   Most consumers prefer steel to plastic components because of their durability.

   (B)   Prototypes of vehicles with carbon tubing have not been shown at major auto shows.

   (C)   The manufacturing process for plastic frame components and carbon tubing is quite different than for traditional steel frames.

   (D)   Automobile manufacturers have not yet resolved certain quality control problems in production of carbon tubing in high volumes.

   (E)   Carbon is more expensive than steel.

19. Which of the following, if true, would most strengthen the argument against the automobile manufacturer's claim?

   (A)   When carbon tubing was introduced in the market place, it was not yet commercially viable to produce it in large volumes.

   (B)   Automobile companies are reluctant to invest in high volume industrial technology to produce carbon tubing until profits from the sale of small scale commercial carbon products, such as bicycle frames, have stabilized.

   (C)   Some types of carbon tubing for sports equipment are in such high demand that there is a back log of several weeks for orders.

   (D)   Because carbon tubing has entirely different chemical properties from plastic frame components, new construction techniques will be required for automobiles.

   (E)   Any valid comparison among steel, plastic and carbon frames must be based on identical performance measures.

20. An electric piano designed to have perfect frequency for each note would sound different than the best Baldwin or Steinbach Grand Piano currently available.

To professional pianists, a piano that sounds different from the best Grand Pianos sounds less like a piano and therefore worse than the best-sounding existing pianos.

Professional pianists are the only accepted judges of the quality of pianos.

Which of the following would be best supported by these statements?

(A) Only amateur pianists should be asked to judge the sound of electric pianos.

(B) Professional pianists assist in designing electric pianos.

(C) The best sounding grand pianos have been around for over one hundred years.

(D) It is currently impossible to create an electric piano that accepted judges will evaluate as being an improvement on existing grand pianos.

(E) It is possible to create an electric piano that sounds better to everyone except a professional pianist.

21. Icarus Airline Manufacturing Corporation has continuously made greater profits by supplying airlines with quality airplanes which are equipped with increased seating capacity. In an effort to continue this financial trend, the company is set to launch a double-decker jumbo jet.

The plan of the company as described above assumes all of the following EXCEPT:

(A) The demand for air travel will increase in the future.

(B) Increased production expenses for the new jumbo jet will be offset by increased revenues.

(C) Passengers have no preference between the new double-decker jumbo jet and the previous models in the market.

(D) The new jumbo jet will be technologically unreliable once in operation, resulting in unexpected costs or unrealized revenues.

(E) The new jumbo jet will not require substantial new training of the pilots or building new parking space at the airports.

22. Many airlines have been pushing the federal government for assurances of greater security in case of terrorist attacks onboard flights. One of these airlines expects the improved security to help increase revenue by $20 million a year, mostly from people who...

Which of the following most logically completes the statement above?

(A) are afraid of traveling by plane because of terrorist attacks

(B) travel by train in the summer

(C) spend more money on traveling

(D) spend less money on traveling

(E) travel by plane when they are pressed for time

23. A teacher in an English literature class analyzed answers given by her students on a written test and concluded that their answers for a given essay were right, on average, 60% of the time.

The conclusion above depends on the presumption that _____

(A) literature classes can teach students successfully even if they are only right a fraction of the time.

(B) teachers that analyze the success of their students are just as good teachers as those that don't.

(C) teachers consistently teaching literature must be careful in giving essay tests to avoid the presumption that their point of view is always correct.

(D) answers to essays on a literature exam are just as likely to be correct as they are to be incorrect.

(E) it is possible to classify an answer to an essay question as being either right or wrong.

24. John, an expert in game theory, predicts that negotiations cannot be resolved unless one party is willing to concede a symbolic step. He also believes that when a symbolic step of concession is taken, negotiations will be resolved. Other game theory experts, however, believe that these results do not take other variables into account.

Which of the following, if true, best supports the contention in the last sentence?

   (A)   Predicting the success of a particular negotiation requires specifying the goal of the negotiation.

   (B)   Judging the outcome of a particular negotiation requires knowing about other negotiations that have taken place in the past.

   (C)   Learning whether a certain negotiation strategy is good requires observing how that strategy works through several negotiating sessions.

   (D)   Parties who are willing to take a symbolic step are more likely to complete negotiations successfully for other reasons.

   (E)   Making a negotiation successful requires knowing the context of symbolic steps that a party in the negotiations might desire.

25. When a major fire occurs in the city of Springfield, the number of media reports about fires increases, a fear-factor response that often lasts many months after the original incident. These media sources also include discussions about fire safety. Emergency response officials in Springfield claim that the fear frenzy whipped up by the media is responsible for the increased number of reports that appear in the city's media outlets, rather than an increase in the number of actual fires causing the reports.

Which of the following, if true, would seriously weaken the claim of the emergency response officials?

   (A)   The publicity surrounding fires is largely limited to the city in which the accident happened.

   (B)   Fires tend to occur more often during certain summer months when it is dry and hot.

   (C)   News organizations do not have any guidelines to help them decide how severe or close a fire must be for it to receive coverage.

   (D)   Fires receive coverage only when news sources find it advantageous to do so.

   (E)   Studies by the government show that the number of fires in Springfield is almost the same every month.

26. During the harvest season a farmer collects 45 kilos of apples per week from his orchard. The farmer claims that he sorts his crop and rejects 10 kilos from this quantity to ensure the same quality of apples every week.

Of the following, the best criticism of the farmer's plan is that the plan assumes that:

   (A)   Grocery shops cannot accept all the apples that are harvested.

   (B)   The overall quality of the apples would not be improved if the total number of apples collected were reduced.

   (C)   Each apple that is sorted is worthy of being sorted.

   (D)   It is difficult to judge the quality of an apple.

   (E)   The 35 kilos of apples that are accepted will be of the same quality from week to week.

27. Save-a-Tot Corporation is a manufacturer of safety seats for bicycles and automobiles. Children often die unnecessarily in collisions because they were not properly fastened into seats that conform to their fragile bodies. Save-a-Tot has recently designed a new type of safety seat that is able to conform more closely than ever to curves in the spines and necks of small children. This new design also cushions the head in a better way. Save-a-Tot claims that the usage of these safety seats will decrease child mortality rates in serious collisions by up to 60 percent.

Which of the following, if true, represents the strongest challenge to Save-a-Tot's claim?

(A) The child safety seats that Save-a-Tot has designed are made of a lighter plastic compound that turns brittle during a collision.

(B) The government demands that Save-a-Tot produce these child safety seats to very strict specifications.

(C) By providing Save-a-Tot seats free with new cars, automobile sales will increase.

(D) The proposed child safety seats will add too much weight to bicycles.

(E) As production costs increase, Save-a-Tot will have to raise the price of its safety seats.

28. Lately many people in a certain post-communist country have decided to emigrate for economic reasons. The people who want to leave the county in search of a job or a better life are those who have no money, or who know many foreign languages.

Of the following people, who is LEAST likely to emigrate?

(A) A person who knows 2 foreign languages, but doesn't have any money.

(B) A person who knows 2 foreign languages, but is afraid to travel.

(C) A person who has no money to travel and knows a second language at an elementary level.

(D) A person who knows no foreign languages and has a suitable quantity of money.

(E) A person who has money to leave the country, but is happy about his/her present situation.

29. Among those automobile mechanics who own their own garages and completed a qualifying course at Main Street Technical School, 35% earn above $80,000 a year. Among those who own their own garages but did not complete the qualifying course at Main Street Technical School, only 10% earn above $80,000 a year. These figures indicate the importance of technical education in getting a higher salary.

The argument above depends on which of the following assumptions about the people mentioned in the statistics?

(A) At least one-third of the group of people who did not complete the qualifying course would today be earning more than $80,000 a year if they had completed the course.

(B) The group of people who did not complete the qualifying course and the group who did are comparable in terms of factors that determine how much people are paid.

(C) Most of those people who did not complete the course did so entirely because of the cost of the course.

(D) As a group, those persons who completed the course are more competent as mechanics than the group that did not.

(E) The group of people who did not complete the qualifying course and who today earn more than $80,000 a year are more capable than the group that completed the course.

30. Finance Minister: Last year was disastrous for our manufacturing sector, which has traditionally contributed about 75% of our national budget. It is therefore encouraging that there is evidence that the IT sector is growing stronger. Taxes from the IT sector accounted for 15% of our national budget, up from 8% last year.

On the basis of the statements above, what best supports the above conclusion?

(A) The increase in taxes from the IT sector could have merely been the result of new laws imposed on the IT sector.

(B) The profits of the IT sector remained at a steady level despite the fact that it paid more taxes to the national government.

(C) The rise in the percentage of taxes that the IT sector contributed to the national government was insignificant in actual dollar terms.

(D) It is difficult to determine whether the jump from 8-15% tax contribution by the IT sector will be ongoing.

(E) The information given above does not fairly compare the contribution of taxes paid by different industries to the national government.

The following two questions are based on the following text:

Industrialists argue that because there is no evidence that links high-voltage electric wires with cancer among children, legislation banning high voltage transmission lines near school districts cannot be implemented on health hazard grounds.

31. The argument reported above would be most seriously weakened if it were true that:

(A) Living under high-voltage transmission lines increases the incidence of headaches and minor ailments in previously healthy children.

(B) Most children who live in areas away from high-voltage transmission lines do not like the way electric poles look.

(C) High-voltage transmission lines interfere with other radio devices such as antennas, satellites and cell-phones.

(D) Most children would prefer to live in areas that are away from high-voltage transmission lines.

(E) Legislation banning high-voltage transmission lines around school districts is easy to enforce.

32. Of the following, which is the best criticism of the argument reported above?

(A) It ignores causes of cancer other than high voltage transmission lines.

(B) It neglects the damaging effects that high voltage transmission lines might have on groups of people other than children.

(C) It fails to mention the role played by other factors, such as diet and water, in the development of cancer in children.

(D) It does not consider the possibility that residents who currently live under high voltage transmission lines might be concerned about exposure to potential carcinogens.

(E) It does not consider that areas far away from high voltage transmission lines are generally less safe to live in.

The following two questions are based on the following text:

Politician A: We must make a strong moral statement against the government of Qarnak. Only a complete military intervention to rid that country of its oppressive government can do this. Therefore, we must go to war.

Politician B: Our aim should be to encourage the government of Qarnak to change its policies and become more open. An embargo, as opposed to a full-scale military intervention, is the best way to achieve this. Therefore, we should only buy products from other countries and do as much as possible to encourage other countries to boycott Qarnak.

33. Politician A's and Politician B's arguments differ in which of the following ways?

   (A)   They state the same goal but propose different ways of achieving it.

   (B)   They state different goals but propose the same way of achieving them.

   (C)   They state different goals and propose different ways of achieving them.

   (D)   They disagree about whether the government should do anything at all.

   (E)   They disagree about whether Qarnak's policies are objectionable.

34. Which of the following, if true, would be the best evidence that the economy in Politician B's country would not be materially harmed if Politician B's recommendation is followed?

   (A)   Many of the major corporations in the Politician B's country buy products from Qarnak.

   (B)   Some of the companies from the Politician B's country that have factories in Qarnak would be able to out-source their production to other countries for little cost within a short period of time.

   (C)   Some companies that do business with Qarnak have instituted fair treatment policies for their workers.

   (D)   Based on the past statistics, the projected financial loss in Politician B's country incurred as a result of the boycott would be negligible.

   (E)   If the government were to go to war against Qarnak, the stability of many its companies would be undermined by possible terrorist activity.

35. Environmental activists: The appearance of three-eyed fish in the river is the result of radioactive material produced at your plant.

   Nuclear Power Plant Management: Our study indicates that the number of three-eyed fish is abnormally high throughout the entire valley because water sources in the area are polluted.

   Which of the following, if true, most weakens the Management's claims?

   (A)   The study does not differentiate between different types of pollution.

   (B)   Communities in the valley have not changed their fishing locations.

   (C)   Toxic chemicals discharged at the plant find their way into local water sources.

   (D)   The plant both uses and produces nuclear waste that has been shown to cause mutations.

   (E)   There had been incidents of three-eyed fish reported on several occasions before the nuclear power plant was built.

36. Recently, there was a huge flood in Hunan, China, during the rice-growing season. This will double the price of rice this season, which means that the cost of making rice-cakes will be more expensive. Unfortunately, rice-cake consumers in Hunan will now have to pay more for rice-cakes.

Which of the following, if true, MOST weakens the argument above?

(A) The recent flood was not as severe as scientists predicted.

(B) Regions other than Hunan also supply rice to rice-cake manufacturers in Hunan.

(C) Ingredients other than rice are used in the production of rice-cakes.

(D) Last year the price of rice was actually lower than the average price over the past ten years.

(E) The price of rice will eventually be too high for most consumers because of inflation.

37. Each time X grocery store raises the price of goods by 10%, sales drop by 20%. However, when the price of apples increased, the quantity of apples sold was the same as before the price increase.

Which of the following conclusions can be properly drawn from the statement above?

(A) Whenever there is a price increase, the amount of a certain product sold must drop.

(B) Shop assistants should take care to try to interest clients in other fruit besides apples.

(C) The drop in sales is consistent with quarterly trends forecast by the grocery store.

(D) Apples are, on average, not as expensive as other fruit in the grocery store.

(E) The sale of apples is dependent not only on their price, but on other factors.

38. Acme University receives 2,000 applications a year from high school students who wish to attend college. The university's admission committee would like to ensure constant standards of quality in the incoming class each year. The admissions committee has decided, therefore, to accept for admission each year only the best 200 students, selected on the basis of the quality of their personal statements.

Of the following, the best criticism of the admission committee's plan is that:

(A) Universities cannot accept all of the students who seek admission in a given year.

(B) The total number of applications will remain at approximately 2,000 in future years.

(C) Each applicant deserves to be considered seriously for admission.

(D) The best 200 personal statements will be difficult to assess.

(E) It is difficult to judge the quality of an applicant based on personal statements alone.

39. The fact that many large women's rights organizations consist almost entirely of white middle-class women has led many black feminist critics to question the seriousness of those organizations in speaking out on behalf of the needs of all women in general.

Which of the following generalizations, if true, would support the criticism implied in the statement?

(A) The ideology of an organization tends to supersede the particular desires of its members.

(B) The needs of black women are substantially similar to the needs of white middle class women.

(C) Organizations are more capable of resolving issues that individuals alone cannot.

(D) White middle class women are more likely to join feminist groups than black women are.

(E) People tend to join organizations which serve their own interests.

40. In the 1860's the majority of states did not permit women's suffrage. Although it might be assumed that the cities of the East Coast would have been the first to grant suffrage, the first area to do so was rural Wyoming in 1869.

Which of the following, if true, best explains the fact mentioned in the article?

(A) After 1869 the suffrage movement grew rapidly and spread to the big cities.

(B) Support for the suffrage movement was strong in the frontier west where women were needed to build up the economy and contribute to the construction of civil society.

(C) Many young urbanites supported women's suffrage.

(D) The most fervent opponents of women's suffrage included cowboys and western industrialists.

(E) In one of the major cities on the East Coast, a woman sat on the city council.

41. Companies that launch asteroid mining robots from the moon have a distinct advantage over earth based asteroid mining robotic systems because of the moon's low gravity. The higher the gravity of the object from which the company launches, the more money it has to spend on fuel and on rocket systems that can carry the extra fuel required to enter orbit. In order to be as competitive as the lunar based Apollo Mining Company, Terra Now Mining Corporation, located near the equator in South America, has decided to build a space elevator that will connect an orbiting artificial satellite with the ground via a super-thin, super-strong cable.

Which of the following, if true, most seriously weakens the argument above?

(A) The cable is composed of a carbon-based material that is not susceptible to drastic thermal changes.

(B) The high cost of building the cable will negate any cost-savings in launching mining robots into orbit for the foreseeable future.

(C) Over its expected lifetime, the cable will cut the cost of placing robots in orbit by 95%.

(D) The mining robots are flexible enough to be sent up and down a thin cable.

(E) The market for elements mined from asteroids is expected to decrease in size over the next fifty years.

The next two questions are based on the following:

42. Investing in the Jones & Weston Munitions Company would be a great way to increase the value of one's stock portfolio at the current time. 'Clock and Roll', a gun enthusiasts' magazine, conducted a survey which indicated that 75% of its readers want to buy a second gun within a year. This is a great time for the gun industry. The new study also shows that the gun industry could only provide 55% of the total population with a new gun each year.

Which of the following, if true, reveals a weakness in the evidence cited above?

(A) The manufacturing of guns requires very precise industrial processes.

(B) Gun manufacturers are not evenly distributed across the country.

(C) The number of people who want a second gun has been increasing each year for the past ten years.

(D) Readers of 'Clock and Roll' magazine are more likely than most people to want a second gun.

(E) Gun magazines include articles about owning a gun as well as articles about hunting.

43. Which of the following, if true, would undermine the validity of the investment advice in the paragraph above?

(A) Some gun owners are satisfied with only one gun.

(B) About half of the people who buy guns also purchase large cartridge magazines.

(C) About half of the people who buy guns do so to protect their families.

(D) Only a quarter of the guns that are made are sold within the first four weeks.

(E) Only a quarter of those who claim that they want a second gun actually end up purchasing one.

44. Many small children have problems with nightmares. Recent studies made by psychologists show that these nightmares can be reduced by letting the children fall asleep with the light on. Two groups of children took part in one of these studies. The group that fell asleep with the light off indicated that they had more nightmares than the group that fell asleep with the light on.

Which of the following, if true, provides evidence for determining whether falling asleep with the light on helps children deal with nightmares?

(A) Nightmares are more prevalent among children than among adults.

(B) Teenagers who fell asleep with the light on had the same number of nightmares as before.

(C) Children who play violent computer games are more likely to have nightmares.

(D) Teenagers who previously had problems with nightmares showed a markedly decreased incidence of nightmares after five months of falling asleep with the light on.

(E) Children with a high level of self-esteem have fewer problems with nightmares than children with average levels of self-esteem do.

45. A list of the best football players was posted at Benjamin Franklin High School in Philadelphia. According to the list, Paul is one of the seven best athletes on this list. Jake is in the top three, just like his friend Greg. Tom is not in the top three, but he is in the top fifteen.

If the information above is true, which of the following must also be true?

(A) Paul is a better athlete than Greg.

(B) Paul is a better athlete than Tom.

(C) Jake is a better athlete than Tom.

(D) Greg and Tom are both better athletes than Paul.

(E) Jake and Paul are both better athletes than Tom.

46. Statistics demonstrate that children who are beaten usually grow up believing it is appropriate to beat their children as well. This cycle is just one instance of violence perpetuating violence. A certain religious sect claims, however, that beating children is a form of discipline, not violence, and that this discipline is necessary to develop certain good habits in children, because children are too emotional and not capable of responding to situations with reason and logic until they reach adolescence.

Which of the following, if true, most seriously weakens the argument above?

(A) Young children often, for no apparent reason, burst into fits of tears or laughter.

(B) If beaten properly, there should be no permanent marks left on children.

(C) Even at an early age, children are capable of differentiating right from wrong and understanding why things should or should not be done.

(D) Children who are more intelligent are beaten for different reasons than less intelligent children are.

(E) Child-beating is an acceptable social practice in many countries.

47. In a bold attempt to go beyond the traditional one-on-one date as a means of finding a partner or having a relationship, a dating service has created a system whereby anyone who signs up for the service gets to attend 'group dates'. This system is supposed to allow the client to compare possible partners with respect to their interpersonal skills that cannot be fully observed from one-on-one situations.

Which of the following, if true, casts the MOST serious doubt on the value of the group date system indicated above?

   (A) One-on-one dates occasionally permit interpersonal skills to be assessed.

   (B) The group-date system could become awkward if too many people are present.

   (C) The more perceptive the client, the more revealing the group date will be.

   (D) There are certain personal traits that only a group-date can bring out.

   (E) The unnatural stress associated with a group date distorts most participants' normal interpersonal skills.

48. Mitchell Motor Company recently had a big jump in pick-up truck sales after hiring a new design team to give their pick-up trucks a more upscale look designed to appeal to a more affluent clientele. The company is now planning to launch a new line of sub-compact cars using the same concept.

The company's plan assumes that

   (A) other sub-compacts with an upscale look do not yet exist in the market

   (B) an upscale clientele would be interested in a sub-compact

   (C) the same design team could be employed for both projects

   (D) giving sub-compacts an up-scale look requires a design team

   (E) customers who bought older pick-up trucks would be just as likely to buy the new upscale looking ones

49. Many high schools send students to special courses to prepare them for language exams. Some language teachers criticize these courses and point out that high schools which do not send their students to special courses have reported a higher average score than those which do since 1995. The language teachers say that the courses are a waste of time and money.

Which of the following, if true, is the MOST effective challenge to this argument?

   (A) Those schools which do not send students to the courses have better knowledge of the exams since they are the only schools which participated in the exams prior to 1995.

   (B) Schools that have sent students to the courses since 1995 have experienced a greater drop in their scores than they had prior to 1995.

   (C) The cost of these courses run by outside teachers has risen dramatically since 1995.

   (D) The poor design of courses to prepare students for the language exams is not the only reason for their ineffectiveness.

   (E) Since 1995, the number of students who passed the language exams has risen by twenty percent.

50. Six months after the city of Nodlin began a traffic safety experiment to decrease red-light runners at its main intersection by installing cameras to catch would-be violators, the program was discontinued. The city claims that the program led to an increase in the number of red-light runners, citing the fact that, following installation of the system, an increase in the number of traffic violators was reported.

Which of the following, if true, MOST seriously weakens the claim of the city that the program led to an increase in traffic violations?

   (A) The intersection chosen for the system had a higher frequency of traffic violations than other intersections in the city.

   (B) The rate of increase in traffic violations was higher in the intersection with the system than at other intersections.

   (C) The number of all traffic violations at the main intersection reported increased as a result of the ability of the system to catch traffic violators who might have otherwise gone unnoticed.

   (D) The six months period during which the system was in place was not representative of regular traffic violation statistics.

   (E) Such systems installed on highways have also been helpful in catching motorists who drive too fast.

51. Instead of blaming an automobile accident on driver error, insurance companies should first try to figure out why the error was made by analyzing flaws in road design, automobile designs and in criteria to determine eligibility for a driver's license. Only then will the insurance companies be able to effectively issue guidelines to prevent future accidents, instead of merely punishing the incidental driver.

Which of the following is a presupposition of the argument above?

(A)   Driver error is not a significant factor in most automobile accidents.

(B)   Automobile manufacturers should be the agents who investigate automobile accidents and not insurance companies.

(C)   Stricter government regulation of the automobile and highway construction industries would make automobile travel safer.

(D)   Investigation of automobile accidents should contribute to the prevention of future accidents.

(E)   Most drivers who make errors in driving repeat those errors unless they are retrained.

52. Some experts in the Sepharian Federation believe that an embargo by Kalistan of a certain petroleum derivative, if implemented, would drive up the price of that derivative in Sepharia by a factor of 20. They also point out that few other countries have the particular derivative and that, with an embargo, Sepharia might have to depend on yet unproven synthetic fuel technologies to acquire a reasonable substitute for the derivative.

Which of the following, if true, constitutes the MOST serious objection to the analysis above?

(A)   Kalistan's economy relies on earnings derived from the export of the petroleum derivative to other countries.

(B)   There are economic steps that Sepharia could take to negotiate with Kalistan and perhaps avoid the embargo.

(C)   Petroleum experts believe the derivative might possibly exist in yet unexplored regions of Sepharia

(D)   Only a small portion of Sepharia's import expenditure is devoted to acquiring the derivative from Kalistan.

(E)   In case of an embargo, Sepharia could buy the same amount of the derivative indirectly on the world market at a less than one-fourth increase in price.

53. Residents of Delta City want to have a cleaner environment in their city and a higher quality of life. This means the construction of more parks and greenways in the city center. If they build more parks and designate certain areas as greenways, however, housing prices will go up in the long term as less land becomes available for habitation. The rise in housing prices will then have a negative impact on their quality of life as they will have to pay more for the same amount of space.

The answer to which of the following questions would be least relevant to evaluating whether the residents indeed face the choice the author says they do?

(A)   Could park and greenway developments be carried out under an alternative plan without increasing the cost of living?

(B)   Would development of parks and greenways benefit the residents of other cities?

(C)   Would the jobs created to develop the parks and greenways be filled by the residents of Delta City?

(D)   Do residents of Delta City support or oppose development of these parks and greenways?

(E)   Will the cost of housing remain at current prices without development of parks and greenways?

54. Recent studies show that people between the ages of 13 and 55 produce 65 pounds more garbage per year now than they did in 1995. This increase has led to a higher percentage of the total garbage produced by all age groups. This age group constitutes a growing percentage of the population, so it partially explains this rise.

Which of the following can be concluded from the passage above?

(A) People over the age of 55 produce less garbage than children below the age of 13.

(B) The population has risen since 1995.

(C) People between the ages of 13 and 55 are more than half of the current population.

(D) Before 1995 people below the age of 13 and over the age of 55 produced a higher percentage of the total garbage than they do now.

(E) People between the ages of 13 and 55 produce more garbage than those that are younger or older.

55. Recently many people in a certain county have stopped buying new apartments. This has happened because of high taxes that have been introduced by the county tax office and the high rate of unemployment that has hit the county. However, the average price of a new apartment has almost doubled in the county.

Which of the following, if true, best explains the increase in the average price of a new apartment?

(A) The price of used apartments has climbed steadily over the past five years.

(B) There will be a tax reduction later in the year which is expected to aid moderate and low income families.

(C) The market for new apartments has been unaffected by current economic conditions.

(D) Economic conditions are expected to get significantly worse before the end of the year.

(E) In anticipation of low demand for new apartments there has been a large decrease in construction.

56. Weather records indicate that the temperature in Linden, a major metropolis, is always 2 to 3 degrees higher than the temperature in Ipswich, a smaller city close by Linden. Experts say that this situation is caused by heavier smog and pollution in larger cities. However, during the last five years, there were 25 days when the temperature was the same in both cities.

Which of the following conclusions can be properly drawn from the statement above?

(A) The temperature can change very quickly in the course of one hour.

(B) Experts neglected the smog and pollution in smaller cities.

(C) These 25 days of symmetric temperatures were due to different atmospheric fronts.

(D) These 25 days are not representative of normal temperature measurements.

(E) Higher temperatures in larger cities are caused by factors other than smog and pollution.

57. Two different cages of rabbits were given injections of mild toxins. In addition, the first cage was also exposed to cold temperature; three-fourths of the rabbits in this cage became sick. Only one-fifth of the rabbits in the normal temperature cage became sick. The lab technicians concluded that cold temperature increases the likelihood of illness in rabbits.

The technicians' conclusion logically depends on which of the following assumptions?

(A) The exposure to cold temperature acted as a catalyst for the toxins which made more rabbits in the first cage sick.

(B) The toxins given to the rabbits in the two cages were of varying strength.

(C) Injecting the rabbits with toxins made them sick.

(D) Even without the exposure to cold temperature, the rabbits in the first cage would have probably gotten sick.

(E) Even exposing rabbits to slight variances in temperature is likely to induce illness.

58.   The government of Akhlazia should stop permitting mafia run opium companies to subtract shipping expenses from their revenues in calculating the amount of kickbacks that go to the central government. These opium companies would have to pay a higher kickback. As a consequence they would have to raise the price of opium and this price would then discourage buyers on the world market from purchasing Akhlazian opium.

Which of the following is an additional premise required by the argument above?

(A)   Opium companies would not be able to offset the payment of extra kickbacks by reducing other operating expenses.

(B)   Opium companies would need governmental approval before they can change the price of opium.

(C)   Buyers on the world market have no other suppliers of opium other than Akhlazia.

(D)   The money the government would earn as a result of increased kickbacks would be used to educate the public about the dangers of drug addiction.

(E)   The increase in kickbacks would be equal to the additional income generated by the rise in prices.

Chapter 3

Verbal Training Set III - Reading Comprehension

3.1   Standard Reading

Passage 1

In 1990, a Harvard Medical Practice study came to the conclusion that ninety-five thousand deaths a year in the United States are attributable to medical malpractice. Not surprisingly, an additional several hundred thousand individuals are subject to injury as a result of medical malpractice. These numbers can jar even the dispassionate observer. A jumbo jet would have to crash every day for a year to reproduce these casualties. Despite the multitudes of people who die or suffer as a result of medical malpractice, fewer
5 than 2100 doctors a year are disciplined in connection with a malpractice claim. Of those providers that do come under scrutiny and censure, the lion's share of them are subject to sanctions on the premises of substance abuse or fraud, rather than malpractice. These facts resurface at a time when federal legislators are considering measures to limit the monetary amount a patient can claim as compensation for damages incurred as a result of medical malpractice. It is the hope of lawmakers in capping jury awards to plaintiffs that it may be possible to reverse the tide of rising health care costs. Since those costs are ultimately imposed on patients
10 in the form of insurance premiums, the reigning logic dictates that limits on awards will save the patient money, and bring the cost of high quality healthcare within the reach of more Americans.

However, the soundness of this approach is called into question when we consider that a Congressional Budget Office report found that only one percent of national health care costs results from the expense of malpractice insurance premiums being passed on to the patient. However, accidents, misdiagnosis and conflicting prescriptions cost the nation nearly sixty billion dollars a year. Even
15 with these losses imposed on patients and on taxpayers yearly, less than half a percent of all civil cases in state courts sought to charge doctors with medical malpractice. The 2000 plus doctors who are disciplined each year amount to hardly one percent of all acting providers. Thus the amount of money going back into the hands of victims is a relatively inconsequential contribution to the overall cost of health care in America when compared to the cost of making good the harm of malpractice. Rising health care costs may more predictably be driven back by improving the way in which the health care industry polices itself and removes unreliable
20 doctors from practice.

1. The main theme of this passage can be summarized as:

  · (A)   Widespread policing is the answer to cutting health care costs

   (B)   Health care costs are the result of too few of the guilty being held accountable

   (C)   The source of high health care costs is difficult to localize

   (D)   Rising health care costs have more to do with the behavior of doctors than with the behavior of patients

   (E)   Traditional government approaches to the health care issue have disappointed

2. The main purpose of comparing the number of malpractice victims to the number of jumbo jet accident casualties is:

   (A)   To exemplify how a dispassionate observer could be caught off guard

   (B)   To show that even if we do not consider the several hundred thousand injured, the number of people who die from malpractice every year is absurdly high

   (C)   To compare the gravity of airline accidents to the seriousness of medical malpractice

   (D)   To note the disparity between airline safety regulations and health care oversight

   (E)   To point out the similarity between the number of people killed in air crashes and the number killed through medical malpractice

3. The main concern voiced over the penalties levied on rogue practitioners is:

    (A) Penalties are given out for the wrong reasons

    (B) Penalties are not severe enough

    (C) Too few penalties are given out

    (D) Penalties are given out to the wrong offenders

    (E) Not enough charges are filed for the penalties to be a threat

4. The implication of the Congressional Budget Office report is that:

    (A) Awards from malpractice claims are not a substantial source of health care costs

    (B) Placing a limit on malpractice claims will significantly reduce the cost of health care to the end user

    (C) Malpractice insurance premiums are not as high as they could be

    (D) Congressional research is polarized and thus often contradictory

    (E) Insurance companies only charge what is fair based on the size of claims and the number of claimants

5. The author of this passage would most likely agree with the argument that:

    (A) Insurance companies will try to inflate their rate of return on premiums

    (B) The cost of health care is inflated by the availability of expensive treatments

    (C) Doctors are compelled to reduce their services in order to cover their own expenses

    (D) Patients could reduce the cost of health care by being more careful in the home, using generic drugs and seeking a second opinion

    (E) The cost of health care is increased by the negligence of doctors

6. The effect of the sentence beginning with "Despite the multitudes..." in line 4 and the later sentence beginning with "These facts resurface" is to:

    (A) Demonstrate the underlying logic for capping jury awards

    (B) Remind readers that those who do not remember history are doomed to repeat it

    (C) Note that this subject is contemporary and topical

    (D) Show that Congress is operating under a false premise

    (E) Show that things are not always as they appear

7. The conclusion that greater policing of doctors will reduce the incidence of malpractice and drive down costs assumes that:

    (A) Most doctors are not up to their responsibilities

    (B) Many more doctors are guilty of substance abuse and fraud than the portion accused

    (C) Doctors can improve their performance and policing will encourage them to do so

    (D) Doctors will never protect one another from investigation on the grounds that they believe they are best equipped to make decisions for the patients

    (E) There is unchecked corruption among doctors

8. The notion of reducing jury awards places the blame for high health care costs most directly on:

    (A) Patients

    (B) Medical malpractice

    (C) Controlling doctors

    (D) The inability of the justice system to work with the health care system

    (E) Class action

Passage 2

Whistleblower laws, as the moniker might imply, are pieces of legislation existing at the federal and state level that are intended to encourage employees to bring a stop to corruption and mismanagement. On the typical assembly line, a person may physically pull or blow a whistle to halt production in order to correct a faulty production process. Likewise, the federal government has passed legislation to provide incentives, as well as protection, to government employees who witness coworkers, and, now more than ever,
5   managers, who are behaving in ways that can be construed as an abuse of their position, or as an outright violation of the law.

Increasingly, the term whistleblower has come to be associated with somebody who informs on a group of trusting coworkers. However, it is exactly this type of connotation that whistleblower laws seek to remove from the mind of the public. Government bureaucracy and state-financed corporations can at times appear to operate above the law, outlasting administrations, evading the discipline of elective review, and oiling their machinery while largely hiding from the public eye. Therefore, it is especially important
10 to make it possible for courageous employees who find themselves entangled in a business or department with its own agenda in mind to be able to speak out on behalf of the larger interests of voters, to whom these entities are responsible. Since an employee who decides to report illegal or unreasonable behavior to the authorities regularly finds himself to be the subject of intense scrutiny, or even fabricated accusations, if he continues to stay at his place of employment, it is necessary to make the act of bringing unethical performance to light appealing enough to outweigh the disincentives posed by angry coworkers, punitive bosses, and a national
15 culture that can frown on disloyalty, even if it is for all the right reasons.

In line with this reasoning, whistleblower laws often provide the employee with a percentage of the money considered 'saved' by his honesty. Moreover, a settlement or court award reached as a result of the disclosure of these problematic issues is often paid to the successful whistleblower to compensate for the risk he has assumed. From another perspective, the employee is simultaneously given protection against undue dismissal and other retaliatory measures that a corporation or department might privately take against
20 the plaintiff after official investigations are underway. These incentives were meant to make whistleblower laws both a progressive reform and effective legislation, so much so that the lucrative prospects of being a whistleblower has not only brought many reluctant employees forward, but also has encouraged some to go into the business of poaching through phonebooks for dubious employers with an eye towards reporting them to government investigators and collecting their prize once a decision is reached.

1. Whistleblower laws were put in place:

   (A) to discourage employees from reporting corruption in the workplace

   (B) to foster the connotation that employee reporting is disloyal

   (C) to ensure that all corrupt practices are discovered

   (D) to save money

   (E) to protect employees from the negative consequences of reporting malfeasance

2. The added measures to provide whistleblowers with pecuniary incentives and protection against unfair dismissal implies that:

   (A) Lawmakers were concerned that legislation aimed at reforming bureaucracy would be ineffective without financial inducements

   (B) The government should offer corporations more funding in exchange for reducing internal costs through better management and quarterly reviews

   (C) Many lawmakers were whistleblowers themselves at one point

   (D) Co-workers will be more understanding if they realize that reporting is not the product of disloyalty but of business acumen and private incentive

   (E) Government bureaucracies do not need to respond to legislative pressure

3. The need for whistleblowers to help control the behavior of bureaucracy is a result of the:

   (A) Independent third party review process

   (B) Lack of competition with other bureaucracies

   (C) Inability of bureaucracy to be well understood by lawmakers

   (D) Operation of bureaucracy outside the discipline of elective review

   (E) Bureaucracy's organizational mission being separate from the mission of the federal government

4. In the passage, the effectiveness of whistleblower laws is demonstrated by:

   (A) The number of corporations on federal contracts who have adopted the cost plus system

   (B) The high prosecution rate of managers who abuse their power and embezzle money

   (C) The inclusion of practical measures to make the legislation realistic

   (D) The willingness of most people to consider whistleblowers as patriots

   (E) The eagerness of a few employees to become freelance investigators of corrupt corporations

5. It can be inferred from the passage that lawmakers viewed a need for so many practical incentives to be part of whistleblower legislation because:

   (A) There have been laws passed but not necessarily followed

   (B) Federal employees make decisions out of self-interest more readily than out of a sense of purpose

   (C) Corrupt bureaucracies result in a culture of corruption among all employees

   (D) Federal bureaucracies are large and unwieldy

   (E) The federal government may be able to change a bureaucracy's leaders but not all of its employees

6. In line 9, the phrase 'oiling their machinery' is probably a metaphor for:

   (A) Refusing to obey federal mandates

   (B) Writing laws

   (C) Proposing laws

   (D) Pitting state governments against federal governments

   (E) Running the day to day operations of an organization

7. The attitude of the author towards whistleblower legislation can be described as:

   (A) Suspicious but relenting

   (B) Supportive and objective

   (C) Agreeable but nonplussed

   (D) Implacable but journalistic

   (E) Prohibitive and histrionic

8. In line 20, the word 'plaintiff' most nearly means

   (A) Applicant

   (B) Pretender

   (C) Claimant

   (D) Dissenter

   (E) Litigator

Passage 3

The size of the European Union market is exponentially larger than it was in the 1950's, when European integration was first proposed. While today the European Union is the only region with the economic might to challenge the United States for meaningful influence over international trade policies, the United States is noncommittal on E.U. proposals calling for the alignment of labor regulations, the opening of consumer forums and the offer of an audience to environmental groups. As the constituencies calling for
5 these developments have been relegated to peripheral positions in the dialogue over trans-Atlantic economic unification, those with an interest in these groups see a trend towards liberalizing the rules for corporate advantage in the economic coordination that has sprung up between the United States and Europe. Much of the current communication between the United States and the European Union is focused on establishing an agreement that codifies the rules of trans-Atlantic trade and that acknowledges the extent of trade conducted between the U.S. and Europe, greater in bulk than between any other pair of regions in the world, without disregarding
10 the efforts European producers must make to satisfy interest groups and regulations.

The heated dialogue between the United States and the European Union on this issue has come hard on the heels of the joining of the U.S., Mexico and Canada in the North American Free Trade Agreement. This agreement seeks to standardize industrial and labor regulations between the United States and its neighbors so that tariffs can be reduced, international transport encouraged, and corporate investment diversified. While bringing standards of production into alignment is a goal that ought to raise the quality of
15 production and the level of cooperation across the continent, it also creates an opportunity to establish a standard contra to European expectations of international regulation. As a solution, the E.U. has proposed TAFTA, the Trans-Atlantic Free Trade Agreement, but the United States has repeatedly hesitated at the proposal, seeking to protect its dominance in the Western Hemisphere. This dominance is secured by its ability to protect its factories and corporations from sources of comparable European production and demanding practices of review and concessions popular in Europe as a nod to social consensus. These issues have resulted in
20 the plethora of interest groups with a voice in the matter simultaneously accusing the U.S of brinkmanship, protectionism, callous deregulation, third world exploitation and anti-competitive practices. The route to economic expansion is a prominent issue in both the U.S. and the European Union, and some with a say in the matter repeat these protests as a screen for their own plans to tip the balance of economic advantage towards their own region at the expense of all other involved parties in the process of exploring for parity.

1. The intent of the author in noting the size of the European Union in the first sentence is to:

    (A)   Demonstrate the difference between the past E.U. and the present E.U.

    (B)   Clarify the number of parties in trans-Atlantic trade

    (C)   Establish the importance of one of the leading parties in world markets

    (D)   Show that the E.U. can not be exploited for U.S. self-interest

    (E)   Demonstrate why the United States is non-committal about cooperation

2. Which of the following could exemplify the concern of peripheral groups over the move to emphasize corporate advantage?

    (A)   The alignment of labor regulations

    (B)   The provision of schooling for the children of migrant workers

    (C)   A suspension of necessary corporate taxes to respond to threats of capital flight

    (D)   Raising the cost of entry to a market for new businesses

    (E)   The standardization of European currencies

3. Which of the following words best substitutes for the term 'heated dialogue' in line 11?

    (A)   Impasse

    (B)   Dispute

    (C)   Shuttle diplomacy

    (D)   Brinkmanship

    (E)   Banter

4. The main concern of the European Union regarding NAFTA is that:

   (A)   North America will have a higher standard of living than Europe

   (B)   North America will improve its standard of living at the expense of Europe

   (C)   North America will adopt production standards that are incompatible with Europe's

   (D)   North America will flood Europe with cheap, low quality goods

   (E)   North America will promote the exploitation of labor

5. It can be inferred from the passage that less stringent production and environmental standards than those of North America are unfavorable to the European Union because:

   (A)   They unfairly lower the quality of life in Europe

   (B)   They reduce the amount of cheap labor entering Europe from the third world

   (C)   They damage the European environment

   (D)   They encourage European workers to move to the United States

   (E)   They make it more difficult for European industry to compete with the lower costs of North American industry

6. In the sentence beginning with the words 'These issues have' in line 19, the term 'callous deregulation' is meant to imply:

   (A)   Deregulation driven by an uncaring attitude

   (B)   A well-reasoned desire for deregulation

   (C)   An insatiable drive towards deregulation

   (D)   Balanced deregulation

   (E)   Inconsistent deregulation

7. It can be inferred from the passage that the author believes the range of accusations against the United States made by groups on the periphery of trade talks is:

   (A)   Credible but lacking influence

   (B)   Credible but irrelevant

   (C)   Biased

   (D)   Well-balanced

   (E)   Incredible but accurate

8. The unwillingness of the United States to upset trade relations with Europe is demonstrated by:

   (A)   The U.S. unwillingness to engage in any new agreements

   (B)   The U.S. insistence on avoiding future talks

   (C)   The U.S. back-up plan to secure relations with Mexico and Canada

   (D)   The U.S. decision not to turn down TAFTA while avoiding any commitment to it

   (E)   The U.S. willingness to parrot the cries of its own social groups

Passage 4

For seventeenth century Europeans, the history of Eastern monarchies, like everything else in Asia, was stereotyped and invariable. According to accounts of Indian events, history unfolded itself with the predictable rituals of heavy-handed folklore. Typically, the founder of a dynasty, a brave soldier, is a desperate intriguer, and expels from the throne the feeble and degenerate scions of a more ancient house. His son may inherit some of the talent of the father; but in two or three generations luxury and indolence do their
5   work, and the feeble inheritors of a great name are dethroned by some new adventurer, destined to bequeath a like misfortune to his degenerate descendents. Thus rebellion and deposition were the correctives of despotism, and therefore, a recurrence, at fixed intervals, of able and vigorous princes through the medium of periodical anarchy and civil war, occurred. It was this perception of history that allowed Britain's rulers to lay claim to the governance of the subcontinent. The British claimed to be interested in avoiding these periods of bloodshed. This claim justified British policy, as well as dictated how they thought about gaining the favor
10 of India's local Raj.

British armies and British administrators were able to insinuate rule over India by setting up native princes in positions of power. Their methods took advantage of existing "doctrines of lapse", and made use of what was already the declared law in cases of heredity. By intervening on behalf of one prince or another, both of whom may have been equally suited to claim the right to the throne in cases in which the rights to leadership lapsed, they put themselves in a position to support a leader they selected, and to
15 maintain his power as long as it was in their interests. In this way the princes became practically obliged to cooperate with the British. The result was two generations of petty despots, insulated from the consequences of misrule by British bayonets. The despots spent their lives in listless debauchery, broken by paroxysms of cruelty and oppression.

1. It can be inferred from the passage that the author is an advocate of:

    (A)   The random nature of Indian rule

    (B)   The rise of Britain to absentee rule over of India

    (C)   The resemblance between folklore and history

    (D)   The need for rebellion as a corrective of despotism

    (E)   The interruption of the Indian cycle of rule by British intervention

2. The passage intimates that Britain was better able to rule on the Indian subcontinent because of:

    (A)   A language in common with that of the Indians

    (B)   A lack of corruption within the British administration

    (C)   The presence of well-trained British soldiers

    (D)   Superior weaponry

    (E)   The use of preexisting laws

3. The author of the passage would be likely to agree with which statement:

    (A)   British intervention in India left it no worse off than when the British arrived

    (B)   British intervention in India requires closer monitoring than the British have since given it

    (C)   British intervention in India was a positive influence on India

    (D)   The system of rule in India before the British arrived had no faults

    (E)   India would have been better off to carry out its cycle of lapse and renewal without British influence

4. The attitude of the author towards the reported cycle of rule in the Asia can best be described as:

    (A)   Resignation

    (B)   Despair

    (C)   Skepticism

    (D)   Matter of fact

    (E)   Approval

5. The damage caused by British rule to the subcontinent was effected by:

    (A)   The refusal of the people to be ruled

    (B)   The inability of the people to choose their leader

    (C)   The inability of the people to resist oppression

    (D)   The demoralization of the Indian identity

    (E)   The exploitive nature of the relationship between Britain and the Princes

6. One judgment of the British offered by this passage might be:

    (A)   They never pretended to undertake socially responsible activity

    (B)   They were interested exclusively in exploiting India's resources

    (C)   They got involved in governing colonies which they know are beyond their powers of governance

    (D)   They had a benign influence on India

    (E)   They sought practical opportunity when their self-interest matched local rulers' objectives

7. The "doctrines of lapse" which positioned princes against one another for regional thrones gave Britain a foothold in India by:

    (A)   Allowing them to exchange a little influence at a critical time for significant influence later

    (B)   Offering an opportunity to take over the leadership role in these areas while no one was in charge

    (C)   Letting the British act as arbitrators in discussions between the dueling princes

    (D)   Positioning the British as an impartial party in Indian politics

    (E)   Ensuring there were no local candidates for leadership

8. From the passage, the attitude of Britain towards Indian politics can be described as:

    (A)   Conflicted

    (B)   Hypocritical

    (C)   Opportunistic

    (D)   Fair

    (E)   Unbiased

Passage 5

The 1996 Telecommunications Act served three groups in the U.S. national framework: government regulators, industrial developers and groups interested in public infrastructure. The transformative reform of U.S. telecommunications law required, plainly, the writers to reinterpret past legislation (the 1934 Communications Act and the 1978 Communications Act) taking into account the technological realities of the day. The reform also offered an opportunity for interests from corporate America and the public
5 sector to be involved. Innovators in these fields had long been looking for an opportunity to enfranchise the public, at last, with electronic and spectrum commons. The troika of groups involved tells something about the plethora of ways in which Congress forms and then advances legislation. Telecom legislation shows how difficult it is to determine whether the success of this legislation better exemplifies Congress as a group of self-interested practitioners of pork-barrel politics, or as an elite group of specialized representatives divided into committees to perform different roles. The Act seems to be a technical formulation of an old law, and,
10 according to its nature, is dependent on the expertise needed to interpret the past legislation to meet the challenges of new technology.

With a great deal at stake for large media corporations, as well as for local broadcasters, interests battling for control over spectrum and broadband created compelling arguments to accept their demands. With that to consider, it is understandable that the passage of the Act in Congress may be viewed as a form of pork-barrel politics. Yet, national parties and the government bureaucracy were given the goal to address a national interest by creating a national telecommunications policy which resolves the arguments among
15 battling interest groups. It is important to consider how a broad national law with immediate effects will affect interest groups. The expertise and professionalism of these groups can not be discounted in the process of review of such technical legislation. The legislation will inevitably determine, one way or the other, the type of national telecommunications market and the nature of the relationships among participants such as business groups, local groups and the public sector. It can be said that the 1996 Act provides very strong backing for both interpretations of how Congress works. Yet, realistically, it seeks to extend a fundamental
20 public resource, the spectrum, while considering the upcoming role media will play in the formation of the civic attitudes of people.

1. The passage observes that the 1996 Telecommunications Act highlights which two interpretations of the functioning of Congress:

   (A) Process and Passage

   (B) Expert Review Versus Constituency Satisfaction

   (C) Voter Satisfaction versus Pork Barrel

   (D) Civic attitudes Versus Consumer choice

   (E) National markets and public space

2. The passage implies that local and national groups:

   (A) Unite to garner more pork

   (B) Have the same interests

   (C) Are divided by their different interests in telecommunications law

   (D) Represent the same interests in the areas of consumer politics and public sector politics

   (E) Cooperate

3. Professionalism, as described in the passage, regarding the 1996 Telecommunications law, is necessary because of:

   (A) The need to reinterpret the law for the technical realities of today's market

   (B) The need for networking among large national media conglomerates with influence over Congress

   (C) The eagerness of committee members to provide valuable opportunities to their home states

   (D) The availability of a specialized elite

   (E) The influence of lobbyist

4. In the sentence beginning with 'The troika of groups' in line 6 the term 'advances' most nearly means:

    (A) Introduces

    (B) Pushes through congress

    (C) Prevents from moving forward

    (D) Declines

    (E) Eliminates constituency objections

5. The relevance of the 1996 Telecommunications Act to the nature of the telecommunications field is connected to:

    (A) Providing large corporations with the opportunity to own many forms of media

    (B) Consumer utilitarianism

    (C) The nature of the relationship between corporate and civic actors in telecommunications

    (D) The restriction of a public good

    (E) Politicians' futures

6. Innovators in the telecommunications field, according to the passage, entered into the debate over telecommunications principally because:

    (A) They sought to play a critical role in the passage of the law

    (B) They had long sought to return spectrum commons to the public

    (C) They wanted to serve as advisors to Congress on the redesign of the telecommunications law

    (D) They viewed corporate interests as leeches

    (E) They are in charge of deciding how telecommunications policy should be developed

7. It can be inferred from the passage that the author views telecommunications legislation as best served by:

    (A) Corporate lobbyists

    (B) Expert committees

    (C) Innovators in the field

    (D) Constituency interests

    (E) Members of Congress

8. It can be interpreted from the passage that both large media corporations and local broadcasters seek primarily:

    (A) The conservation of the old laws and the complete rewriting of the laws respectively

    (B) A change in the laws for their own private interests

    (C) Only technical updates of the old laws rather than risking allowing the other any more influence in the market

    (D) The elimination of the other from the market

    (E) A role in providing their own expertise in the modernization of the laws

Passage 6

For 200 years until World War I, French-speaking Wallonia was a technically advanced, industrial region, while Dutch-speaking Flanders was predominantly agricultural. This disparity began to fade during the interwar period. When Belgium emerged from World War II with its industrial infrastructure relatively undamaged, the stage was set for a period of rapid development, particularly in Flanders. The older, traditional industries of Wallonia, particularly steelmaking, began to lose their competitive edge during this
5   period, but the general growth of world prosperity masked this deterioration until the 1973 and 1979 oil price shocks and resultant shifts in international demand sent the economy into a period of prolonged recession. In the 1980s and 1990s, the economic center of the country continued to shift northwards to Flanders. The early 1980s saw the country facing a difficult period of structural adjustment caused by declining demand for its traditional products, deteriorating economic performance, and neglected structural reform. Consequently, the 1980-82 recession shook Belgium to its core—unemployment rose, social welfare costs increased, personal debt
10   soared, the government deficit climbed to 13% of GDP, and the national debt, although mostly held domestically, mushroomed. Against this grim backdrop, in 1982, Prime Minister Martens' center-right coalition government formulated an economic recovery program to promote export-led growth by enhancing the competitiveness of Belgium's export industries through an 8.5% devaluation. Economic growth rose from 2% in 1984 to a peak of 4% in 1989. In May 1990, the government linked the franc to the German mark, primarily through closely tracking German interest rates. Consequently, as German interest rates rose after 1990, Belgian
15   rates increased and contributed to a decline in the economic growth rate.

Although Belgium is a wealthy country, it overspent income and under-collected taxes for years. The Belgian government reacted to the 1973 and 1979 oil price hikes with poor macroeconomic policies: it transferred workers made redundant in the private sector to the public sector and subsidized ailing industries—coal, steel, textiles, glass, and shipbuilding—in order to prop up the economy. As a result, cumulative government debt reached 121% of GNP by the end of the 1980s (versus a cumulative U.S. federal public
20   debt/GNP ratio of 31.2% in 1990). However, thanks to Belgium's high personal savings rate, the Belgian Government managed to finance the deficit mainly from domestic savings. This minimized the deleterious effects on the overall economy.

1. An appropriate title for this passage might be:

    (A)   The Rise of Flanders to domestic Leadership

    (B)   Managing the Challenge of Structural Adjustment in the Post-War Belgian Economy

    (C)   Dead Weight: How Greater Belgium Lost Flanders the Industrial Advantage

    (D)   Fiscal Rally: How P.M. Martens Found his Legs

    (E)   Which Way: Fickle Government Starves a State with Too Many Choices

2. The information in the beginning of the passage concerning the rise of Flanders over Wallonia serves to:

    (A)   Introduce the protagonist of the author's text early in the passage

    (B)   Foreshadow the counterpoint between successful and unsuccessful policymaking

    (C)   Introduce and demonstrate the idea of a compositional sea-change in the greater Belgian economy

    (D)   Show how runaway development was ready to take hold of the Belgian economy before it was mismanaged and eventually recouped

    (E)   Provide the reader with the factor responsible for driving away development in the greater Belgian economy

3. The oil price hikes of the 1970's can be most accurately considered:

    (A)   A structural problem in the Belgian economy.

    (B)   A pivotal turning point leading to an immediate improvement in economic policymaking

    (C)   Comparable to the fictional child telling the emperor he has no clothes

    (D)   An unpredictable stroke of bad luck reversing Belgian economic momentum

    (E)   A wasted opportunity to focus on pre-emptive export-driven reform

4. The phrase "grim backdrop" in line 11 is used by the author to:

    (A) Show that no matter how bad things are, a politician can make them worse

    (B) Make light of Martens' genuine but misspent efforts to turn around the economy

    (C) Show that Martens brought real change in the face of formidable challenge

    (D) Pardon Martens by showing that even the most expert of handlers could not have changed the hand Belgium was dealt

    (E) Imply that there was no hope for Belgium

5. The genre of the piece can be categorized as:

    (A) Apologetic

    (B) Historical

    (C) Polemical

    (D) Argumentative

    (E) Encyclopedic

6. In the passage, the author's use of the phrase "poor economic policies" in line 17 and the word "prop" in line 18 in regards to government subsidies suggests what about his opinion of government intervention in the economy?

    (A) The government should not intervene in economic issues that can be handled privately

    (B) The government should not support industries that are ailing

    (C) The government can encourage sustainable progress without working with market forces

    (D) The government must be more decisive in its decision-making

    (E) The government cannot avoid being at the mercy of market fluctuations

7. The author's critical portrayal of the Belgian government's reactions to the oil crises in the 1970's does not necessarily make its officials economically malfeasant because:

    (A) No economist could have done better

    (B) Economists are academics; politicians are pragmatists

    (C) This economic review of the Belgian economy is retrospective; the decisions made at the time were without the benefit of hindsight

    (D) There are no right or wrong answers in economics

    (E) Administrators were giving the public what they wanted

8. In the end of paragraph one (line 13), the author notes that linking the franc with the German mark raised interest rates in the Belgian economy, setting off a decline in the rate of growth. However, in the last sentence of the second paragraph (line 21), the passage states that abundant personal savings made it possible for Belgium to pay off its debts. If higher interest rates lead to higher personal savings from which debts can be paid off, what is the best way to describe the tone of the passage regarding high interest rates:

    (A) Ambivalent

    (B) Skeptical

    (C) Foreboding

    (D) Accepting

    (E) Defeatist

Passage 7

Recent evidence from scientists has shown that eating "fast food" can be addictive in much the same way as using controlled substances can be. According to researchers, "fast food" such as hamburgers, processed sugar, and a wide range of deep fried foods can trigger a dependency in the brain that perpetuates a habit of further use. It is a view that is increasingly supported by scientists who see a codependence between people's decisions and environmental influences (including the wide availability of "fast foods")
5   that have structural effects on human development. The proposed conclusions contend that the brains of overeaters experience chemical changes in response to unbalanced diets with a high content of processed sugar, salt, and saturated fats.

In time and in some cases, if people continue a pattern of consumption containing too much unhealthy food, their intake of this food will initiate changes in the brain that elevate the minimum level of ingestion the brain needs for satiation. Moreover, since high consumption of "fast foods" stimulates opiates in the brain (substances which act as natural pain relievers), large, recurrent
10   doses of "fast food" can mimic the effects of opiates, albeit in a less intense form. Scientists raising rats on a diet of twenty-five percent sugar found that upon suddenly eliminating glucose from the rats' food supply, the animals experienced all the symptoms of withdrawal attributed to reducing traditional addictive opiates, including shivering and chattering teeth. Later, by treating rats with drugs that block opiate receptors, scientists were able to lower the amount of dopamine in the nucleus acumen of rats' brains, an area linked with the dynamics of reward. Such neurochemistry can be seen in heroine addicts coping with withdrawal. By this
15   reasoning, obesity, like other addictions, can be viewed as a disease beyond the control of those afflicted by it.

This has brought lawyers to argue that civil society has a responsibility to regulate food and educate people about the abuse of "unhealthy foods" in a way that is comparable to society's control of opiates and narcotics. Corporations that target this vulnerability in human beings can then be held liable for the sicknesses that result from the poor eating habits overwhelming their customers. Still, some scientists scoff at the lengths to which their colleagues seek to separate the decision making process from people's behavior.
20   For these researchers, the distinction between a habit and an addiction is not quantitative but qualitative. Their consensus is that individuals can still moderate their behavior to control the effects of what they eat on their systems.

1. The passage seems to suggest that scientists who see a co-dependence between people's decisions and environmental influences would affirm that:

    (A)   Human decision-making has unconscious, chemical influences
    (B)   Human beings have a responsibility to control their surroundings
    (C)   Overeaters are not responsible for their behavior
    (D)   Obesity is a public health crisis
    (E)   Overeaters continue to eat because they are unable to overcome the difficulties of withdrawal

2. Based on the information provided in the passage, the relationship between administering drugs that block opiate receptors and dopamine levels can be considered:

    (A)   Dependent
    (B)   Directly correlated
    (C)   Related
    (D)   Co-dependent
    (E)   Unrelated

3. Lawyers defending corporations against the findings of researchers on the effects of "fast food" would most likely argue:

    (A)   Obesity is a pre-existing condition in individuals
    (B)   Obese people must treat their disease with medication that blocks opiate receptors
    (C)   The distinction between a habit and an addiction is "not quantitative but qualitative"
    (D)   Corporations were not aware that "fast food" caused chemical dependency because the science confirming it is so new
    (E)   It is the responsibility of consumers to stay informed about their choices

4. By labeling obesity as a disease, the scientists in the passage seek to point out that:

   (A)   The obese need to obey a strict diet

   (B)   The obese are more vulnerable to the health hazards of chronic consumption of "fast food" than those who are not obese

   (C)   Obesity is a condition that targets those with a genetic precondition to it

   (D)   Obesity is a result of factors that cannot be understood solely as the results of the behavior of individuals

   (E)   Obesity exists in an individual whether or not they overeat

5. Researchers in the passage who dispute the conclusions of their colleagues who link obesity with chemical factors find fault with their colleagues':

   (A)   Findings

   (B)   Controls

   (C)   Assumptions

   (D)   Method

   (E)   Comparisons between data

6. The phrasing of dissenting scientists that notes "the distinction between habit and addiction is not quantitative but qualitative" in line 20 objects to the assumption:

   (A)   That linking a chemical process to a behavioral pattern is sufficient to categorize someone as diseased

   (B)   That there is only one factor which determines a person's behavior

   (C)   Overlooking the cumulative effects of behavior which contribute to chemical changes in the brain

   (D)   That any amount of fast food is bad for people

   (E)   That people should only eat foods without sugar

7. From the passage, the role of dopamine in the rats' brain seems to:

   (A)   Reduce food intake

   (B)   Block opiates

   (C)   Replace opiates when they are blocked

   (D)   Punish rats when opiates are received

   (E)   Instruct the rat to eat more

8. As presented in the passage, lawyers who would seek to take "fast food" restaurants to court for damaging the public health would agree with which of the following:

   (A)   The government is not knowledgeable enough to safeguard public health

   (B)   Corporations are responsible for the consequences of their products

   (C)   The responsibility to determine what a good product is should be determined by the market

   (D)   People who suffer from obesity are victims of governmental incompetence

   (E)   People should take responsibility for their own diets

Passage 8

In the 1580's, England sent Sir Francis Drake on an expedition to the East Indies' Hispaniola, which he facetiously called "singeing the King of Spain's beard". This expedition rendered it impossible for the Spaniards to attempt the invasion of England during that year, as they had fully intended. They had considered themselves fully prepared to invade, whilst England hardly was. The number of transport ships, and the quantity of stores, provisions and other equipment that Drake had destroyed in their ports was so great that

5   it required a year to replace them. In the meantime, the Prince of Parma, on behalf of Philip of Spain, and certain commissioners on behalf of England's Queen Elizabeth, took this as their opportunity to hold meetings in the Netherlands, something which amounted to a farce of negotiating for a treaty of peace; it was a mere pretense on both sides.

In actuality, it is believed that the Queen of England began these talks as a ruse to divert the hostile preparations of the King of Spain. In turn, the show was continued by the Spanish who welcomed the chance to attach their own plans to this duplicity. The Spaniards

10 had not concluded their plans to overtake their rival. They used these meetings to conceal their own peacetime mobilization towards war. Spain sought to use England's diversion as a passive shield with which to take her by surprise, by "sewing the fox's skin to the lion." However, the build-up by Spain and her intent to conquer England became public knowledge before the discourse was spent.

The potential benefits of stealing upon England were nullified by the tolls stemming from seeking Papal approval of a just war against the excommunicated English Queen. That approval had to be unambiguously communicated to the world of Christendom, done in

15 a way that made the war on England out to be a rebuke for the crown's heresy and royal arrogance. However, that fanfare gave Sir Francis Drake the impetus and the cover to savage the Spanish port towns before Spain took on the English navy, eliminating the initial advantage Spain had traded for popular support and resulting in an unobstructed attack on her wartime posts.

1. Sir Francis Drake's name for his mission to Hispaniola suggests:

   (A) That he was unaware of the full scope of its success

   (B) That he would strike very near the King of Spain himself

   (C) That his attack was at the heart of the Spanish empire

   (D) That he sought only to make the King of Spain look bad

   (E) That he suspected his success could only disadvantage Spain, not eliminate her as a threat to England

2. It can be inferred from the passage that continental Spain:

   (A) Had an important reliance on products from its colonies

   (B) Was easily taken in by English duplicity

   (C) Lacked competent military leaders like Drake

   (D) Was prevented from winning by the demands imposed by a larger empire

   (E) Was at a military disadvantage to England because of its large percentage of coastline and island colonies

3. Since neither Spain nor England had any intention of declaring peace, the sham peace talks can be seen as:

   (A) An agreement to disagree

   (B) Competing diversionary tactics

   (C) Hedging bets in case either nation needed to fall back on a peace treaty

   (D) A show for international audiences who wanted to prevent war in Europe

   (E) Proof that each nation interpreted the real intentions of its opponents poorly

4. The main strategy of defense by the English against the Spanish seemed to be:

    (A) Bogging Spain down in international politics

    (B) Surprise attacks

    (C) Its geographic isolation

    (D) Spying

    (E) Intimidation

5. The phrase "Sewing the fox's skin to the lion" in line 11 implies what about Spain's use of the peace talks:

    (A) Spain used the peace talks to tie up English resources necessary for an early English attack

    (B) Spain used the peace talks to make itself seem weaker than it was

    (C) Spain used the peace talks to find out how powerful the English were

    (D) Spain used the peace talks to gather international support for a just war

    (E) Spain had nothing to lose by engaging in the peace talks

6. The term "spent" in line 12 most directly means:

    (A) Completed

    (B) No longer valuable

    (C) Beyond the control of the Spanish

    (D) Exchanged for something valuable

    (E) Wasted

7. In line 17, the term "advantage" refers to:

    (A) The opportunity for peace

    (B) Popular support

    (C) Naval superiority

    (D) A surprise attack

    (E) A well defended coastline

8. If not for England's early surgical attacks against Spain, it can be concluded that:

    (A) England would have been forced to make peace

    (B) The Spanish would never have taken revenge on England

    (C) There would not have been popular support to attack England

    (D) Spain would have fought and won a war against England

    (E) Spain could have kept its war against England a secret until it was time to attack

Passage 9

The Big Dig is the unofficial term for the Central Artery/Tunnel Project, a massive undertaking to replace the existing elevated Central Artery (Interstate 93) through the heart of Boston, Massachusetts, with an underground highway. The design includes a new tunnel to Logan Airport. Due for completion in 2004, it is the most expensive highway project in American history (roughly $15 billion, or more than $1 billion per mile). The Zakim Bunker Hill Bridge at the project's northern end has already become a
5   new symbol of Boston. Reworking such a busy corridor without seriously restricting traffic flow required a number of state-of-the-art construction techniques. Because the old elevated highway (which remained in operation throughout the construction process) rested on pylons located throughout the designated dig area, engineers first utilized slurry-wall techniques to create 120 ft. deep concrete walls upon which the highway could rest. These concrete walls stabilized the sides of the site, preventing cave-ins during the excavation process. Other challenges included an existing subway tunnel crossing the path of the underground highway. In order
10 to build slurry walls past this tunnel, it was necessary to excavate under the tunnel and build an underground concrete bridge to support the tunnel's weight.

The Zakim Bunker Hill Bridge, designed by Swiss designer Christian Menn, represents the terminus of the project, connecting the underground highway with I-93 and Route 3. The bridge is a distinctive suspension bridge supported by two forked towers, which are connected to the span by cables and girders. On January 17, 2003, the opening ceremony was held for a 1.3-mile tunnel section
15 of the Dig, connecting the Massachusetts Turnpike to Logan International Airport. The westbound lanes opened in the afternoon of January 18 and the eastbound lanes early January 19. The tunnel is expected to reduce the trip from downtown Boston from 45 minutes in traffic to 8 minutes. The next phase, taking the elevated Interstate 93 and putting it underground, will be completed in two stages: the northbound lanes are scheduled to open in March 2003 and the southbound lanes by early 2004.

1. One factor that made the Central Artery Tunnel Project labor intensive overall was:

   (A)   Accommodating the flow of existing traffic

   (B)   The need for state-of-the-art construction techniques

   (C)   The shortage of funds to cover the project

   (D)   The extent of money spent on the project

   (E)   Lowering the pylons onto a support wall

2. Referring to the Zakim Bunker Hill Bridge as a new symbol of Boston suggests that it is important because:

   (A)   It brings the aesthetically conservative tunnel onto the aesthetically progressive bridge span

   (B)   The project represents a long unrealized unification of Boston with the surrounding suburbs

   (C)   It physically makes future progress and growth possible for Boston

   (D)   It is a physical demonstration of Boston's ability to progress and grow

   (E)   The bridge connection between the airport and the city shows how Boston has finally become a global city

3. The Zakim Bunker Hill Bridge is to the Central Artery Tunnel Project as:

   (A)   The Reichstag is to German independence

   (B)   The Petronas towers are to the Malaysian economy

   (C)   The Berlin Wall was to German unification

   (D)   Red Square is to the Kremlin

   (E)   The spire is to the Eiffel Tower

4. When the passage mentions how the engineers "first" used state-of-the art slurry wall techniques in line 7 it most nearly means:

   (A)   This was the first time the slurry wall technique was used

   (B)   It was the initial step in shoring up the elevated highway

   (C)   Slurry walls were used for the elevated highway before they were used for the subway tunnel

   (D)   Slurry walls were the best option for preventing cave-ins

   (E)   Slurry walls appeared to work on paper but could not be used in practice

5. The practical benefit of the tunnel to city drivers is:

   (A)   The ability to reach parts of the city previously inaccessible

   (B)   Its ability to attract more business and jobs to the Boston region

   (C)   Its ability to reduce the time to commute to downtown Boston

   (D)   Its ability to eliminate traffic in the downtown area

   (E)   The opportunity to use the westbound lanes while the eastbound lanes are still under construction

6. The mood of the passage is:

   (A)   Biased

   (B)   Unbiased

   (C)   Declaratory

   (D)   Extemporaneous

   (E)   Scathing

7. The word "excavate" in line 10 most directly refers:

   (A)   To weakening the stability of the subway tunnel

   (B)   To digging out the underlying dirt and rock

   (C)   To sinking the anchors for the underground bridge

   (D)   To running the Central Artery Tunnel through the subway tunnel

   (E)   To making the subway tunnel unnecessary

8. The Central Artery Tunnel will replace:

   (A)   The Central Artery

   (B)   Stretches of Boston's subway

   (C)   Massachusetts Turnpike

   (D)   The tunnel to Logan airport

   (E)   An underground bridge

Passage 10

Many games of deceit designed to extort material from unsuspecting targets are often as old as the history of contracts and arbitrage. At best, many modern scams pour time-proven combinations of treachery and connivance into new molds. Still, the characters, the motives and the techniques roll through well-worn courses, and today's confidence games simply show that while one classic conman's style can grow all too recognizable, the core plot of a con can survive changes in times and in peoples.

5 Classical, or ad hoc, cons are talked about in two ways: big or short. Both take aim at a "mark" or an unwitting victim, and require preparation, theatrics and near metronomic timing. Both cons are actually relatively short-lived. Their distinction lies in what is taken from the victim. The short con seeks to relieve the mark of what he has on him, while the big con "puts the mark on the send", or sends him out for more than he has on his standing person. A big con requires a large outlay of money, people and time, and generally requires more extravagant showmanship as well as more precise coordination of the basic characteristics. Often, a

10 big con will require the con man to create a whole perimeter of relationships with which to surround his mark. The target is left to wonder at the web of relationships, but would be overwhelmed if he considered the possibility of premeditation, and the staggering organization of time and people that is aimed squarely at him. Still, a con generally relies on the fact that the mark is unsuspecting from the start.

For the con man, the job of distracting his mark from the possibility that he is being corralled into a controlled environment lies
15 in the rigors of preparation. That early work requires several steps, including finding a victim worth the unavoidable risk of being discovered. The rewards of success must also be sufficient to repay the costs of setting up the stage-work of the con. This work is shared by a "roper" and an "insideman", with the roper lassoing the victim into the con, and turning him over to the insideman, who plays the role of the legitimate businessman with something to offer. Such conmen succeed by playing characters that are seemingly in opposition to each other. Their tactics are preemptive, predicting the movements of their victim and taking steps together,
20 beforehand, to make everything appear to their mark like a game of chance with the odds in his favor.

1. The main difference between modern confidence games and older ones is the:

(A) Style

(B) Plot

(C) Approach

(D) Roles

(E) Combinations of elements

2. The distinction between a short con and a big con is primarily:

(A) The outlay of money

(B) The degree of preparation

(C) The type of item sought

(D) The location of the item sought

(E) The quality of the "mark"

3. A successful con most likely requires a "mark":

(A) To have experienced cons before

(B) To have never experienced a con

(C) To be carrying a large amount of money

(D) To be carrying little money

(E) To be overwhelmed if he considered the possibility of a con

4. The most appropriate title for this passage is:

    (A)   A Short History of Scams

    (B)   The Art of the Con

    (C)   Taken In: How to Protect Yourself from Fast Eddie

    (D)   Comparing Cons

    (E)   What Snake Oil's Good For: How to Turn Their Deceit into Your Advantage

5. The author of this passage would most likely agree with which assessment:

    (A)   Confidence scams are examples of the inefficiencies of transactions

    (B)   Confidence scams require traditional business acumen

    (C)   Confidence scams are unlikely to work

    (D)   Thespians are no less skilled than con artists

    (E)   Most people deal fairly because the returns on a successful con are slim compared with its preparations

6. The comparative phrase "Classical or ad hoc" in line 5 is used in the sentence beginning with the same phrase to:

    (A)   Show the durability of time tested cons across a range of styles

    (B)   Demonstrate the universality of the upcoming definitions

    (C)   Show that cons can take on more than one form

    (D)   Point out that modern cons, though successful, are less prepared

    (E)   Link modern cons to ancient Greece

7. According to the passage, the oppositional roles played by the "roper" and "insideman" are used to:

    (A)   Give the mark an inaccurate picture of the chances of being successful

    (B)   Disguise their complicity

    (C)   Increase the apparent likelihood of profit for the mark

    (D)   Present the "roper" as a victim

    (E)   Encourage the "mark" to feel sympathy for the "roper"

8. If all these sentences follow this passage, which would come first?

    (A)   "Obviously, many things can go wrong when planning for the future, so it is the availability of contingency plans which separate good cons from failed ones."

    (B)   "It is very difficult to persuade a victim to relinquish the advantage to the insideman, taking up a considerable portion of a con's run time."

    (C)   "Often conmen feel no remorse for their behavior, making victims all the more vulnerable to harm."

    (D)   "It is at this stage that all the participants in the con seek their payment."

    (E)   "The legal framework of American justice allows this duplicity to succeed because people rely excessively on the law to reclaim their property, rather than avoiding these situations in the first place."

Passage 11

The attack on Pearl Harbor by the Japanese introduced America to the world theater of World War II. What was unique about this battle was that American citizens experienced it as the first attack on American soil in what was then recent memory. Throughout World War I, Americans mostly felt secure in their homes. However, the changing times and the audacity of nationalistic world powers, raised questions as to the need for civilian defense.

5 The highest priority was the protection of children from possible attack. The escalation of World War II already involved lengthy campaigns of civil terror waged by opposing powers. No power with a soldiering part in the war was immune or blameless. Germany unleashed the lengthiest bombing campaign of the war on the people of London primarily to weaken British morale. Later, the Allied Forces would fire-bomb on the German city of Dresden. Dresden had housed an almost entirely civilian population and had incidental wartime production.

10 Early on, Britain and the United States enacted an emergency measure to protect their youth population. A leading concern was the exposure to gas attack, an effective measure against unwitting urban dwellers. Immediately after Pearl Harbor, thousands of military training masks were rushed to people living on the islands. However, the available equipment was unsuitable for protecting children. Instead, Hawaiian officials produced an expedient made up of bunny ears and a hood. This would lead to further improvisation in the protection of the child civilian population. The Sun Rubber Company designed a mask based on the universal Walt Disney cartoon
15 figure Mickey Mouse. The Mickey Mouse gas mask was then approved by the Chemical Warfare Service of the U.S. Department of Defense, with the assumption that other winning designs could follow the success of this first run. The popularity of these masks was dependent on internalizing their use in children by making their presence part of a perceived game. This potentially reduced the element of fear that the masks conveyed on their recipients. If the element of fear could be diminished, gas masks might be employed by their owners more quickly in the event of an attack, and also worn without interruption. All of this would increase the
20 chances of survival of the youth population, of no small concern to a nation with large numbers of its working age males facing the perils of combat overseas.

1. According to the passage, the main distinction between World War I and World War II for Americans was:

   (A) the lengthy campaigns of civil terror

   (B) the blame shared by all participating powers

   (C) the mobilization of civilian factories for military use

   (D) the first violation of national security in several generations

   (E) the threat of nationalism from foreign aggressors

2. The purpose of national armies engaging in civil terror is presented by the passage as being:

   (A) the destruction of the civilian wartime infrastructure

   (B) to reduce the number of potential reinforcements for dwindling armies

   (C) to keep armies and pilots active during long periods without confrontation

   (D) to destroy the enemy's willingness to continue fighting

   (E) to kill key people

3. The design of gas masks to look like cartoon characters was intended to:

   (A) make the war seem less omnipresent to children

   (B) make children less afraid of a foreign attack

   (C) induce children to learn how to use the mask properly

   (D) increase sales of gas masks to families

   (E) bring a level of normalcy back to everyday life

4. The passage observes that the special efforts taken to consider the need to protect the youth population were based on concerns that:

    (A)   they may be needed to replenish the lines of men in the trenches

    (B)   they would be needed to repopulate the country if the men overseas do not return

    (C)   they may have been the only ones available to work jobs throughout the economy after the war

    (D)   they were the main concern of parents who vote

    (E)   once children get sick, they are the most difficult to bring back to health

5. The topic of the passage can best be described as:

    (A)   the coordination of the wartime economy to meet civilian defense

    (B)   the special efforts to protect children in response to heightened civilian vulnerability

    (C)   the need for all nations to engage in civilian terror tactics

    (D)   the incorporation of popular images in the tools of war

    (E)   the resourcefulness of the American military machine in meeting wartime production

6. In the sentence beginning with 'Instead, Hawaiian officials', the word 'expedient' most nearly means:

    (A)   to execute quickly

    (B)   a cleaning agent

    (C)   a response to an urgent need

    (D)   a terror tactic

    (E)   a placebo

7. The benefit of internalizing the use of these masks in children was that:

    (A)   they would wear them to bed

    (B)   they would take the masks to school

    (C)   they would encourage friends to use them

    (D)   they would not be afraid

    (E)   their lack of fear would keep them from hesitating

8. It can be inferred from the reading that a significant avoidable danger of a wartime terror attack is:

    (A)   enemy propaganda

    (B)   the youth of the civilian population

    (C)   poor decisions on the part of unprepared civilians

    (D)   the damage to civilian morale

    (E)   the lack of warning of an attack

Passage 12

What had once been considered the just and predictable result of western capitalist decadence now confronts the Russian Federation as a sobering reality: the widespread proliferation of illicit drug abuse and the accompanying illnesses of addiction. The factor most responsible for the startling abundance of drugs in parts of Russia, where once cannabis and opium derivatives had been considered curious finds, is fundamentally the diversification of the supply points.

5 No longer must the overwhelming proportion of hard drugs reach Russia's interior through St. Petersburg or Moscow. Whereas under Soviet leadership, Moscow and St. Petersburg were reliable bottlenecks between the western European and even Asian sources of illicit drugs, post-Soviet Russia has seen the development of supply lines to almost all of its interior regions from ambitious suppliers all along Russia's borders, now shared with independent, unstable republics that were once encompassed by the Soviet Union.

That reality has meant that in regions where once vodka, glue, acetone, gasoline and anesthetics were the alternatives to sobriety, all 10 forms of illegal psychoactive substances can now be had. Canvassing of the Russian people seems to demonstrate that psychoactive substances are used in high quantities. The challenges to Russian officials, surprised by this boom in drug abuse, have been not only convincing the public against making these choices but also obtaining credible data on Russian drug use. Because the rise in illegal consumption may be regarded as evidence of ineffective or corrupt police practices, underreporting of abuse has been standard practice by regional agents of the government on whom officials in Moscow rely for information. Therefore, the job of 15 reclaiming the health of the Russian people will start not just with convincing the Russian people of the drawbacks of narcotic use, but in informing government employees throughout the country of the need to share in the view that frequent drug consumption is the precursor of a public health crisis, not the calling card of bad police work.

1. The first sentence in line 1 directly suggests what about the perception of drug use by Soviet officials:

    (A) Widespread narcotic abuse is the result of wealth

    (B) Widespread narcotic abuse comes from open borders

    (C) Widespread narcotic abuse is a sign of social decay

    (D) Widespread narcotic abuse is most likely to occur where rules pertaining to it are lax

    (E) Widespread narcotic abuse is the predictable result of inequality

2. The second sentence in line 2 and the following paragraph serve to invalidate the presumption of the opening line by:

    (A) Taking the blame away from Russian officials

    (B) Showing that Russian officials were not prepared for the drawbacks of a diverse economy

    (C) Removing the blame from drug suppliers

    (D) Showing that drug use needs to be understood in economic terms

    (E) Showing that Russia has become much like western capitalist powers

3. According to the passage, the ability of Soviet leadership to suppress drug abuse in the Soviet Union was linked to:

    (A) Soviet influence on the values of the populace

    (B) Price supports for alternatives to hard drugs

    (C) The ability to police all republics of the Soviet Union

    (D) Prevailing wages being too low to make abusing drugs an option

    (E) A unified public with solid values

4. The passage would most likely describe the problem of underreporting from Russia's officials and police as an example of:

   (A)   Compliance

   (B)   An organizational pathology

   (C)   Unrealistic expectations

   (D)   A failure of executives

   (E)   Honesty

5. It can be inferred from the passage that the difference between drug use in the Soviet Union and post-Soviet Russia is that:

   (A)   Soviet Union did not experience drug abuse, while post-Soviet Russia is plagued with drugs

   (B)   Drugs were highly regulated in Soviet Union; they are unregulated in post-Soviet Russia

   (C)   Soviet Union experienced drugs as a problem in major urban centers; post-Soviet Russia sees drugs as a more universal problem

   (D)   Cases of drug abuse in Soviet Union were well reported; cases of drug abuse in post-Soviet Russia are underreported

   (E)   The now-independent republics of the former Soviet Union see Western Europe as a target for drugs produced in the Central Asian region

6. The main concern of the passage regarding the use of hard drugs in Russia seems to be:

   (A)   The deterioration of social values

   (B)   The rise of an underclass

   (C)   The strengthening of unstable independent Republics

   (D)   The unleashing of disease

   (E)   The inability of the police to control the paths of drugs into Russia

7. The passage attests that the increase in hard drugs consumed by Russians can be observed because:

   (A)   Though police underreport discoveries of narcotics, the numbers they are reporting have still increased

   (B)   The power of the independent Republics seems to be inexplicably growing

   (C)   The price of drugs has decreased throughout Russia

   (D)   Russian people admit it

   (E)   Russian people must regularly be caught with drugs on them

8. Solving the drug crisis in Russia requires:

   (A)   Reliable information sources

   (B)   More police

   (C)   Closing borders

   (D)   A television campaign

   (E)   Making Moscow and St. Petersburg the bottlenecks they once were

Passage 13

The relationship between consumers and business in the U.S has been delineated by mass production, proprietary models and in-
house managerial hierarchies. These systems have benefited from the movement of capital between companies, and used the gains to
assure the dominance of the United States by building a national distribution network with a standardized product aimed at universal
appeal. A sociologist of capitalism would remark that in order for many of these industries to have survived, whether they were
5   canning meat or pre-fabricating houses for sale by catalog, they would not only have had to set up the physical distribution links,
but also have had to convince the public to patronize their unfamiliar product instead of a local or regional product. Since existing
markets are linked to coveted notions of local culture, independence and highly specialized tastes, using mass producers instead of
regional craftspeople would not simply entail selling cheaper staples as a substitution for what was regionally available. Indeed the
large-scale producers redefined the American economy in the early twentieth century, although this redefinition involved a certain
10 degree of political wrangling and influence to gain control of a national market with a standardized product. The government made
some business associations, such as cartels, illegal and advocated centralized, legal monopolies and holding companies, tailored for
the capital markets. This process assured centralized management and a group of producers willing to put up a high fixed investment
for single purpose machinery.

While there are different versions of this brief history of 20th century U.S. capitalism, the success of the mass production model,
15 resting on a standard and interchangeable product, has been at odds with the specialized production of individual craftsmen since the
U.S. market matured into a producer of goods in two ways. Eventually, mass producers became the de-facto standard. Depending on
one's view, the public's entitlement to regulation of business, and especially monopolies, has much to do with the amount of political
influence that created this original dualism in the economy and defined the outcome of this influence. If one holds the contention that
the passage of the anti-trust law and the emergence of legislation legalizing the holding company made mass production 'politically
20 feasible' and boutique production (heavily reliant on associations of laborers and merchants) illegal, one can make the argument that
the large corporation owes something of its success to government.

1. It can be inferred from the passage that if the U.S. government had not passed legislation regarding collusion that:

    (A) Monopolies would dominate the political sphere in the United States

    (B) Many industries in the United States would be under federal control

    (C) Small business would be far more successful

    (D) The stability of American markets would not be what it is today

    (E) Workers would be better off

2. The author's attitude towards proprietary mass producers is:

    (A) Neutral

    (B) Dismissive

    (C) Aggrieved

    (D) Negative

    (E) One of Consternation

3. According to the passage, canned meats would be least likely to penetrate which of the following markets:

    (A) A prison population

    (B) Military purchasers

    (C) Overseas markets

    (D) An immigrant enclave

    (E) A company town

4. In the beginning of the second paragraph, the phrase "While there are different versions of this brief history" in line 14 implies the author:

   (A)   May be wrong

   (B)   Is in doubt

   (C)   Does not know the whole story

   (D)   Has a political rather than a historical perspective

   (E)   Considers but dismisses other arguments

5. One argument the author would most likely make regarding the future of government intervention in business is:

   (A)   The government is an unnatural actor in market transactions

   (B)   The government increases the costs of doing business for market actors

   (C)   Intervention could have contributed to the success of large corporations.

   (D)   Intervention is an inevitable reality in a stable market economy

   (E)   Intervention is the result of political power interests competing with one another

6. A central concern of the author in arguing that mass producers benefited from a particular legal framework is:

   (A)   To show that small business networks may experience resurgence

   (B)   To defend the perspective of those in favor of government intervention

   (C)   To belittle the role of corporate business in America

   (D)   To point out a historical fact

   (E)   To credit the government for having the foresight to regulate the economy

7. The turning point in the rise of mass production for the American economy is portrayed by the passage as being:

   (A)   Mass producers becoming the default standard for the economy

   (B)   The increase in the variety of goods on the market

   (C)   Dissatisfaction in the workforce

   (D)   Criminalizing collusion among small producers

   (E)   Declining production standards

8. According to the passage, the actors with the most to gain by ushering mass production into the American economic framework were:

   (A)   Immigrants with low-level skills in need of reliable jobs

   (B)   Federal regulators seeking to extend their control over a fractured proletariat

   (C)   Overseas corporations

   (D)   Actors willing to risk a great deal on fixed investment

   (E)   The unemployed

Passage 14

Lord Dalhousie is credited with the creation of the modern postal system in India. Dalhousie, who held many roles in the administration and internal development of the region, contributed to the Indian postal system by sweeping away the fabric of its past obstructions and levying a uniform rate of postage.

All letters weighing less than a prescribed amount in weight would require the same postal fee (half an ana) regardless of their
5 destination or origin. This idea of instituting a uniform unit of weight and of charge for the whole of the vast Indian empire seemed to many orthodox financiers of his time to be sheer folly. It was, they said, pushing Rowland Hill's scheme of a penny postage for England to an extreme. For these onlookers, Dalhousie's plan was not so much an extension of the English penny postage scheme, as a reduction ad absurdum of the reform that had been effected in Great Britain. What could be more extravagant or more unjust than to levy the same charge on two letters, one of which was to be delivered to the adjoining street, and the other to the opposite
10 side of India.

Lord Dalhousie was not significantly deterred by the criticism. Because of the uniform rate of postage, the old wrangle over the payment for delivery of every letter, from which the rural postman invariably managed to squeeze something additional for himself at the expense of the recipient, could be replaced by a simple system of postage stamps. The system was more reliable for the person mailing the letter, and encouraged increased patronage.

15 The proof of his success was the renewal of the postal system as a self-sustaining organization rather than its continuance as a chronic drain on British colonial finances. The social results were even more important. It has been said that the half-penny post that Lord Dalhousie put in place in India was more consequential than the telegraph, the railway and even Public Instruction for reversing the isolation which predated it.

1. The objections to the uniform postal rate in India were related to:

    (A) The fact that it was not fair to charge the same rate for different degrees of service

    (B) The fact that it was an unproven method

    (C) The fact that it conveyed a lack of trust in postal workers

    (D) The inability of the letter delivery service to handle a flood of cross-India mail

    (E) An attempt by critics to put their own recommendations in place

2. According to the passage, the main benefit of the half-penny post scheme to India was:

    (A) An increase in the rate of communication throughout the subcontinent

    (B) Increased rates of literacy

    (C) Reduced corruption among the postmen

    (D) Its independence from British financial support

    (E) A tradeoff between reliability and patronage

3. It can be assumed from the results of Dalhousie's revisions of India's postal system that:

    (A) The only way to see if something will be successful is to put it into practice

    (B) That if something works on a small scale, it should work on a large scale as well, if executed properly

    (C) That disorganization and unreliability may be more costly than charging at rates below expenses

    (D) That Britain's financial support of the postal system gave it no incentive to improve

    (E) India was a single, coherent state in a way no one had anticipated

4. One lesson that can be taken from Dalhousie's success is:

   (A) Personal experience can be more informed than extensive theoretical knowledge

   (B) Postal systems are one example of a good that is not subject to supply and demand curves

   (C) There had been British mismanagement

   (D) Long term social gains can compensate for short term capital losses

   (E) For Britain's purposes, the penny postage scheme should have preceded the telegraph, the railway and Public Instruction

5. In line 8, the term "reduction ad absurdum" most closely means:

   (A) To misunderstand the purpose of an idea

   (B) To simplify an idea while losing its key elements

   (C) To extend an idea to a scale beyond which it is practical

   (D) To make a functional premise seem ridiculous

   (E) To apply an idea to an unrelated problem

6. The passage specifies that simplifying the mail system compensated the post office for the costs of uniform postage by:

   (A) Reducing staff

   (B) Increasing patronage

   (C) Increasing reliability

   (D) Creating postage stamps

   (E) Creating a market for written communication

7. The most decisive evidence of Dalhousie having made the right decision in instituting his postal scheme is:

   (A) Increased patronage

   (B) Reduced corruption in India

   (C) Its previous success in England as Rowland Hill's postal scheme

   (D) The attainment of a financially sound postal system

   (E) The quieting of critics

8. The experience of Lord Dalhousie in the passage demonstrates that:

   (A) Larger markets may experience increased transaction costs

   (B) Transaction costs are negligible

   (C) Postal workers are always corrupt

   (D) Letters are the most efficient means of communication

   (E) Standardization has the ability to reduce transaction costs

Passage 15

There is a perception among many legislators in post-industrial economies that there is a worn path to economic prosperity that leads to an increase in the standard of living. This perception is embodied in the common language which compares nations competing with one another to 'big corporations' competing with one another, an idea Bill Clinton used in trying to establish a path towards an information services economy in America. However, this perception, that there is a specific, and even predictable, direction
5 growth must go in, and that it must be done at the expense of manufacturing industries, as well as to the detriment of other countries, overlooks the way in which social groups, productivity and technology interact. Moreover, it overlooks the fact that, as economist Paul Krugman favors saying, countries are not direct competitors with one another. In fact, the term 'competitive', in regards to national economies, begins to lose all useful meaning when it is applied to rival states. As such, quickly removing a manufacturing sector in order to encourage the growth of an information and service sector can unnecessarily remove jobs from an economy
10 and destroy the balance that is necessary, even in a post-industrial economy, between the manufacturing sector and the information processing sector. Seeing this sort of move as the inevitable path to technological development can be presumptuous and misdirected, especially if the goal is seen as economic growth at the expense of a perceived competitor, with whom one must continue to trade goods and purchase economic inputs.

Thus, innovation does not define a set path on which a national economy must embark to take full advantage of its resources. Indeed,
15 matching the skills of the labor force and the present resources of the country with demand in the international market is not a policy that can be discounted or that is devalued in the face of technological advances. The standard of living within a country is not a function of the size of the white collar workforce, but of how well an economy matches the skills of its workers to its productive activities, and how well it fulfills the demands of global markets. Institutions within a country can help improve and direct the skills of a national workforce, while accommodating quality of life considerations, without an economy having to be at a disadvantage
20 compared to a foreign managerial or information economy. This does not assume that an information economy does not give a nation certain political, military and status advantages over other nations, but the relationships among nations do not have to be limited to equalizing their information processing sectors.

1. One drawback stated in the passage of attempting to spur the economy of a nation through premature service sector concentration is:

    (A) States are not in competition with one another

    (B) Growth is not predictable

    (C) A decline in manufacturing output

    (D) The loss of jobs

    (E) The threat to the military from a decline in manufacturing

2. The passage views Bill Clinton's comparison between nation states and big corporations to be:

    (A) Premature

    (B) Anticipatory

    (C) Inaccurate

    (D) Plausible

    (E) Hyperbole

3. One reason the passage offers for why it is inaccurate to view national economies as competitors is:

    (A) Lack of statistical proof

    (B) Inability of nation states to conform to the tenets of game theory

    (C) The ineffectiveness of viewing economic actors as competitors

    (D) The need to purchase key inputs from one another

    (E) Cultural similarities

4. It can be inferred from the passage that one reason the economies of nations might be considered to be competitors is because:

  (A) As one nation's economy improves another's deteriorates

  (B) There are finite resources in the world

  (C) Economies seek to draw talented labor from one another

  (D) Certain types of economies facilitate military strength

  (E) It is the only explanation that matches modern political events

5. The passage suggests that which of the following would best correspond with the suggested measures a nation should take to improve its economic outlook:

  (A) Cutting luxury taxes to encourage the construction of residential high-rise buildings

  (B) Establishing a close relationship between educational institutions and businesses

  (C) Phasing out agricultural production for cheaper imported crops

  (D) Permitting a trade deficit in order to increase eventually the export of intellectual goods

  (E) Eliminating manufacturing

6. From the passage which of the following can be concluded:

  (A) Growth is predictable

  (B) Social groups are not involved in technological growth

  (C) Manufacturing is not detrimental to the service sector

  (D) Manufacturing is the key sector in an economy

  (E) Manufacturing should be subsidized by government

7. An appropriate title for this passage might be:

  (A) How to Reinvent an Economy

  (B) Corporate Competition among Nation States

  (C) The Shoe That Fits: Wearing the Success that You Have

  (D) No Losers: How All the World Economies are One World Economy

  (E) Homegrown Success: Rusting Factories and Knowledge Mints

8. The purpose of this passage is to:

  (A) Answer a question

  (B) Outline a problem

  (C) Provide a set of directions

  (D) Dispel a myth

  (E) Compare two possible solutions

Passage 16

However inventive Newton's clockwork universe seemed to his contemporaries, by the early twentieth century, it had become a sort of smugly accepted dogma. Luckily for us, this deterministic picture of the universe breaks down at the atomic level.

The clearest demonstration that the laws of physics contain elements of randomness is the behavior of radioactive atoms. Pick two identical atoms of a radioactive isotope, say naturally occurring uranium 238, and watch them carefully. They will begin to decay
5 at different times, even though there was no difference in their initial behavior. We would be in big trouble if these atoms' behavior were as predictable as expected in the Newtonian world-view, because radioactivity is an important source of heat for our planet. In reality, each atom chooses a random moment at which to release its energy, resulting in a nice steady heating effect. The earth would be a much colder planet if only sunlight heated it and not radioactivity. Probably there would be no volcanoes, and the oceans would never have been liquid. The deep-sea geothermal vents in which life first evolved would never have existed.

10 But there would be an even worse consequence if radioactivity were deterministic: after a few billion years of peace, all the uranium 238 atoms in our planet would presumably pick the same moment to decay. The huge amount of stored nuclear energy, instead of being spread out over eons, would all be released simultaneously, blowing our whole planet to kingdom come. (This is under the assumption that all the uranium atoms were created at the same time. In reality, we have only a general idea of the process that might have created the heavy elements in the gas cloud from which our solar system condensed. Some portion may have come from
15 nuclear reactions in supernova explosions in that nebula, some from intra-galactic supernova explosions and others still from exotic events like the collisions of white dwarf stars.)

The new version of physics, incorporating certain kinds of randomness, is called quantum physics. It represented such a dramatic break with the previous, deterministic tradition that everything that came before is considered classical, even the theory of relativity.

1. The main theme of this passage discusses:

   (A) How Newtonian physics is irrelevant

   (B) The difference between supernova explosions and star collisions

   (C) The worldly benefits of uranium 238

   (D) How randomness is a fundamental principle of modern physics

   (E) The danger of accepting an idea without continuing to challenge it

2. The author discusses the activity of uranium 238 atoms to show:

   (A) That no two atoms are exactly alike

   (B) The dangers of nuclear power

   (C) How sunlight alone could never heat the planet

   (D) How Newtonian physics can explain all aspects of the physical world

   (E) How randomness exists in the most basic constructs of the physical world

3. According to the passage, identical radioactive isotopes:

   (A) Were overlooked by Newton

   (B) Can have different chemical properties

   (C) Are subject to different physical events

   (D) Decay at different rates

   (E) May begin to decay at different times

4. According to the passage, the Theory of Relativity is considered:

   (A)   The pinnacle of quantum physics

   (B)   A Newtonian explanation of randomness

   (C)   Incorrect

   (D)   Deterministic

   (E)   A bridge between the classical tradition and quantum physics

5. The passage demonstrates how central randomness was to the development of life on Earth by saying that if it had not existed the most important consequence would have been that:

   (A)   Deep sea vents could never have evolved

   (B)   Light would travel at different speeds depending on its point of origin

   (C)   Uranium 238 atoms would decay simultaneously and destroy the earth

   (D)   The earth would not have a way to store the sun's heat

   (E)   Genetic mutations

6. An appropriate title for this piece might be:

   (A)   Randomness and Supernovas: Theories and Events Which Lead to Life

   (B)   A Review of Classical Physics and Newtonian Tenets

   (C)   Revising the Model: The Most Basic Principle of Physics

   (D)   Einstein's Dice: The Classic-Quantum Debate

   (E)   Renaming Physics: Accepting the Role of Randomness in the Principles We Learned

7. The style of this piece can be best regarded as:

   (A)   Journalistic

   (B)   Extemporaneous

   (C)   Hortatory

   (D)   Encyclopedic

   (E)   Considered

8. The author presents quantum physics as:

   (A)   The incorrect interpretation of physical events

   (B)   A way of explaining events using Newtonian physics

   (C)   An explanation of the rules of the physical world

   (D)   The replacement of Newtonian physics

   (E)   The missing piece of Newtonian physics

Passage 17

Synergetics is an epistemology for interpreting concepts in life through geometric relationships. Buckminster Fuller, a multi-disciplinary scholar and inventor, coined the term synergetics to describe what he considered a "coordinate system" for the physical universe, summoning the language of the Cartesian coordinate plane with which mathematicians graph physical space. Synergetics has come to serve as a method for describing the behavior of whole systems whose behavior cannot be predicted from independent
5   analyses of their parts. In Fuller's conception of synergetics, this coordinate system seeks to map not only the physical characteristics of the universe, but also the rationale structuring mankind's heuristic interpretations of the world. The basis of Fullers' model is that all observable phenomena can be codified as interactive systems, and those systems can be principally understood as a geography of spherical networks comprised of interrelated points of interest. Those interrelationships then equate with the morphology of observable phenomena.

10 At its most discrete, Fuller understood a "system" as being the first division one could make of the universe. That logic could then be applied to all things that existed. It follows that conceptual thoughts themselves are synergistic systems. Not the least of his intentions was to have a better way of speaking about the dynamics of the universe by understanding the structure of thinking, man's tool for hashing through observation, and composing it in relational terms. This would then lead to a model that demonstrated the nature of the paradigms that enveloped thought. If the known laws of the universe could be said to be bottled in thoughts, then Fuller
15 sought better carafes in which to carry and relay the derived logic of empirical knowledge. His immediate language for contending with these ideas, and creating a fluid, interactive metaphor for the activities of observable phenomena (in the form of physical energy, or ideas, or knowledge) was what came to him most readily, geometry. The unit of that geometry was the tetrahedron. It became the unit of his explanations.

Ultimately, Fuller offers a science of sociological networks and the internal riggings of the mind in order to construct a system of
20 rules for otherwise unruly occurrences. His subject matter was the pattern of all activity. Synergetics sought to create an explanatory model for experiencing natural occurrences by pointing to the underlying order of activity that is universally in harmony with mathematic rationality.

1. Synergetics can best be described as:

    (A)   A hard science

    (B)   A mathematical revolution

    (C)   An interpretation of knowledge

    (D)   A reorganization of the laws of physics

    (E)   A new lexicon for an unprecedented discussion

2. Synergetics can be termed "heuristic" in

    (A)   That it acts as a model for absorbing and inter-relating information

    (B)   That it is a model for better teaching of complicated relations

    (C)   That it serves as a model for social networks

    (D)   That it is both a real world and hypothetical application of knowledge

    (E)   No way. It is tautological not heuristic.

3. In line 8, "morphology" refers to:

    (A)   The empirical characteristics of the world

    (B)   The theoretical relationships of phenomena

    (C)   The changing relationships of matter

    (D)   The science of categorizing matter

    (E)   The nomenclature of taxonomy

4. Through Fuller's epistemology a "system" can best be understood as:

   (A)   A series of related mechanisms

   (B)   A unit

   (C)   A subgroup

   (D)   A component

   (E)   A conceptual thought

5. Fuller's most basic device for teaching synergetics as a model for thinking about empirical reality geometrically was:

   (A)   The system

   (B)   The pattern of all activity

   (C)   Mathematical rationality

   (D)   The tetrahedron

   (E)   Logic

6. Fuller would likely consider synergetics a scientific way of making sense of:

   (A)   Unobservable phenomena

   (B)   Inexplicable relationships

   (C)   Unpredictable outcomes

   (D)   Unrealistic undertakings

   (E)   Uncharted space

7. Fuller's "carafes" refer to:

   (A)   Transmitters of knowledge

   (B)   Laws of physics

   (C)   Uses of language

   (D)   Arabian cisterns

   (E)   Geometrical shapes

8. Synergetics would be least useful in explaining:

   (A)   How drosophila seem to defy the laws of aerodynamics

   (B)   The variations in the stock market

   (C)   Patterns of voting and the rise of a global political culture

   (D)   The changes in the Amazon ecosystem

   (E)   Why the sun rises in the east

Passage 18

The rise of the modern national debt, in seventeenth century England, was the result of a political process that placed France and England, long time saber-rattlers, in a swap of political support for financial struts. The financial disorders of the reign of the English King Charles II are believed to have been the source of his unpatriotic aberrations in foreign policy. These aberrations resulted in advantages for France over Holland. Indeed, Charles would not have been the slave of France in its schemes against Holland had he
5 not been obliged to depend on the subsidies of Louis, the French monarch.

The rise of the modern treasury system owes its breeding to this turn of events. The modern treasury system might have lingered much longer before separating from the exchequer system, in which it had been swathed, if it had not been for the dislocation of that exchequer system as a result of political unrest, which, in turn, arose from Charles' financial straits. Much of the blame for the creation of England's national debt falls on Charles himself. But a correct estimation of the financial difficulties of Charles'
10 government will almost inevitably lead posterity to reconsider its adverse verdict on Charles, and to transfer some part of the blame from him to the House of Commons. The truth was that Charles II returned to a bankrupt inheritance. The country had been exhausted by the financial demands made upon it by the strong policy of Oliver Cromwell, England's martial leader, and by the maintenance of the army at home for repression and of the navy on the high seas for aggression.

The taxable capacity of the country had been exceeded, with the twofold result that on the one hand the material and monetary
15 resources of the country had been exhausted, and that on the other the administration had been forced to borrow. From the moment of his accession Charles II was compelled to adopt the system of financing the government through private bankers. This system was not a novelty. The same bankers who financed Charles II had previously financed the Commonwealth not merely in London, but also in Dublin and Edinburgh. But what was novel was the intervention of Parliament to try to reform government expenditures through careful review of the exchequer's books, expecting to save the government from specie scarcities not by allocating it more
20 money, but by reordering the King's revenue.

1. The origins of the English national debt can be found in:

   (A) the use of foreign banks

   (B) the corruption of Charles II

   (C) the intervention of Holland

   (D) the policy making of Oliver Cromwell

   (E) overspending by Charles II

2. The passage dates the origin of England's national debt to the reign of Charles II by drawing which distinction between the debt of past governments and that of Charles?

   (A) the use of a system of financing by private bankers

   (B) the heavy military spending and low tax income

   (C) the exchange of political support regarding Holland for French money

   (D) the attempts by Parliament to regulate the King's books and assign responsibility for repayment

   (E) the unwillingness of the population to pay taxes

3. The factor presented by the passage as most responsible for Charles II's spending was:

   (A) the development of complex administration

   (B) exhaustive military spending

   (C) aberrations in his foreign policy

   (D) a reduction in the amount of freely available national currency

   (E) an inability to support the strong military presence England had established abroad

4. The author of the passage would most likely agree with which of the following notions?

    (A)   all history is revisionist

    (B)   it is a nation's people who determine its fiscal success more than its leader

    (C)   events coincide around leaders, placing credit or blame disproportionately in their hands

    (D)   leaders command events to occur and thus make their careers by spurring others to action

    (E)   the world climate created by the histories of opposing nation states outweighs the influence of their individual leaders

5. It can be inferred from the passage that the author considers the development of the modern treasury system in England:

    (A)   to have been a unique outcome of seventeenth century international politics

    (B)   to have been an advantageous occurrence

    (C)   to have been of dubious value

    (D)   to have been the intention of the House of Commons because of its pursuit of Cromwell's military policies

    (E)   to have been a reaction to Charles II's financial policies

6. Modern aspects of the treasury systems enacted under Charles II exclude:

    (A)   a treasury system separate from the exchequer

    (B)   officially presenting estimates and appropriation of supply

    (C)   private bankers financing the government

    (D)   parliamentary review of the exchequer's books

    (E)   reducing royal expenses

7. The decision of the House of Commons to take fiscal action only in response to foreign policy inconsistencies is relevant because:

    (A)   Parliament was responsible for military matters while the King assessed taxes and decided on spending

    (B)   Parliament may have contributed to the English debt crisis by being sympathetic to Cromwell's expensive foreign policy ambitions

    (C)   Parliament left too much responsibility to Cromwell and the King

    (D)   Parliament was unwilling to tax the people while it spent money on the army and navy

    (E)   Parliament had sought this scenario to advance constitutional rights

8. From the passage, it can be inferred that the term 'unpatriotic aberrations' in line 3 is used by the author to indicate:

    (A)   traitorous leanings of the king

    (B)   the perception of the people regarding his foreign policy

    (C)   a dislike of Holland

    (D)   a criticism of Cromwell's policies

    (E)   the king's opposition to French designs on his crown

Passage 19

If the reader consults any standard history of the Evangelical revival in Britain during the eighteenth century, he or she will probably conclude that the part played in the movement by the Moravians was almost entirely confined to their well-known influence over John Wesley, the famous horseback evangelizer and founder of the Methodist Church. This was, however, far from being the case. From the day when Wesley left the Fetter Lane Society (the original band of English Moravians adopted this name when they became
5 too numerous for their original meeting house, and moved to the Great Meeting House on Fetter Lane) in July 1740, the influence of the Moravians in England began, not to decrease, but to increase.

For the next fifteen years they were busily engaged in various parts of the country in vigorous evangelization. The Fetter Lane Society, the group that originated as an Anglican sit-down seminar group, developed a distinct faith with its own rituals. While for two years it still preserved its avowed character as an ordinary religious society, its zeal took on a more Moravian feel as it grew and
10 reorganized. The Moravians, a religious group who had first impressed Wesley on a sailing ship to the Americas, had inspired these men to come together and speak and act in a different way. However, the men were of Anglican stock. Although the society was supposed to be Anglican, the Moravian type of teaching became the order of the day. The public was admitted to the meetings and the services took a more stereotyped form. New societies were founded in other parts of the city. Finally, owing to mob disturbances, the chapel in Fetter Lane was licensed, and the brethren took upon themselves the name of "Moravian Brethren, formerly of the
15 Anglican Communion."

In one sense this was a dangerous step. As soon as the brethren asked for a license they practically, in the eyes of the law, assumed the position of dissenters. The next step was more important. A number of the members of the Fetter Lane Society applied to its leader for full admission to the Moravian Church. This was perplexing for Fetter Lane. There was not actually a Moravian congregation in England. However, the Fetter Lane "lot" gave a favorable answer, and seventy-two applicants joined to form the United Brethren of
20 England.

Nevertheless, this group did not consider itself departed from the Church of England. They spurned the title "Dissenters". They professed loyalty to the Anglican Church, and, doubtlessly, they were sincere.

1. The development of the United Brethren of England as a group separate from the Anglican Church can best be described as:

   (A) Inevitable
   (B) Calculated
   (C) Unintentional
   (D) Forced
   (E) Orchestrated

2. An important early step which moved these men of "Anglican stock" towards the Moravian faith was:

   (A) Evangelization
   (B) The adoption of the Moravian teaching style
   (C) The request for a license to be an independent organization
   (D) Turmoil in the Church of England
   (E) Papal conflicts

3. The passage seeks to dispel the common assumption that:

   (A) The Fetter Lane Society was not Anglican
   (B) The Moravians were insincere about their loyalty to the Anglican Church
   (C) The origin of the Moravian Church was the Fetter Lane society
   (D) John Wesley was more important to the Evangelical Revival than the Moravians
   (E) The Moravians only influence on the evangelical Revival was through John Wesley

4. The main topic of this passage is:

   (A) The role of the Moravian Church in the Evangelical Revival

   (B) The role of John Wesley in the founding of the Moravian Church

   (C) The rise of the Moravian Church from Anglican Roots

   (D) The reasons behind the similarities between the Anglican Church and Methodist Church

   (E) Religious organizing in 18th century England

5. What was responsible for the confusion as to what to do with the seventy-two applicants to the Moravian Church?

   (A) The large number of applicants

   (B) Concern about being labeled dissenters by the English crown

   (C) The inability to train the applicants in Moravian ritual

   (D) The lack of a Moravian church in England

   (E) The competition with other Religious Societies for legitimacy

6. The tone of the piece is best described as:

   (A) Encyclopedic

   (B) Polemical

   (C) Hortatory

   (D) An example of historiography

   (E) Extemporaneous

7. In the passage, the wariness of the English government to recognize the Moravians can be seen from what exchange between Moravians and the English government:

   (A) The unwillingness of the Moravians to be labeled as dissenters

   (B) The title granted in the License "Moravian Brethren formerly of the Anglican Communion"

   (C) The granting of the license owing to mob disturbances

   (D) The fleeing of Moravians to America

   (E) The confusion of Moravians about what to do with the seventy two applicants

8. The progression of the Moravians from a religious society into a recognized independent congregation followed what order:

   (A) Anglican Church-Fetter Lane Society-Moravian Brethren, formerly of the Anglican Communion-United Brethren of England

   (B) Anglican Church-Fetter Lane Society-Moravian Brethren, formerly of the Anglican Communion, Methodists, United Brethren of England

   (C) Anglican Church-Moravian Brethren, formerly of the Anglican Communion-United Brethren of England-Fetter Lane Society

   (D) Anglican Church-United Brethren of England-Moravian Brethren, formerly of the Anglican Communion-Fetter Lane Society

   (E) Anglican Church-United Brethren of England-Fetter Lane Society-Moravian Brethren, formerly of the Anglican Communion

Passage 20

The positioning of human beings as one of the species with the largest biomasses on earth, and as the leading influence on earth's ecosystems, is the result of the ecological processes which brought their migration from the African Savannah, and geographically dispersed them throughout the world. It can be said the most rudimentary measure of the success of the species is its position near the top of the aggregate biomass scale. Biomass is the total mass of all living members of a species. For human beings, it is a reflection
5 of their claim on territory, and their consumption of resources as a species. It might be short-sighted to belittle the success of an emerging species or breed for being small in number if it is evident that the members of the species are elegant and well-adjusted. However, the ability to adapt one's habitat to the largest ecosystem, while still retaining the flexibility to deal with local demands on the population may be considered high art in the annals of successful adaptation. It is here that human beings have had nearly unparalleled success (insects being larger in worldwide biomass). As a result human beings exist in huge numbers. It is the fact that
10 human beings have remained in a generally undifferentiated form that allows them to rank highly as a single successful species.

The whole world has been tenanted with life. Human beings are considered unique as they retain their form as they travel from environment to environment. Historically, human beings, like all organisms, may be driven into new areas, or a new environment may spring up around them as a result of drought, competition or geological changes. Still, human beings have been able to adjust their behavior sufficiently to avoid having nature make such extensive piecemeal adjustments to them that entirely distinct workable
15 alternatives of the same model occupy the new space. It was through such piecemeal adjustments that dinosaurs yielded to pigeons, primitive fish to amphibians and then eventually to whales, even Homo sapiens partially to Neanderthals for a time. In all cases, these offshoots and also-rans of each species had to co-exist alongside their preceding heritage. Thus, it can be said that many species, through one of their members, were able to succeed in carrying the genetic information of the group into another ecosystem. But eventually, each derivation became classified as something other than its ancestor. In this way, the transfer of genetic material
20 circles the globe, and a species takes on scientifically unique identities at different times and in different places. Humans thus remain distinct not because they are the first to exist in so many habitats, and take advantage of so many resources, but in that they have become one of the relatively few organisms to accomplish widespread population of different habitats while being able to exchange genetic material with others from their group, even if they had been largely geographically isolated over many generations.

1. According to the passage, the high ranking of human beings on a planetary biomass scale directly demonstrates which aspects of their success:

   (A) Their position at the top of the food chain

   (B) Their ability to eat almost anything and engineer their environment

   (C) Their ability to navigate their evolution

   (D) Their consumption of resources and claim on territory

   (E) Their mobility

2. What makes human beings unique in their colonization of the Earth is that:

   (A) They have existed at the same time in several genetic forms

   (B) Genetically they followed a similar path to that of dinosaurs

   (C) They withstood dispersal while becoming the only surviving species in their genus

   (D) They are the highest ranked organisms on the biomass scale

   (E) They carried their genetic code to all parts of the world

3. According to the passage, what characteristic has allowed human beings to avoid splitting into different species?

   (A) Their ability to reproduce with all the members of their species

   (B) Minimal exposure to geographic isolation

   (C) The death of all their competing species

   (D) Their ability to adjust their behavior to fit their environment

   (E) The presence of a very diverse genetic code with many permutations in a large population

4. The passage quantifies success in terms of:

    (A)   The length of time a species has been in its state

    (B)   The population density of a species

    (C)   The population size of a species

    (D)   The global dispersion of its genetic code

    (E)   The degree of adaptation to its environment

5. In the passage, an important factor in the success of a species is:

    (A)   Geographic dispersion

    (B)   The elimination of all but a few members of an original species

    (C)   The age of the preceding species

    (D)   Mutation

    (E)   Sexual selection

6. In the sentence beginning with 'In all cases' in line 16, the word 'preceding' means:

    (A)   Existing at the same time

    (B)   Receding from

    (C)   Diminishing with every generation

    (D)   Previous

    (E)   Migratory

7. The passage discusses genetic material in regard to which of the following:

    (A)   Consumption

    (B)   Mutations

    (C)   Spiral form

    (D)   Migration

    (E)   Disease

8. The style of this piece may be considered:

    (A)   Biased

    (B)   Polemical

    (C)   Balanced

    (D)   Vague

    (E)   Idealistic

3.2 Supplementary Reading

Passage 21

Beginning with Darwin's publication of the *Origin of Species*, the topic of evolution and speciation of organisms has emerged as a science within biology that is subject to considerable branching and reinterpretation. *Origin of Species* introduced the notion of fitness within a specific environment as the determinant in the success or failure of a new species. For Darwin, fitness supplied some of the organisms of a species with a competitive advantage. Thus some members of a species were able to propagate while others
5 slowly were outmaneuvered for food, territory, security, and the opportunity to mate. As intuitive as Darwinian logic has come to be, and as sensibly as it interprets the empirical behavior and location of similar species, Darwinian adaptation has had to weather much reinterpretation focusing on the precise processes that transform competitive advantage into speciation. The notion of punctuated equilibrium is one such challenge to Darwinian 'elegance'.

Punctuated equilibrium is a theory akin to Darwinian logic, but which asks specific questions as to just how fitness turns a minority of
10 an organism's phenotype into a separate non-impregnable species altogether. Darwin's logic expects species to rise from a beneficial perforation of the line of continuity of that species. Darwin states if one organism contains all the elements of its breed of organisms, but also some uncommon advantageous trait, it will successfully reproduce, and spawn progeny who enjoy an iteration of that process as long as their permutation makes them more fit for prevailing conditions. Punctuated equilibrium takes another approach to the conditions necessary to turn an organism tailored by mutation or another differentiation into an out and out species.

15 Punctuated equilibrium views Darwinian gene flows and causation to be overly ambitious, or simplistic. In actuality, say its proponents, any comparative advantage acquired by the member of a species would, under most conditions, be re-absorbed and 'averaged out' among a sizeable number of members of the species before it had time to be visible, a gradation too subtle for Darwin and his naturalists to observe outside the isolation of the tiny Galapagos islands. P.E. updates Darwin by noting that the sudden emergence of a differentiation, endowing an organism with more fitness than its former species, would not usually give that organism or its de-
20 scendants a significant degree of independence in the absence of disastrous conditions. For the evolution reformers, this comparative advantage only leads to a speciation event if the conditions in which it occurs are cataclysmic for the species as a whole, including massive geographic reformations (such as the flooding of the Mediterranean basin) or unexpected ecological devastation. What this says is that in order for a deviation to turn into a species, conditions surrounding that deviation must always be sufficiently harsh to drive the evolutionary pressure of speciation. This creates a timescale for speciation that is better represented by a pendulum swing
25 in one swift motion, than by seeping growth and petty attrition of a Darwinian forbear fanning out over successive generations.

1. The most appropriate title for this passage might be:

   (A) Debunking Darwin: Why Fitness Was Never an Issue

   (B) One Better: Coming Closer to the Makings of Fitness Hence Species

   (C) Taking Turns: How Fitness Became a Proxy Issue for Second Line Darwinists

   (D) Repairing History for Darwin and His Apologists

   (E) Making an Honest Man Out of Darwin

2. The primary difference between Darwinian evolution and Punctuated Equilibrium is:

   (A) The number of supporters of each theory

   (B) The possibility of cataclysmic events as a contributing factor in evolution

   (C) The areas of the world providing support for each theory

   (D) Punctuated Equilibrium simply fills in unexplained aspects of Darwinian evolution

   (E) Darwin views mutations as the source of new traits while Punctuated Equilibrium considers ecological disasters to be the source of new traits

3. According to the passage, the principal objection of Punctuated Equilibrium's supporters to the Darwinian theory of fitness and speciation is that:

   (A) It moves too slowly to account for the progress of the fossil record

   (B) Darwin does not consider that ecological disasters often drive speciation

   (C) Species is a relative term for a collection of individual gene permutations

   (D) It is contingent on microclimates or controlled circumstances

   (E) It assumes the principles it sets out to prove

4. Punctuated Equilibrium may be best described as:

   (A) A Corollary to *Origin of Species*

   (B) An Abbreviation of *Origin of Species*

   (C) A Refinement of *Origin of Species*

   (D) A Contradiction of *Origin of Species*

   (E) A Continuation of *Origin of Species*

5. In line 7, the sentence beginning with 'The notion of', advocates of Punctuated Equilibrium would be likely to fault the 'elegance' of *Origin of Species* for being:

   (A) Unproven

   (B) Unscientific

   (C) Discursive

   (D) Oversimplified

   (E) Deceptive

6. Punctuated Equilibrium would be likely to describe the occurrence of speciation as:

   (A) Unpredictable

   (B) Malefic

   (C) Plodding

   (D) Unrealistic

   (E) Inevitable

7. According to the theory of Punctuated Equilibrium, which of the following events would be less explicable than the others?

   (A) An increase in the hardness of the beak of a certain bird in response to all the local soft fruit being lost in a fire

   (B) Darkening in the color of the fur of the Belgian bilge rat upon landing in a polluted foreign country

   (C) An increase in the muscle density of a dingo allowing it to run faster than others in its pack

   (D) The thickening of the skull and general size of some members of Homo Sapiens at the onset of the ice age

   (E) The disappearance of a species following a tsunami

8. In the sentence beginning 'For the evolution' in line 20, the word 'unexpected' is used to mean:

   (A) Epidemic

   (B) On a large scale

   (C) Immediate

   (D) Unforeseen

   (E) At once

Passage 22

The question of legalized abortion in America has largely been considered in terms of moral objections resulting from competing perceptions of human rights and freedom of choice. While the representatives of these views have been influential actors for whom lawmakers must tweak any legislation pertaining to abortion, economists now offer tangible evidence that the abortion issue must be evaluated with some very practical considerations as well. While the importance of the life of a fetus brought-to-term is never a
5 forgotten aspect of the debate on abortion, the relevance of the abortion issue to the lifestyle opportunities for all of society has yet to be weighed heavily in the debate.

However, in their retrospective examination of many years' evidence, John Donahue and Steven Levitt, researchers from Harvard University and the University of Chicago, have pointed out that a suggested correlation between the passage of Roe vs. Wade, the integral piece of abortion empowerment legislation, and reported crime statistics twenty years later can in fact be noted. This is
10 because the period during which most perpetrators engage in the majority of any society's illegal activity is when they are in their late teens and early twenties. Adolescent and young adult males are considered to be the most likely to engage in illegal activity. Their relative inexperience in the world, the paucity of opportunities and their group relationships make them more prone to violence and defiance than women or older males. The researchers note that within a few years of the U.S. Supreme Court Roe vs. Wade decision, up to a quarter of all pregnancies in the United States resulted in abortions. Also, they observe that crime rates between 1985 and
15 1997 declined. The researchers note that children who would have otherwise been born in the early years after the Roe vs. Wade decision would be reaching their late teen years between 1985 and 1997. However, they were not born, and crime decreased in this time frame. These researchers interpret the termination of an unwanted pregnancy as the rational response of a woman who is not prepared to care for a child. Going forward with an unwanted pregnancy presumably confers on the woman too great a challenge in raising a child she is poorly prepared for, and provides the child with an upbringing that is suboptimal, making him more vulnerable
20 to be party to illegal conduct.

These numbers signify less crime as a result of letting more mothers choose when to have a baby. Crime is financially costly to taxpayers as well. Lawmakers may take heed of this evaluation if they consider Donahue and Levitt's calculation that the economic benefit to society from the termination of unwanted pregnancies may be as high as 30 billion dollars annually. As the ideological arguments over abortion refuse to abate, it may be time for hamstrung legislators to consider new sources of information to simplify
25 their decisions about reopening the question of abortion reform and government aid.

1. The primary difference presented by the passage between the original abortion debate and the present one presented by the researchers is that:

   (A) The original debate was subjective while the present debate is objective

   (B) The previous debate was based on ethics while the present debate is based on religion

   (C) The original debate was between completely oppositional parties while the present debate has more heterogeneous discussants

   (D) The previous debate was phrased ideologically while the present debate is concerned with practicality

   (E) The original debate was supported scientifically while the present debate does not involve science

2. The style of the passage may be considered

   (A) Persuasive

   (B) Encyclopedic

   (C) In the style of historiography

   (D) Scientific

   (E) Journalistic

3. One fact which would strengthen the claims of the researchers would be if:

   (A) There was also a sharp decrease in white collar crime during the period of reported statistics

   (B) There was a decline in the economy during the period of reported statistics

   (C) States which legalized abortion first saw earlier decreases in crime during the period of reported statistics

   (D) Young males were shown to be avid watchers of violent programming

   (E) States which legalized abortion first saw increases in crime during the period of reported statistics

4. The implication of the passage regarding unwanted pregnancies is that:

   (A) They are more common in poor families

   (B) They are more likely to yield males

   (C) They are more common to women likely to be criminals

   (D) They are unwanted for a good reason

   (E) The children resulting from unwanted pregnancies are raised by women

5. What is the presumption of the author regarding the historical abortion debate when presenting Donahue and Levitt's research as the premise for legislative decisions?

   (A) It is that both sides were equally wrong.

   (B) It is not the role of the state to make decisions based on the personal politics of its citizens.

   (C) The research is weighed as heavily as either of the ideological arguments in the debate.

   (D) It is more important to establish a useful policy on future abortion discussions than to be mired in debate.

   (E) Legislators view the ideological abortion debate as politically irresolvable for practical purposes.

6. In the sentence beginning in line 2, the author seeks to do what to the abortion debate:

   (A) Confine the debate to a small audience

   (B) Emphasize its complexity

   (C) Increase the influence of narrow interest groups

   (D) Argue for a return to a debate on ideological grounds

   (E) Simplify the dialogue

7. The practical consideration of the researchers is that:

   (A) More abortions will result in less crime

   (B) Crime decreases and money is saved when women have freedom of choice

   (C) Crime is a function of population growth

   (D) Abortions of non-violent females are an unavoidable consequence of allowing women the right to an abortion

   (E) Crime increases when there is a right to abortion

8. In the line 19, the word "suboptimal" could be replaced with which of the following without changing its contextual meaning:

   (A) Inadequate

   (B) Almost perfect

   (C) Inefficient

   (D) Economically advantaged

   (E) Second best

Passage 23

The creation of Israel as the home of Jews worldwide, a legacy revived after 1400 years of dispossession and Diaspora, is a topic which, for all its chronicles and celebrated developments, falls into varying interpretations of rightful entitlement and ownership. The contrasting interpretations of ownership and the presence in Israel of different groups, each presenting lawyerly versions of the cycle of events and rights of possession, has led to a certain amount of doubt on the part of historians seeking to model the conflict.
5 History may choose to see the Israeli-Arab conflict as a situation of ethnic strife, as a confrontation of nationalist sentiments, as the learning process of self-determination, or even as an apartheid government in violation of human rights. Producing a work which chronicles the events that have led to present-day Israel may necessitate considering the difficulty of modeling changes using new and old theories of international relations and balancing the concerns of multilateral non-governmental agencies over human rights with traditional concerns of nation states such as imperialism, state building and the formation of military coalitions.

10 Amid the many potential models, a history of the development of Israel must still contend with the nineteenth and twentieth century phenomenon of nationalism. Whatever factors are pointed to as the most important causes of Israel's creation, the period in which the political motions which began to bring Israel to international attention coincided with the age of nationalism. According to Israeli historians, it is nationalism that was the first inspiration for Leon Pinsker in *Auto-Emancipation* and then for Theodore Herzl, author of *The Jewish State*. They were the founders of Zionism. These works were a departure from the previous calling for the
15 uniting of all Jews to fulfill a religious mission. The books called for unity among Jews to achieve nationalist goals, including the establishment of a homeland. However, the difficulties that have persisted in securing Israel as a Jewish National Home may seem, at times, not to be the problems that would arise from a nationalist cause, but rather the difficulties which come from a minority seizing power, or more simply put, as the trials of colonialism.

The contrasting views of the legitimacy of Israel's claim to its land and its statehood by historians rise from doubt as to whether the
20 actions of the first settlers and pioneers were done in a way that was in accordance with international law. Usurping the land of a native people was thought of by some not as an infringement of sovereignty, but as the establishment of a protectorate. The credibility of each side in the modern negotiations in the Middle East between Israel, Palestine and their Arab neighbors, is heavily linked to understanding what rules applied in international law and warfare. This necessitates an understanding of formal international agreements with the Arab people, as well as the land brokering done by the Great Powers on the brink of a world war.

1. The one element that all historical interpretations of Israel must address is:
   - (A) Human rights
   - (B) Non-governmental organizations
   - (C) Movements in International relations
   - (D) Imperialism
   - (E) Nationalism

2. According to the passage, a difficulty with characterizing the Arab-Israeli crisis for historians could be:
   - (A) A lack of information
   - (B) The unavailability of interpretations of rightful entitlement
   - (C) A lack of interest in the topic
   - (D) The applicability of models from different periods in International Relations
   - (E) The political sensitivity of the topic

3. It can be inferred from the passage that 'Auto-Emancipation' addressed which of the following issues:
   - (A) How to expel indigenous peoples from the Persian Gulf
   - (B) How to secure religious freedom
   - (C) How to unite Jews to address purely religious goals
   - (D) The continuation of Jewish communities worldwide
   - (E) The uniting of Jews to achieve nationalist goals

4. One problem the passage sees regarding the rise of the Jewish State is:

    (A)   The lapse of time in which the Jews did not occupy the land of Israel

    (B)   The ambiguity of 19th century international law

    (C)   The role of Jews as a minority seizing power

    (D)   Incompatible agreements made by the Great Powers during their war

    (E)   The financial viability of the new state

5. In the passage, the difficulty in establishing a national home is explained by the effects of:

    (A)   Warfare

    (B)   Social democracy

    (C)   Labor unrest

    (D)   Protectorates

    (E)   Colonialism

6. The passage states that the credibility of participants in the modern crisis in the Middle East is related to:

    (A)   Justifying the circle of violence that has ensued

    (B)   Predicting what is yet to come

    (C)   Denying the existence of history

    (D)   Having an understanding of international law

    (E)   Preventing the occurrence of a similar crisis

7. The passage portrays the 19th century perceptions of usurping native land to establish dominance in a region as being:

    (A)   Benevolent

    (B)   Conflict-creating

    (C)   Incidental

    (D)   Illegal

    (E)   Inadmissible

8. The passage implies that land claims may be justifiable if:

    (A)   The occupation was established in accordance with principles of international law

    (B)   The occupiers continue to hold their land successfully on their own

    (C)   There was no legal right to land

    (D)   Justice was no longer a useful instrument given the choices that had to be made

    (E)   The occupation was condoned by the majority of the Great Powers

Passage 24

Success of the high tech industries in the developed countries has been a function of the demand for their products in international markets, and the adaptability of those industries in responding to changes in market demand and the emergence of flurries of competitors. Equally important to the success of the high tech industry in the United States, Britain and several other industrial powers is the willing supply of international labor: job-hungry immigrants, who fuel the technology revolution in the hubs of
5 industrial design and redesign.

Cognizant of the need for educated, compliant labor, the U.S. Congress has sought to give preferential treatment to skilled foreign professionals. Yet, within the United States and other tech powers, there are circles among which such initiatives prompt contempt, not stemming from the usual grievances begrudging the leeching of local jobs, but because of developed countries' facilitation of a brain drain from the developing countries. These provisions have created a crisis in technology policy in countries such as India,
10 where taxpayers in the country regularly finance the education of many young people at elite institutions for math and science so that these students can play a crucial role in supporting or creating national industries. However, the highly technical nature of their training is said to leave them lacking in allegiance to their native country, and willing to trade insularity for higher salaries abroad.

The consequence has been that voracious technology industries in those developed countries, principally the U.S., have engulfed an outpouring of Indian graduates who would never 'redeem their pledge,' as New Delhi politicos put it, to improve 'Mother India's'
15 own post-industrial future. An added source of fright for Indian politicians is the defection every year of a select one hundred plus exceptional individuals upon whom the prospect of industrial revolution may very well rest, as reported by researchers at the India Institute of Technology. All this threatens stagnation and decline, with tax dollars wasted and educated, opportunistic youngsters chasing foreign advantage. Now, non-resident Indians (NRIs), so-called by those who remained in the motherland, have accepted citizenship in America only to find their own politics changing. Wealthy, and with dual loyalties, they are suspicious of several
20 national policies that make it possible for countries, not just companies, to poach developing countries' talent on a wholesale basis. In response, they remind fellow NRIs of the value their Western business experience can provide if it were to be filtered back into India's own technology sectors. These middle and upper class NRIs are also principal contributors to a large remittance economy which is a much needed source of support for destitute regions in India. Politically these uprooted Indians now object to what they find in national policies: windfall profits for their adopted country at the expense of their homeland. Nevertheless, they are aware
25 that these complaints will amount to little since the challenge of raising India's standard of living is too broad for the remittance economy to achieve.

1. The style of this piece can be considered:

    (A) Argumentative

    (B) Encyclopedic

    (C) Editorial

    (D) Biased

    (E) Flippant

2. The best reason supporting an argument for transferring subsidies from private corporations to India is:

    (A) Holding labor purchasers hostage in a sellers market

    (B) The lack of alternative sources of capital for India

    (C) Punishing taxpayers in developed countries

    (D) Restitution for Indian taxpayers

    (E) The right of NRIs to vote against the expansion of foreign economies with Indian talent

3. In line 14, the phrase 'redeem their pledge' is best said to suggest:

    (A)   Bearing an obligation

    (B)   Fulfilling a written contract

    (C)   Accepting foreign offers

    (D)   Refusing of a request

    (E)   Achieving a dream

4. The author portrays the American NRIs as:

    (A)   Disloyal

    (B)   Saboteur-minded

    (C)   Uncaring

    (D)   Conscientious

    (E)   Fickle

5. In the sentence beginning with 'these provisions' in line 9, the term 'crisis' refers to

    (A)   The change in direction of an incendiary device

    (B)   Second thoughts

    (C)   A temporary problem

    (D)   Severe consequences of a plan of action

    (E)   The calculated aggression of a foreign power

6. In the sentence beginning with 'Politically these...' in line 23, the term 'windfall' implies:

    (A)   A zero-sum game

    (B)   Consistent success with negligible costs

    (C)   Unexpected success

    (D)   Migration of currency across borders

    (E)   Negligible

7. The passage faults Indian technology policy for which of the following:

    (A)   For not indoctrinating students with an appreciation of their homeland

    (B)   For taking place in a largely underdeveloped country

    (C)   For not producing enough technically-qualified graduates

    (D)   For not encouraging a remittance economy that reduces the incentive to work

    (E)   For not charging corporations enough to set up offices in India

8. The passage implies what about the relationship between India's standard of living and remittances?

    (A)   If India had a higher standard of living it would not expect remittances

    (B)   India actually owes capital to developed countries for helping it modernize during its post-colonial reconstruction

    (C)   The notion of restitution for Indian taxpayers is a thinly-veiled plea for the redistribution of wealth

    (D)   The widening gap between the rich and the poor will make it impossible for India to keep educating its youth

    (E)   The remittance economy is not large enough to raise India's standard of living significantly

Passage 25

The use of groundwater is a topic that is responsible for bringing many types of seemingly unrelated groups to the table with a common interest. The use of such water is categorized as a "tragedy of the commons" paradox. Since groundwater is typically a resource that is found on public property, its usage can be difficult to quantify on a user-pays basis. Standard classical economics suggests that since every rational participant seeks to maximize his own returns, the plurality of individual users for any 'commons',
5   such as a groundwater well, is motivated to make use of that resource as extensively and as quickly as possible, or else they lose their share to a more aggressive consumer of the resource, such as a neighbor seeking to improve irrigation. However, while this attitude may seem to maximize the benefits for any single participant, collectively these participants are disadvantaged by their overlapping actions. In the case of groundwater, simultaneous, competitive exploitation of a seemingly free resource can result in squandering groundwater in the short term and great expense in the long term when vital demands will be impossible to meet with the remaining
10 short supply. For these reasons, groundwater usage is under review in arid regions of the United States.

The rule of open competition for groundwater collection is known in many parts of the United States as 'the rule of capture.' Various areas which have relied on this laissez-faire principle to manage the resource are now rethinking the danger of letting free market principles trump collective agendas. The primary danger in allowing the rule of capture to prevail is less relevant to neo-classical short-term maximization calculations made by competing landowners with similarly sized farms. While 'the rule of capture' has
15 been dubbed 'the rule of the biggest pump' at times, in places like East Texas, where scarcity is an issue, tempers have flared not in response to the competition between scores of similarly sized farms vying for the output of one water source. Rather, current conflict is the result of very different types of users emerging as competitors in the exploitation of local aquifers. For instance, groundwater ranching comes into direct opposition to the habits and rights-of-way established by local agricultural farmers, ranchers and rural communities. These groups, with the help of environmental watchdogs, are seeking to modify the old rule of capture as a result of
20 the concern about the sustainability of groundwater, coining the term 'Correlative Rights'.

These rules seek to bring the rights of neighboring users into balance with one another by establishing a Doctrine of Reasonable Use to limit groundwater withdrawal from the land with an eye to local purposes. While in possession of a practical strategy for reforming groundwater usage, these groups have not been totally successful. In East Texas, groundwater conservation districts have emerged as one solution to appease these locals. However, government still finds it difficult to prevent groundwater ranchers
25 from legally exporting the local supply to other regions for private profit. As a result, the threat to fair use of groundwater and its sustainability remains a sticking point for different users with very different relationships to the land.

1. A situation that might be categorized as a 'tragedy of the commons' paradox is:

   (A) a corporate leader selling his stock on the open market and precipitating a steep drop in corporate confidence

   (B) a manufacturer reducing the quality of its product in face of significant price reductions by a competitor with a better-marketed, though inferior product

   (C) a borderline student failing his class because all the other borderline students dropped out before the final exam

   (D) a large corporation selling below cost in a regional market to drive its competition out of business

   (E) developing nations refusing to enforce international air quality standards because of worries that such standards would allow neighboring nations to industrialize faster

2. It can be inferred from the passage that for the author, maximization equations in neo-classical economics:

   (A) Do not produce the best possible average returns for individuals who must manage usage of a commons

   (B) Do not apply outside John Locke's model of demarcated property

   (C) Are the best way to manage water resources

   (D) Are most important in East Texas

   (E) Have no benefits for anyone

3. In the passage, the main objection communities have raised to groundwater ranching is/are:

   (A) The fact that some parties use the resource unequally

   (B) Wells may run completely dry in some areas

   (C) Water charges may have to be implemented

   (D) The fact that some parties improve their current position while diminishing the availability of the resource locally

   (E) Movement of water to areas far from its source leads to water loss through leakage

4. It can be inferred from the passage that users with similar demands and comparable objectives:

   (A) experience less conflict than very different users of a common resource

   (B) experience more conflict than very different users of a common resource

   (C) are less capable of managing the long term viability of a common resource

   (D) are more likely to undervalue a common resource through under-use

   (E) negotiate with one another to determine who is most capable of making the best use of a common resource

5. The phrase 'not been totally successful' in the final paragraph most closely means:

   (A) An admission to a problem without definitive solutions

   (B) The understanding that the problem exists but is not resolvable

   (C) The inability of government and locals to coordinate their interests

   (D) Failure of a plan to solve the problem

   (E) To pursue a solution that is more destructive than the problem

6. The lack of legislation to revise the 'rule of capture' in the past implies that:

   (A) Farmers did not seek out more water than absolutely necessary

   (B) Farmers agreed on how much water everyone should extract

   (C) The competitive usage of groundwater did not give one farmer more net benefit than another

   (D) Farmers had not felt the resource was threatened by the past rate of unregulated use

   (E) Farmers are more interested in keeping outsiders away from their community than in saving water

7. It can be inferred from the passage that the government created 'groundwater conservation districts' in order to:

   (A) Drive water ranchers out of their districts

   (B) Demonstrate to farmers that water ranchers and locals have common interests

   (C) Deceive locals into assuming the government will turn away the tax dollars from water ranchers in pursuit of environmental headlines

   (D) Demonstrate to locals that the government is attempting to address the problem

   (E) Remove concerns about groundwater sustainability

8. In the passage, the differences between local interests and water ranchers serve as an impediment to groundwater management because:

   (A) they prevent locals and water ranchers from discussing their interest in water management

   (B) they place locals and water ranchers in opposition to one another regarding their relative positions towards water sustainability

   (C) they make it possible for water ranchers to completely overwhelm the local interests, thus making it unnecessary to negotiate with them

   (D) they result in proxy battles which complicate the issues at hand

   (E) they distract both sides from the real issue of water sustainability

Passage 26

While clandestine observation has always played a part in investigation, the most important difference between modern database surveillance and traditional legwork is the proliferation of surveillance of the systems of mundane transactions and of social behavior. No less foreboding is analysis through calculations of regression and methods of associated comparison, to broaden scientifically the range of 'suspicious' behavior in order to justify the oversight of new types of actors, and an increased number of actors. These abilities are being incorporated into a policy about which the public is not aware, and one which is outside the scope of current legislation.

Given that most people regard themselves as 'law abiding,' and that the avoidance of crime, drug abuse and other quality of life infractions rates highly in citizens' priorities, the development of improved surveillance systems is widely seen as a benign invasion that improves policing. This sort of perception has led the U.K., after it was able to pinpoint two young men as being the culprits in the murder of a young boy, to be the country with the most widespread use of surveillance cameras. The impracticality of, and lack of interest in, prosecuting every transgression caught by the system obscures its threat to individual liberty. But while this may keep the disadvantages of surveillance from bringing people to vocal dissent, what should be raised in the public consciousness is that what surveillance changes is the amount of leverage a minority of actors (authorities, bureaucrats, or system managers) receive over the general population. In any encounter in which one individual must confront the state, the state achieves an advantage by having so many more 'leads' on the individual with which to use bullying tactics, and by engaging in non-judicial activities such as Secret Service searches, the disbanding of rallies, and the detention of political and foreign activists. Compiling a file of criminal activities engaged in by a subject under surveillance is routine. But there can also be an insinuation of an activity that a government uses politically to undermine the position of a subject. That action changes the direction of prosecution, reiterating the importance of, and the reasoning behind, such safeguards as the Miranda acts, designed to protect suspects from incriminating themselves in the absence of their lawyer. The greatest danger is that the rules of criminal justice can be controlled by a bureaucratic, authoritarian organization to prolong detention, and to control the flow of information under conditions of the confinement of a subject, in order to improve the ability of investigators to aid the prosecution. The monopoly which public bureaucracies have on prosecution and investigation allows them to use or disregard official rules in ways that are not transparent to a defendant. It has been shown that increasing the level of surveillance in the public arena does not improve the ability to identify offenders, but improves the ability of the government to operate extra-judicially. This offers authorities the opportunity of manufacturing opportunities for themselves to control behavior in ways that are beyond redress.

1. The main concern of the passage regarding improvements in surveillance is

   (A)   The ability to record the activity of everybody

   (B)   The lack of knowledge many people have regarding their surveillance

   (C)   The ability of the government to remove the obstacles to prosecution

   (D)   The disbanding of rallies and detention of political prisoners

   (E)   The fact that surveillance is technically illegal

2. The passage suggests that which of the following is true of most people:

   (A)   They have consented to surveillance

   (B)   They are told that surveillance is no more widespread than in the past

   (C)   They do not consider themselves law abiding

   (D)   They are unaware of the details of surveillance

   (E)   They consider surveillance to be beneficial

3. According to the passage, which of the following is the most important benefit of improved surveillance for the state?

   (A)   It makes it possible to identify and punish criminals far more effectively than before

   (B)   It makes it possible to improve the case against suspects

   (C)   It makes it possible to track down many more criminals

   (D)   It increases the number of jobs available in the public sector

   (E)   It limits the power of the police

4. The author would be most likely to agree with which of the following:

   (A)   Government should be able to police itself to avoid overstepping its powers

   (B)   Government has a need to protect itself from criminals

   (C)   Government power lies partly outside the law

   (D)   Government is only as trustworthy as its people

   (E)   Government fulfills the wants of the people its represents

5. In the passage the biggest danger of improved surveillance to the public has to do with:

   (A)   Falsely identifying criminals

   (B)   Allowing the government to act without a process of review

   (C)   Empowering a minority of the public

   (D)   Reversing democracy

   (E)   Increasing costs

6. It can be inferred from the passage that the author believes that the example of the boys from the U.K. collared in the murder case:

   (A)   Validates the use of surveillance

   (B)   Is a good example of the need for surveillance

   (C)   Is not sufficient evidence of the value of surveillance

   (D)   Is an isolated case

   (E)   Is a reproducible result

7. The passage shows that laws that are passed to protect the rights of defendants are intended to:

   (A)   Reduce the role of government in people's lives

   (B)   Acknowledge that a defendant is innocent until proven guilty

   (C)   Allow defendants the opportunity to explain their side of the story

   (D)   Limit the power of government to aid the prosecution

   (E)   Show that the public is more sympathetic to defendants than to prosccutors

8. One problem the passage sees with the capacity of government to contribute to the prosecution is:

   (A)   The unreasonable punishment of offenders

   (B)   The inability of government to prove its case

   (C)   The monopoly of the government over prosecuting offenders

   (D)   The lack of press access to a case

   (E)   The ability of the public to regulate government

Passage 27

Universities in Europe are increasingly under the influence of the globalization movement, with examples of this trend widespread across the continent. European universities must answer the perceived needs of multinational corporations, as these firms aspire to draw on an employee base that is borderless, and highly mobile. The system of German engineering schools provides a lucid example for understanding the logic behind transforming European education from a system of segmented and self-contained schools into a
5 system with much more inter-reliance among institutions. Engineering schools are good examples of the myopia of many European institutions because of the common misreading by these schools that they are safe in exclusively focusing on the engineering content of their programs while claiming independence from political transformations taking place outside their one specific discipline; in outlining the alternative view, a clear example of how closely linked educational environments are to their coursework is provided.

It is the attitude that professional schools only need to be concerned with the immediate issues pertaining to students' core com-
10 petencies that raises objections from corporate onlookers and many international educators across the engineering fields. Leading concerns for critics of the German university system are that there is limited intercourse between different academies, and that too few courses are taught in English. The lack of availability of English courses in German engineering schools contributes to there being a paucity of international students in German programs. In addition, German engineering students can find themselves painted into a corner midway through their studies if they seek to change the direction of their education. This is because they have lim-
15 ited experience in taking courses in other German universities, and taking engineering courses abroad is the exception, never the rule. Moreover, if these students were to transfer to another school, it is commonplace that much of their course history would not count towards a future degree in a different program. For these reasons, engineering education has come under well-lit scrutiny by businessmen, educators and government officials.

In response, engineering administrators have developed a better head for global issues that pertain to their students' desire for
20 varied post-university employment, as well as their students' access to borderless knowledge during their university years. These issues have jointly led educators to identify the need for a new Magna Carta of universities in order to transfer their awareness into solutions. The outcome of this collective attention is the Bologna Declaration. Its recommendations are fourfold: to establish a system of comparable degrees to facilitate international competitiveness, to adopt the two cycle (undergraduate and graduate) system of schooling, to establish a standard credit system for classroom work, and to find a way to ensure the quality of programs
25 offered Europe-wide. These improvements in European education increase the international marketability of matriculating students. However, of equal importance, they also increase the mobility of students during their university years.

1. Mention of German sociology programs was probably not included in the passage because:

   (A) They do not have the same difficulties as other programs

   (B) They are by nature peopled by a diverse and interactive student body

   (C) Their discipline has a heightened focus on external conditions

   (D) One example is sufficient for the purposes of the passage

   (E) Multinational corporations have little interest in the graduates of sociology programs, and exert no pressure on these head of these programs

2. Critics of German university programs seem to prefer that more courses be taught in English in order to:

   (A) Make German students less likely to attend foreign schools

   (B) Make students better qualified to accept employment positions throughout Europe

   (C) Make more research available to German students

   (D) Make it easier for students from abroad to get credit for German university courses

   (E) Encourage more students from abroad to take courses in Germany

3. The term "well-lit scrutiny" in line 17 implies:

   (A)   Criticism that is overdue

   (B)   Critique under the worst of conditions

   (C)   Critique from many sources is the most thorough

   (D)   Critique that is deserved

   (E)   Thoroughly executed critique with many perspectives

4. Which of the following best replicates the use of "paucity" in line 13 in the middle of the second paragraph?

   (A)   Complete lack

   (B)   Small number

   (C)   Significant number

   (D)   Over-abundance

   (E)   Diversity

5. The author would most likely agree with the principle that:

   (A)   The purpose of education is to raise active citizens

   (B)   The purpose of education is to create well rounded individuals

   (C)   Education should provide students with the flexibility they need to function effectively later in life in whatever field they choose

   (D)   Education ought to ease cultural tensions

   (E)   Education should encourage students to work outside of their national origins

6. The Bologna Declaration declares the goal of:

   (A)   Creating educational standards

   (B)   Promoting English in European schools

   (C)   Regulating engineering programs

   (D)   Allowing students to pursue a greater selection of vocational opportunities

   (E)   Decreasing student mobility

7. The author's primary concern about the unlikelihood of engineering students ever changing their course of study is best expressed in which statement?

   (A)   It is important to facilitate a variety of choices for students

   (B)   Engineering degrees should not count towards a variety of credit programs

   (C)   Engineering schools should not be reformed

   (D)   Engineering schools are obligated to prove their competitiveness

   (E)   Engineering schools can no longer overlook the realities of the market

8. According to the passage, the importance of students being mobile during their university years is related to:

   (A)   The need of students to choose a city they like in which to study

   (B)   The attractiveness of engineering as a career

   (C)   The fact that too few cities have engineering schools

   (D)   The desire for an amalgamation of engineering schools

   (E)   The need of multinationals to have access to a wide labor pool

Passage 28

In 1957, the United States invested in mining the atom for its stores of energy, and funneling this cache into an engineering and military revolution. Wartime uses of atomic energy went largely towards the development of more powerful weapons of mass destruction, though the Department of Defense also utilized it as a more efficient means of long-range propulsion for warships and submersibles. At the same time, the United States Atomic Energy Commission (AEC) created what it would later call the "Plowshare
5   Program". This initiative was intended to develop peaceful applications of modern nuclear power, then under feverish development by scientists primarily for Cold War armaments, and to develop domestic energy sources "too cheap to meter".

In August of 1958, scouts from the AEC conducted something of a reconnaissance of Point Hope, in Northwest Alaska. They had selected Ogotoruk Creek in this region as a possible site for the detonation of an atomic bomb. The logic behind the detonation was political and practical. The AEC had decided to bowdlerize the discussion of nuclear weapons by teaming nuclear arms with civil
10 engineering. If the science of Cold War defense could be a proven boon to civil engineering, the AEC felt it could dilute the intense public skepticism towards above ground nuclear testing. Romanticizing their ingenuity, the AEC identified their plan as "Operation Plowshare", alluding to the Biblical panegyric of a world after war when men may someday "beat their swords into plowshares". Atomic technology was presented as being an engineering wonder, the driver of the future instead of the idle sentry needed for John Marshall's Mutual Atomic Destruction policy.

15 The need for something positive to add to the discussion on the nuclear weapons program came as Russia's successful launch of the Sputnik I satellite into space induced shallow breathing in members of America's scientific and engineering elite. The immediate reaction, in the name of one-upmanship, was that "earth excavation" would be the surest demonstration of impressive and beneficial applications of America's existing nuclear capabilities. Their preferred advice was to detonate a 2.4 megaton atomic device on the northwest coast of Alaska, to create a deepwater hole facilitating the shipping of coal, timber and oil, while developing Alaska's
20 coast, with obvious benefits for the 48 mainland U.S. states. This proposal would be accepted by the AEC, who designated it 'Project Chariot'. It was marketed to Alaska's financial community and lawmakers, but they remained unconvinced of the plan's commercial viability. The AEC then attempted to sell the plan to the U.S. Congress as a unique opportunity to uncover scientifically the benefits of nuclear energy. However, local Inuit objected and wrote to President John F. Kennedy of their unease about heavy metals leaching and radiation (a plea backed by detractors in the continental United States). In turn, the AEC came to reconsider the reaction backing
25 their proposed demonstration would realistically earn them. Project Chariot was shelved indefinitely and replaced by less visible undertakings which would be declassified decades later.

1. According to the passage, the AEC's purpose for "Operation Plowshare" was to:

    (A) Find cheaper ways to produce energy for export

    (B) Innovate in the field of mechanical engineering

    (C) Improve the reputation of the nuclear arms program

    (D) Partake in weapons development

    (E) Diversify export industries

2. The phrase "obvious benefits for the 48 mainland states" in line 20 probably refers to:

    (A) A more respectable nuclear arms program

    (B) Better access to Alaska's resources

    (C) Political undermining of the arms program's opponents

    (D) The development of a national market for nuclear arms in civil engineering

    (E) Increased knowledge of the effect of nuclear weapons on geographic landmasses

3. The selection of Ogotoruk Creek as a site for the detonation was the result of:

   (A) Resistance from surrounding populations

   (B) Executive fiat

   (C) A scan of the area in situ

   (D) Cartographic research and topographical comparisons of Northwest Alaska

   (E) Political decisions

4. The passage regards American scientists as thinking of Sputnik I as:

   (A) An international political statement

   (B) A scientific achievement

   (C) Proof of Russia's scientific superiority

   (D) Specious showmanship

   (E) A precursor to the escalation of the arms race

5. The attitude of American voters regarding nuclear weapons testing can be inferred to be:

   (A) Doubtful

   (B) Gung-ho

   (C) Competitive

   (D) Inventive

   (E) Complacent as long as it takes place in someone else's backyard

6. The unwillingness of the AEC to proceed with Project Chariot as planned was the result of:

   (A) Disapproval from President Kennedy

   (B) Its inability to achieve its original purpose

   (C) Financial impracticality

   (D) Better technological opportunities in undisclosed plans

   (E) The threat of heavy metals and radiation to local Inuit

7. The phrase "ready advice" in line 18 implies that:

   (A) A nuclear detonation was the only way to compete with the Russians

   (B) A nuclear detonation was the idea scientists saw as the best option

   (C) A nuclear detonation seemed like the most obvious response

   (D) A nuclear detonation was the first idea scientists could offer

   (E) A nuclear detonation was the only thing scientists were prepared to discuss

8. The decision by the AEC to name their plan "Operation Plowshare" was related to what characteristic:

   (A) Political savvy

   (B) Humor

   (C) Irony

   (D) Anticipation

   (E) An intimacy with leitmotif

Passage 29

The 1870s were a time of drastic technological challenges to industrializing nations. These challenges resulted in stark differences in the path of development pursued by economies organizing themselves for productive capacity. Manufacturing centers reacted differently to the opportunities blooming in these challenges, each assessing the benefits of rationalization and taking stock of their relevance to its production process. But while scores of industries in a variety of countries predicted some benefits from
5   mechanization, the opportunity to increase production while reducing costs was rightly subject to pervasive debate.

German printing and textile firms showed why industrialization was not a cut and dried process. German and Austrian companies appeared to acknowledge certain impetuses to move over to mechanical production of a particular category of printed cotton handkerchiefs. The production of these handkerchiefs was reliant on the handiwork of individual workmen. These handcrafted articles were the pride and joy of certain regional manufacturers who settled in this niche of the international market. Select German firms
10 obtained the ability to double and triple production while reducing their work force. But risks accompanied this methodology. While this rationalization did bring a substantial fall in the total remuneration of labor, it also significantly lowered the sale price and presented risks of overproduction. Head over heels production of items, with lowered regard for the ability of the market to absorb such production, had latent negative features.

The case of 'double printing' of 'Turkish bonnets' provides one example of why the adoption of fast, cheap production techniques
15 was not a forgone conclusion for established manufacturers. In the case of these bonnets, a sudden, unpredictable drop in the demand for these items, faster than producers could react to changed preferences, concurrent with a monetary crisis in eastern markets, produced friction in the industry, opening up public debate as the relationship between bosses and workers became strident.

Reaction to production innovations was regional. It seemed as if the American system of production, from the start, sidestepped some dangers. It was precisely the American system that had drawn European attention to standardized production, which did offer
20 an increase in profits while containing labor costs and unpredictability. American production was synonymous with standardization, mechanization and mass production. But in actuality, the American system was not uniquely immune to the conditions of the world market. Manufacturers of watches in Switzerland, of scarves in Germany and weavers in 19th century Glarus were reserved about their approval of change. Class disparity and capital rigidity would become built-in pressure points on the American economy. These were just the things which also kept many European producers from settling around a consistent, reproducible pattern of
25 mechanization.

1. The central theme of the passage is that:

   (A) the American economy is better equipped to withstand the rigidity of standardization

   (B) negotiation is important in selecting a path of development

   (C) many businesses have failed in their attempt to industrialize

   (D) employed labor is an unavoidable contributor to the development path of companies

   (E) there are many paths to industrialization, and different companies need to be mindful of them when they react to individual innovations

2. The author of this passage would most likely agree that:

   (A) industrial plants should consider their potential contribution to a national war machine before making changes to their assembly line

   (B) the reduced cost of processed sugar makes it a better source of calories than other types of sugar

   (C) protectionism can be a valuable asset in industrial development

   (D) firms should consider the risks of overproduction

   (E) overproduction is not a problem

3. For the author, the proof of the relevance of considering the local situation is communicated by:

   (A) the example of the American Great Depression

   (B) the number of watches produced in Switzerland

   (C) the type of cotton used in handkerchiefs

   (D) the design of Swiss watches

   (E) the problems in the bonnet market because of an Eastern currency crisis

4. In the passage, the threat posed by standardization involves:

   (A) lack of variety in colour

   (B) lack of detail

   (C) elimination of regional differences

   (D) overproduction

   (E) alienation of the workforce

5. The point of the example of the bonnet manufacturers aims to demonstrate:

   (A) that technological advance guarantees success

   (B) the irrelevance of the debate regarding advances in industrialization

   (C) that new technologies should not be used if sales are good

   (D) that there is no need for market research

   (E) the relationship between technological advance and market adaptability

6. The passage presents the difficulties eventually faced by American industrialization as being:

   (A) the quirks that needed to be ironed out of an unprecedented opportunity

   (B) unforeseen by American capitalists

   (C) issues irrelevant to a decision to standardize production

   (D) a danger of standardized industrialization anticipated by some European industrialists

   (E) unavoidable

7. One lesson the author might impart to his readers is that:

   (A) innovation must overcome the resistance of many self-interested parties before it can rationalize work process to cut expenses

   (B) labor will always reduce the rate of progress for socialized countries

   (C) a particular benefit can also be a cost down the line

   (D) national systems of industry are compelled to industrialize by competitive pressure from industrializing nations

   (E) social agendas should not stand in the way of progress

8. An appropriate title for this passage might be:

   (A) American Industrial Pressure on the European Regional Economy

   (B) Examples of Industrial Growth and Industrial Decline

   (C) Discussion on Advantages and Pitfalls of Industrialization

   (D) Avoiding the American Mistake: Why Industrial Innovation Will Create Unemployment and Unrest

   (E) Rationalization: Getting More for Less

Passage 30

Gangsta rap is a genre of rap music, with lyrics based on the violence, hedonism and misogyny inherent in the gangster lifestyle. Gangsta rap is typically identified with the American West Coast, while the broader Hip Hop music phenomenon is a potpourri of different styles. While it is unclear whether the violence in gangsta rap is actually based on real violence, the imagery and "thug" iconoclasm of gangsta rap, when packaged with smooth technical production, enabled West Coast rap to distinguish itself within
5 Hip Hop music.

Gangsta rap brought recognition to California as a legitimate music scene capable of African-American social commentary. Ultimately, Gangsta rap embraced a commercial production style, which differentiated it from the music's roots in East Coast rap. The combination of Los Angeles' advanced technical production methods (Los Angeles had an extensive music post-production industry making wide use of synthesizers) and socio-economic and racial messages effectively branded Gangsta rap as a uniquely West Coast
10 style of music. A brash and militant attitude born out of the experiences of disadvantage and racism differentiated West Coast artists from their East Coast counterparts. While initially all West Coast rap was pigeonholed as Gangsta rap, audiences' appreciation of Gangsta rap as a genre in itself made it possible for Hip Hop to solidify its foothold in American music.

Hip Hop had historically evolved among the economically challenged inner cities of the American East Coast. Previously, music of this style, characterized by a heavy emphasis on rhyming with a syncopated beat, had been universally labeled Hip Hop. This
15 definition was challenged by rap group N.W.A.'s Straight Outta Compton. The album's aggressive, stripped-down sound defied the traditional conventions of rap. The group's lyrical celebration of indulgence and unrelenting criticism of an American society which produced a culture of disadvantage for American blacks indicated that the old categories were not sufficient to classify its style.

Ironically, such social commentary found commercial and critical success despite the music's highly commercial production style. Rap aficionados who valued conventional Hip Hop for its authenticity and "street cred" still respected the music despite its slick
20 production techniques. Rappers were thus able to diversify, continuing to appeal to traditional rap audiences, while courting a mainstream bank of fans. Artists such as Dr. Dre, once a young Turk of West Coast rap and the most enduring of the region's vocalists, made use of funk music, notwithstanding its disco lineage, to find a sound that overlaid his message with the "canned beat" post-production style popular in the region's studios. The combination allowed Hip Hop to reach a more heterogeneous audience, an audience that had already become familiar with West Coast production methods. This coupling allowed audiences to
25 contextualize this style of Hip Hop, facilitating the listener's ability to appreciate Gangsta rap's lyricism and musical production style on its own terms rather than solely against the yardstick of East Coast rap. Once West Coast rap was acknowledged as a unique style, fans were able to compare apples to apples, in evaluating the quality of East Coast and West Coast rap.

1. The main point of the passage is that Gangsta rap became commercially successful because it

   (A) Distinguished itself from East coast rap through rhyming

   (B) Appealed to rap aficionados

   (C) Synthesized commercial production techniques and biting social observations

   (D) Moved from general frameworks into highly contextualized topics for songwriting

   (E) Freed vocalists from the drudgery of post-production work

2. The passage suggests that images of violence associated with Gangsta rap had what outcome?

   (A) They further confused audiences

   (B) They earned rap commercial success but critics were nonplussed

   (C) They made rap solely black art with a surprisingly limited range of topics

   (D) They led to the differentiation of Gangsta rap within Hip Hop

   (E) They coupled indulgence with social activism

3. The militant, misogynistic and self-indulgent imagery of gangsta rap was linked to a machined post-production process with what effect:

   (A)   It made it possible to understand gangsta rap in contrast to Hip Hop

   (B)   It alienated audiences

   (C)   It made it possible to discuss gangsta rap as a new style

   (D)   It did not garner a wide enough audience of followers to achieve critical mass

   (E)   It maintained its street credibility

4. The attitude of the author towards the hedonism and misogyny of rap lyrics seems to:

   (A)   Be in favor of "gangsta rap"

   (B)   View these characteristics as a means to an end

   (C)   Doubt the sincerity of their use in rap songs

   (D)   Dispassionately acknowledge a relationship between the national rise of gangsta rap and its hedonism and misogyny

   (E)   Be a nonjudgmental observation of the way other people live

5. The importance of "canned beats" to the appeal of rap to a more diverse audience implies what about rap's growing listener base:

   (A)   They listen to rap's sound more carefully than its message

   (B)   They are not interested in the challenges facing inner city blacks

   (C)   They prefer to listen to a sound they are familiar with

   (D)   They are only willing to support revolutionary ideas if they are impressed by the even tempered reviews big business can offer

   (E)   They consider the merging of hedonism and politics to be an attack on to their political sensibilities

Passage 31

Sustainable development involves groups and agencies that coordinate efforts relating to the environment or obtain foreign direct investment on behalf of developing countries. Initially, sustainable development was a reference term for environmentalists who discussed alternatives to expendable resources. Planting trees at the pace at which they are cut down can be one example of sustainable development, if it is done without crippling the internal ecosystem. Wind farms are also safely considered an indisputable
5   application of sustainable development. Of course, the range of activities that may be designated as "sustainable" makes policing every invocation of the term more alchemy than science. Whether oil companies who allocate 1/24th of their total profits, while still a princely sum, towards renewable energy deserve to consider themselves backers of sustainable development is not, for example, a reasonable question in the minds of graying 'earth-firsters'. More doubtful uses of the phrase leave veteran environmentalists and radical progressives in the field of both semantics and considerations of authorial intent. Sustainable Development Mutual Funds
10 are a good example. There is some doubt as to what exactly sustainable development is.

The United Nations 1987 Commission on Environment and Development, known as the Brundtland Commission in contemporary UN office-speak, defined sustainable development as meeting "the needs of the present without compromising the ability of future generations to meet their own needs." However, this definition, itself innocently similar to the Chinese proverb "We do not inherit the earth from our ancestors, we borrow it from our children", has encouraged the nettlesome development of "SD" mutual funds.
15 The Brundtland Commission made it possible for groups such as money managers and the "Sustainable Development Consultancy" to market themselves as green, do-good corporations. The Sustainable Development Consultancy even ranks corporations on their sustainability. This lends credibility to the idea of a mutual fund that is sustainable, assuming it invests in these "SD" ranked companies. However, the logic behind such rankings dovetails with the rhetoric of the politically correct movement without upholding the core attributes of sustainable development. This makes for good public relations and a chorus of supporters on the bandwagon,
20 but no real distinction between behavior that protects and renews the environment and Madison Avenue headlines. If green-neutral banks and dirty mining operations can be winners on the "SD" scale provided they compensate for environmental transgressions with equally weighted social props, such as local hiring, or public meetings, then we may have good things to say about these companies, but their sustainability is surely overrated.

There are real benefits in applying the term "sustainable development" to the right actors. However, it becomes the responsibility of
25 heavyweight agencies, such as the UN, to set an example with reasonable and appropriate dialogue on sustainability to prevent the symbolism of the term from being misused for private gain. Without that caution, talking points such as sustainable development become a disorganizing influence on decentralized, grassroots organizations, whereas these talking points once acted as their call-sign, relaying a decisive message and clear intent between collaborating activists.

1. The concerns of veteran environmentalists over the usage of the term "Sustainable Development" have to do with:

   (A)   A traditional right to the term

   (B)   A science of environmental nomenclature

   (C)   Copyright issues

   (D)   Logic

   (E)   The clarity of a message

2. The primary purpose of this passage is to:

   (A)   Identify the actors in the environmental movement

   (B)   Demonstrate the importance of coordinating organizations

   (C)   Elucidate the difficulties of improving environmental problems

   (D)   Cease the reliance on sustainable development

   (E)   Clarify the meaning of sustainable development

3. This passage would be most likely to appear in a/an:

   (A) Company annual report

   (B) Financial magazine

   (C) Accounting textbook

   (D) Pamphlet for expatriates

   (E) Editorial on the misuse of the term Sustainable Development

4. One difficulty raised in the passage with preserving the integrity of the term Sustainable Development is:

   (A) The lack of a proprietary trademark on the term

   (B) The contrived origins of the term

   (C) The lack of interest in sustainable development

   (D) The unwillingness to use the term

   (E) The eagerness of large organizations to adopt the term

5. The problem the passage observes with the definition of "Sustainable Development" composed by the UN is:

   (A) It was irresponsible

   (B) It was influenced by business and politics

   (C) Large, corporate organizations should not make use of the term "Sustainable Development"

   (D) It was ambiguous

   (E) It established a policy for defining the term without a means of policing its use

6. The author uses the term "dovetails" in line 18, to emphasize:

   (A) The unscientific nature of the term "Sustainable"

   (B) The unscientific nature of the term "renewable"

   (C) The method of watering down of the term "Sustainable"

   (D) The wide applicability of the term "Sustainable" for environmental causes

   (E) The accuracy in the use of the term "Sustainable"

7. "Graying 'earth firsters' ", mentioned in line 8, are most likely to view which of the following as an example of "Sustainable Development":

   (A) Burning clean hydrogen for energy while using still more fossil fuels to extract it from water

   (B) Moving people out of green-space consuming suburban enclaves into major cities so that councils may enact improvements in mass transit

   (C) Flying in fuel consuming jet planes while planting trees to compensate for carbon emissions

   (D) Mounting a mission to Mars to transfer excess population to another ecosystem out of concern for the limits on terrestrial stocks

   (E) Providing subsidized transport to poor breadwinners in third world countries to work in richer first world countries for money to send home

8. It can be inferred form the passage that the intention that a person or group harbors in describing behavior as "Sustainable" is considered:

   (A) Irrelevant to environmentalists

   (B) A point of contention between different environmentalists

   (C) Honorable on the part of private companies

   (D) An effort to present the whole truth by otherwise "dirty companies"

   (E) Subject to the review of the UN

Passage 32

In the marketing of any new product, the number of potential consumers is not the only variable that a responsible corporation needs to take into consideration in its analysis of potential profits. Even though a given product may have numerous possible uses and a willing market of consumers, the effect of that product on a corporation's image and the public's good will is not guaranteed to be in direct correlation to its commercial success. While some corporations use loss-leaders to increase the profits of unrelated products
5 through their benefits to branding, corporations are equally wary of successful products that will hamper the sales of other product lines and the ability of the corporation to function politically in its market.

This reality is most striking in the American contraceptive industry, where endless surveys of women reveal that more choices always seem to equate to more satisfied consumers. Still, there appears to be as many as 100 new contraceptives trapped between development and market. Consider that when we speak of research and development in the contraceptive industry, it is products
10 for females that we concern ourselves with almost exclusively. The unwillingness of corporations to supply female consumers with their products of choice makes a statement about the political inferiority of these women as consumers. Undeniably, while men have a single, relatively simple and effective measure for contraception, women are afforded a cornucopia of alternatives that suit their lifestyles, sexual appetites, and personal habits. However, for women's sake, this patchwork of options should never be viewed as too varied or as colorful enough. Since it is women who are at risk of an unwanted pregnancy, not men, women have an interest in
15 protecting themselves from the result of their sexual relations. Being proactive about contraception is a safer course of action than relying on the benevolent consideration of their partner and uncertain availability of his "wallet condom".

However, while American women spend 3/4 of their reproductive lives evading unwanted pregnancies, and 60% of pregnancies remain unplanned, evidence suggests that Americans view sex in political discourse with weak stomachs even as women privately search for options to protect themselves from unintended circumstances. Based on this, it is evident that conservative pharmaceutical
20 corporations are laden with fear over the reaction of extremist pro-life groups, religious organizations and prominent members of the Republican Party to increased research and even successful marketing of contraceptive alternatives. The enormous market of consumers who would welcome convenient alternatives to the daily "pill", such as a patch, monthly hormone injections, or intrauterine devices, continue to wait much longer than necessary for such products on account of the intimidating presence of a minority of well organized non-consumer groups dominating product availability. The solution to this paradox is not only to preach
25 that corporations need to pursue the orthodoxy of their own free market rewards, but also to create open communication about the real sexual lifestyles of women and to organize women around a possible bounty of consumer choices by criticizing their opponents' self-appointed flag-planting missions to a private moral high-ground.

1. The passage states that which of the following can be considered more important than a certain product's profitability:

   (A)   Safety

   (B)   Cost of development

   (C)   Managerial complications

   (D)   Supply chain risk

   (E)   Publicity

2. The implication of the author in the sentence beginning "Still, there appears to be" in line 8 is that:

   (A)   The corporations could bring these products to market but choose not to

   (B)   The products were not likely to be well received by consumers

   (C)   The products are not safe for wide distribution

   (D)   The products would bring a loss for corporations if they were all marketed simultaneously

   (E)   The products are too costly to manufacture

3. The passage presents the decisions of corporations and their marketing campaigns as a function of:

    (A) Corporate responsibility

    (B) Canny marketing

    (C) Risk taking

    (D) A lack of information

    (E) Risk adversity

4. The passage states that women are "politically inferior" as consumers in relation to:

    (A) Males as consumers

    (B) Official governmental organizations

    (C) Corporations

    (D) Organized religion, republicans and pro-life groups

    (E) Contraceptive manufacturers

5. The logic behind the author's presumption that women are underserved by the birth control market is that:

    (A) Women have less disposable income than men do

    (B) Women are unwilling to buy new contraceptive products

    (C) Women are more likely than men to sue manufacturers

    (D) Women are less uniform than men in their contraceptive needs

    (E) Women are not swayed by advertising

6. With which of the following assessments of capitalism would the author likely agree?

    (A) It must be regulated so that women will have all the choices they need

    (B) It is not subject to the political influence of extra-market actors

    (C) It is inherently biased against women

    (D) It could provide women with many of the sources of contraceptives they seek

    (E) It should be abandoned

7. Which of the following would be a plausible step in light of the passage to increase the willingness of pharmaceutical companies to offer more contraceptive products to women?

    (A) Normalizing discussions on sex through televised discussions

    (B) Increased purchasing of available contraceptive products by women

    (C) Passing legislation that would have men take more responsibility for the consequences of sex

    (D) Demand that pharmaceutical companies lower their prices

    (E) Ban advertising of contraceptive products

8. In the sentence beginning "Being proactive about" in line 15, the term "uncertain availability" most nearly means:

    (A) Likelihood

    (B) Poor chance

    (C) Voluntarism

    (D) Good chance

    (E) Reliability

Passage 33

The importance and rapid growth of an American software computing sector in the mid nineteen seventies brought the sector heightened attention from U.S. lawmakers. In order to protect the intellectual property of corporations and producers in the sector, the U.S. government extended copyright law to include products that copied the look as well as the programming code of a product. As the profile of the sector grew, lawmakers found they could enact legislation with popular support. This move brought many
5   individual programmers into conflict with one another. The presiding industrial order of academics, programmers and companies that had nurtured the growth of labor networks in the industry had created much of the working capital of the sector. It had done so according to principles of scientific inquiry, research and review. The working capital in the field was the product of many efforts of individuals, not only corporate investors and producers. Thus, intellectual property would be difficult to protect for contributors on the periphery with laws designating its rightful owner. For most though, the expansion of copyright protection had begun to place
10 corporate investors at cross-purposes with the software programmers by placing the desire to prevent "free riding" at odds with the established benefits of the free and open exchange of information for critique and redesign. This threatened to put a chilling effect on innovation.

The tension between the freedom to modify and the freedom to apply copyright protection had been building throughout the late 1970's as software came into its own in the American marketplace. What remained to be discovered was whether software could be
15 effectively treated as a commodity. Later, the Reagan administration made advances in disassembling the watershed of government funding and grants amassed over the years for a variety of academic and corporate research. These grant programs came to be viewed by the White House as an antiquated and wrongheaded methodology, as relics of post-Depression thinking which were unnecessary in a climate of economic expansion in which businesses could succeed on their own. Lawmakers had already begun to give the software industry the tools to engage in fee-simple transactions, and this meant the Reagan administration increasingly was able to
20 encourage lawmaking that reflected its economic principles.

The Copyright Act of 1976 overhauled U.S. copyright law, extending the legal protection of copyright to software programs. According to Section 102(b) of the Act, individuals and companies now possessed the ability to copyright the "expression" of a software program but not the "actual processes or methods embodied in the program." Translated, programmers and companies had the ability to treat software programs like a story or song. Other programmers could take inspiration from the work, but to make a direct copy,
25 they first had to secure permission from the original creator. Although the new law guaranteed that even programs without copyright notices carried copyright protection, programmers quickly asserted their rights, attaching copyright notices to their software programs. Programmers, particularly those retained by software businesses, began to feel that individual pieces of software needed to be self-sufficient, paying for themselves through market demand.

1. According to the passage, the U.S. federal government is most likely to engage in economic lawmaking:

   (A) If an economic sector outgrows its own institutional rule-making bodies

   (B) When it is economically feasible for the administration to do so

   (C) To increase pre-existing growth

   (D) To safe-guard American property rights

   (E) When a problem is brought to its attention

2. The deconstruction of post-Depression incentive programs by President Reagan's policy makers implies that:

   (A) They valued an American ideal of property over the prospect of immediate economic growth

   (B) They considered corporate producers as more important than individual contributors

   (C) They saw that the computing sector would require explicit property laws in order to continue its growth in America

   (D) The post-Depression programs should never have been put in place

   (E) They believed businesses should be self-sufficient

3. The most significant reason some programmers were against the Copyright Act of 1976 was because:

   (A) It took all programmers' property away from them

   (B) The inability to steal other programmers' work would make them insolvent

   (C) It was an interruption of existing working relationships

   (D) It raised the transaction costs of coding for all programmers

   (E) It would force programmers to switch employers

4. Which choice best describes how the sentence beginning with "Later, the Reagan administration made advances..." in line 15 contributes to the development of the central theme of the passage:

   (A) The consideration of software as a commodity took place in a wider climate of privatization and commercialization

   (B) The consideration of software as a commodity was encouraged by the policy making of the government

   (C) Government policy making can and did influence the behavior of industry by affecting the institutional environment in which industry operates

   (D) Government sponsored incentive programs prevented software companies from operating independent of external support

   (E) Government sponsored incentive programs are essential

5. The opponents of the Copyright law of 1976 would consider the benefit of enhanced property rights:

   (A) A development with negligible impact

   (B) A possible long term benefit with dangerous short term disadvantages

   (C) A benefit for no-one in the software sector

   (D) A microeconomic solution for an irresolvable macroeconomic problem

   (E) A short term economic benefit with long term disadvantages for the software sector

6. The term "chilling effect" most directly refers to:

   (A) Alienation from the means of production

   (B) Slowdown in the rate of innovation

   (C) Greater inequality between owners and producers

   (D) Hoarding of innovations

   (E) Higher transaction costs

7. From the last sentence beginning in line 27, it can be inferred that the author believes that the expansion of copyright restrictions:

   (A) Encouraged many programmers to take a stance against once-tolerated theft

   (B) Compelled programmers to protect their work aggressively only for fear of other programmers copyrighting it

   (C) Gave programmers something they had long been waiting for

   (D) Was not equally advantageous to all programmers

   (E) Caused programmers to focus more attention on independent projects rather than collaborative ones because they could retain exclusive rights to the commercialization of their projects.

8. According to the passage, the major distinction between programmers for and against greater copyright protection is:

   (A) Proponents believe that quality software is fundamentally a corporate or private effort and opponents believe it is too difficult to distinguish who owns a piece of software since everyone benefits from one another's involvement

   (B) Proponents believe that the expanded market for commercial software drives it to be privately developed in order to reap uncontested profits while opponents believe that the software industry is most effective as a collaborative effort and that it remains impossible to enforce fee-simple compensation on a per-piece basis

   (C) Proponents believe that professional programmers were unfairly being held hostage by the greater number of nonprofessionals responsible for simple bug checking while opponents believe that all work that goes into a program deserves equal compensation if it does not limit the quality of the end product

   (D) Proponents believe that the software industry can not succeed in the absence of property relations without government subsidies while opponents believe that they are entitled to government subsidies as long as they are productive

   (E) Proponents believe that the only way to improve the software industry is by eliminating the weaker programmers while opponents believe that programming can effectively coordinate the efforts of those at all levels of expertise

Passage 34

A common surprise for many foreigners experiencing the cultural offerings of Germany for the first time comes after they have nearly finished a hearty meal of bratwurst or kielbasa and started to turn their minds to other delights, such as a stroll or a night on the water. Before the next order of business can be taken up, many tourists discover an unsettling distinction between their trusty comfort stations thousands of miles away and that of their adopted setting. While the flush toilet is originally an American
5 innovation, German flush toilets have a visibly unique construction style, leaving many unprepared inductees biting their fist and wondering what to do first. In particular, the German flush toilet can be distinguished from its North American inspiration by the existence of an 'examination shelf', a platform on which ordure may rest for the purview of its provider. The design is based on the idea of monitoring one's good health by studying the most immediate results of digestion. This is unheard of across the ocean.

In fact, cultural distinctions between the two major modern industrial powers, Germany and America, have called for a startling
10 amount of research by sociologists into the ergonomic details of the respective lifestyles preeminent in each culture. This research often begins in the kitchen but experts do not deny that there are important lessons to be gleaned from all the functions of life. For instance, the original American model of the flush toilet reflecting the associated puritanical American culture, was not considered a wholly practical improvement based on German customs, even though it brought additional hygiene and sanitation. Specifically, American toilets completely submerged effluence in water, reinforcing the social psychology dominant in American culture that
15 regarded corporeal functions to be impure, and thus a form of evil. This model was still not an obvious sell for the 'Volk' in Germany. This is because, unlike Americans, Germans perceived the scrutiny of their dispatch as part of a 'prudent' process of self-diagnosis, recommended by gerfundesvolk as being useful for the maintenance of good health. Thus, the American invention, designed to obscure natural processes from the observer so that the device could function in the cultural manner in which it was conceived, would not have been seen entirely as an improvement in Germany because it overlooked vital cultural practices, inseparable from
20 German dietary habits. The obvious benefits of the American toilet would have been superseded by the cultural and practical preferences of Germans.

There is an important point to be learned from both the original impasse and the subsequent resolution through German redesign. Development specialists should note that cultures must safeguard their styles and traditions for numerous reasons. Yet, ultimately these practices merge together to contribute durability and organization to the society. What one onlooker may see as an improvement
25 to one way of life may in fact have hidden flaws that only local people will notice. In the case of German sanitation, the redesign of the American innovation with the 'inspection shelf' to check for a series of health-related indicators was an easy alternative until the 1940's when modern medicine made such practices largely unnecessary. Over-eager inventors, and environmentally-conscious providers of foreign aid, may reason from this example that they are likely to be servants of their objectives if they herald their own intervention with an onlooker's skepticism, rather than with unchecked enthusiasm for sure progress.

1. What situation most nearly resembles the dynamic that disturbs the author in the above passage?

   (A) Environmentalists putting metal spikes in trees to make it dangerous for loggers to clear cut old growth forests

   (B) Encouraging dense urbanization to decrease the number of encroachments on cropland near cities

   (C) Providing a market for poor people to buy and sell a type of livestock that plays a prominent role in their religion

   (D) Advocating a national immigration policy to attract knowledge workers from third world countries into a growing service economy short on skilled professionals

   (E) Distributing free 'low flow' toilets and showers to save water in large urban centers

2. The author would most likely regard the commitment of the overly enthusiastic inventor or foreign aid provider as:

   (A) unwilling but uxorious

   (B) obvious but insidious

   (C) ambitious but hackneyed

   (D) forward thinking but myopic

   (E) benevolent but egotistical

3. Which statement from the passage would argue against a dam on a large river and the flooding of surrounding villages for the sake of improved irrigation and power capacity downstream from a watershed region?

   (A) "In fact, cultural distinctions between the two major modern industrial powers, Germany and America, have called for a startling amount of research by sociologists into the ergonomic details of the respective lifestyles preeminent in each culture"

   (B) "For instance, the original American model of the flush toilet, reflecting the associated puritanical American culture, was not considered a wholly practical improvement based on German customs, even though it brought additional hygiene and sanitation"

   (C) "The redesign of the American innovation with the 'inspection shelf' to check for a series of health-related indicators was an easy alternative"

   (D) "There is an important point to be learned from both the original impasse and the subsequent resolution through German redesign"

   (E) "What one onlooker may see as an improvement to one way of life may in fact have hidden flaws that only local people will notice"

4. It can be inferred from the passage that the 'inspection shelf' toilet

   (A) did not sell well in America

   (B) was considered by the toilet's original designer but disregarded as unfavorable

   (C) was introduced to overcome low sales of American toilets in Germany

   (D) was viewed as unnecessary given the sanitary improvements provided by the American toilet

   (E) could only sell well if Americans were taught how to use it

5. The theme of this passage can be best described as:

   (A) the misunderstood efficiency of German dietary practices

   (B) the value of redesign

   (C) contrasting industrial successes and ergonomic differences in Germany and America

   (D) individuals responsible for designing influential systems should rely on audience feedback

   (E) technical changes must be coordinated with social factors to improve contemporary conditions

6. According to the passage, the most confusing thing about German toilets for those who are unfamiliar with them is

   (A) How to properly diagnose oneself

   (B) The assumption that hygiene being compromised

   (C) The lack of warning

   (D) The physical design

   (E) Unfamiliarity with German customs

7. The mood of this piece could be considered:

   (A) Persuasive

   (B) Argumentative

   (C) Informative

   (D) Biased

   (E) Humorous

8. An appropriate title for the above passage might be:

    (A)   Asking the Right Question: How to Avoid Interpreting the Third World through the Western Manual

    (B)   Historical Perspectives on Cultural Comparisons: How Cultural Premises Distinguished German and American Development

    (C)   Wing Nut: Unusual Versions of Every Day Items

    (D)   The Continental Shelf: Difficulties in Foreign Product Placement from the Toilet to Micro-development

    (E)   Showing Up: Why a Cautious Entrance is the Way to Head Off a Cultural Impasse

Passage 35

Paradigm shifts in disciplines and professions come into being when a growing minority's resistance to current thinking on a subject usurps the standard methodologies. The minority may succeed by outliving the adherents of the old line of thought, or by recruiting a new wellspring of assenting technicians. Methodologies within the field then change as new advances in techniques or technology are coordinated with the new views of thinkers. This is accomplished as the changes preferred by the dissenters achieve dominance
5   using the tools being developed in the workplace. In this way, computerization was able to evolve into an industry and a science far beyond what was envisioned by the traditional academic side of the discipline. The diverging aesthetics of the computer (the mainframe and the personal computer) are an example of this interpretation of paradigm shifts. Personal computer users were a minority who gained a comparative edge in approaching old problems in a new way. But they benefited most from the style of programming on personal computers. This style encouraged many hobbyists and individuals to begin programming on their own.
10 Computer users, who attempted to apply a less formal logic in developing code, were not only benefited by the proliferation of computers, but by the increased ability of users to reach one another, and to share a working culture based on more malleable rules of programming, as well as common social principles. Thus, they were prepared to take advantage of tools that matched their natural political organization. They were willing to risk their credibility as scientists or professionals on new methodologies through experimentation and they were positioned to take advantage of other paradigm shifts in the culture, in communication and
15 in individualism. These shifts made for a wider dissemination of knowledge and expertise.

These types of changes in scientific orthodoxy show how the development of competing technologies in computing was matched by a change in the way consumers saw their position as users of machines, and how designers perceived the 'right' way of programming computers. The very notion of a 'personal computer' facilitated a paradigm shift in the way computers were used, and thus designed. Largely, it had been believed that computers would continue to be used as cooperative machines for large-scale number-
20 crunching. That perception had led to the understanding of computer science as a discipline that needed to be compartmentalized and standardized with a precise lingua franca across academic, business and governmental sectors. The expense of computers and the need for their input to be the product of numerous individuals or departments had required that code be highly readable, and thus follow a prefabricated style of construction. But new types of users and types of computers would lead to differing attitudes within computer science (a growth in a less formal and less professional group of users). The role of 'tinkering' with the devices
25 would change the direction of the science, and the industry, in a way that educators did not conceive, if only because it posed such an uncharted, locally-directed and self-organizing development in computer-aided design. What made this new culture so significant was that it created the competitive industry of computerization by involving many dedicated individuals throughout the country and across different professional disciplines, acting according to a common understanding. This may be one explanation for the complexity and success of this type of computing. This success was not the result of planned development.

1. According to the passage, standards change because of:

   (A) New educational opportunities

   (B) Technological development

   (C) New publications

   (D) Changing morality

   (E) The agreement of technicians that changes are merited

2. In the sentence beginning with 'This is accomplished', in line 4, 'dominance' most nearly means:

   (A) Expectation of

   (B) Success

   (C) Demand for

   (D) Concern about

   (E) Escape from

3. According to the passage a minority may redirect the field in which it works by:

   (A) Petitioning the leaders of the field

   (B) Popularizing new tools

   (C) Demonstrating how its style is more in line with cultural trends

   (D) Computerizing the methodologies of the workplace

   (E) Limiting the availability of information

4. One thing which the less formal logic of programming benefited from was:

   (A) The suitability of contingency plans in the unpredictable course of development for computers

   (B) The decline of the mainframe

   (C) The scarcity of personal computers

   (D) Educational advances

   (E) Improvements in communication

5. It can be inferred from the passage that a paradigm emerges from:

   (A) The coincidence of changing views and scientific advances

   (B) The alienation of a subculture of loyalists

   (C) The deduction that current methodologies are acceptable

   (D) The democratic negotiation of the rules by which a culture of scientists interacts

   (E) Consumer demand for a new standard

6. Which of the following words would be the most appropriate substitute for the word 'current thinking' (line 1) in the first sentence?

   (A) Fixed minimum percentage

   (B) Perceived wisdom

   (C) Reasons

   (D) Fiat

   (E) Forum

7. The term 'malleable' in the sentence beginning with 'Computer users' in line 10, means:

   (A) Clear

   (B) Quantifiable

   (C) Understandable

   (D) Appropriate

   (E) Flexible

8. The need for mainframes to follow a prefabricated style of construction was related to:

   (A) The high cost of production

   (B) The cheap prices for computers

   (C) The lack of predictability in where the field would go

   (D) The need for code to be easily readable

   (E) Manufacturing constraints

Passage 36

In April of 1986, the Chernobyl nuclear power plant became the subject of worldwide concern. Chernobyl was a nuclear station located in Ukraine, at that time a state of the Union of Soviet Socialist Republics. On April 25, the Chernobyl-4 reactor, one of several operated at the site, was readied for a test to examine the effects of low power on the reactor and turbine behavior. At issue was a question of how long the turbines could spin once the main electrical power supply had been cut, always a possibility for a
5   number of unpredictable reasons. However, it was well known that this reactor became extremely unstable when operated on low power, knowledge that resulted from tests conducted at similar facilities. After disabling the triggers for the deactivation mechanisms in case of instability, Chernobyl operators began the test, reducing the flow of coolant into the reactor and increasing power output. Operators then sought to shut down the reactor, but something irregular about the Soviet reactor design parameters caused power to surge, allowing the fuel elements to break open and letting loose an explosive column of steam which brought the cover plate apart
10   from the reactor. This plate had prevented fissile material from reaching the atmosphere while in place. Another explosion followed, expelling ignited fuel and graphite from the reactor, and mixing air with the graphite moderator to create an eruption of flames. The graphite then burned for nine days releasing most of the radioactive material into the atmosphere that would cause Chernobyl to be regarded as the textbook example of the dangers of nuclear power.

Yet, in truth, those dangers had more to do with the isolation of the Soviet Union and the resulting inadequate emphasis on safety
15   than it had to do with nuclear instability. In this case, five thousand tons of boron, dolomite, sand, clay and lead were airdropped onto the reactor to extinguish the flames and contain the release of radioactive material. Furthermore, two hundred and ten thousand people were resettled to less contaminated areas and Chernobyl unit 4 was enclosed in a large concrete shelter, the construction of which is regarded by some to be qualified as the eighth wonder of the world.

When the most inflammatory damage control was already underway, Western scientists and Eastern personnel realized that the
20   Chernobyl disaster provided a real opportunity to assess all Soviet reactors, and to improve their safety protocols manifold. Improvements were implemented in a process of increased collaboration between design teams and nuclear operators on either side of the now healing East-West divide. Through visits of nuclear plants and the establishment of East-West twinning arrangements overseen by the World Association of Nuclear Power Operators safety has been improved both in the Eastern Bloc countries and in nuclear plants throughout Europe and America. Appreciative of these results, the International Atomic Energy Agency now co-
25   ordinates engineers, from both East and West, to review safety standards. The proof is self-evident; there now exists as much as 1 billion dollars in Western aid for safety-related projects throughout the Eastern Bloc. The fund goes towards training engineers and constructing stations such as the international radioecology laboratory inside the Chernobyl exclusion perimeter. Each such undertaking aims to benefit the future science and management of nuclear energy.

1. According to the passage, the dangers of nuclear power were not as central to the Chernobyl disaster as:

   (A)   Soviet isolation

   (B)   Exceptionally high western standards

   (C)   Safety being presented as something other than a reward for scientists in the East-West competition

   (D)   The media blitz of the event

   (E)   Over-reliance on contingency plans

2. According to the passage, a contributing factor to the Chernobyl disaster was:

   (A)   Computer error

   (B)   Adverse weather conditions

   (C)   Unrealistic demands for energy output

   (D)   Lack of information

   (E)   Human error

3. The passage implies that the domestic Soviet nuclear accident:

   (A) could not happen west of the divide because of extensive safety procedures

   (B) was a result of the militarization of the Cold War

   (C) was the result of engineers with poor training

   (D) will be easier to clean in the future due to research from radioecology laboratories

   (E) would not have occurred if the fissile material did not escape

4. The passage considers which of the following as a positive sign that safety measures were being taken seriously after the Chernobyl Reactor?

   (A) the dumping of 5000 pounds of boron, dolomite, sand, clay and lead on the reactor

   (B) the building of a concrete sarcophagus to house the spent reactor

   (C) the resettlement of people

   (D) the continuation of the nuclear power program

   (E) twinning arrangements between eastern and western plants

5. The author would be least likely to agree with which assessment of the following causal relationships:

   (A) Guns do not kill people, people kill people

   (B) Increasing the size of the hulls of supertankers will not decrease the danger of breeches if it makes captains more brazen

   (C) Automobile air bags will not save net lives if fewer people wear seat belts because of them

   (D) computer storage of grades in Universities is more convenient but less secure than paper bureaucracy

   (E) drilling for oil would be considered less harmful to the environment if all city life relied on extensive mass transit

6. According to the passage, the most important improvement to nuclear power to come out of the review of the Chernobyl-4 meltdown was:

   (A) The healing of the East-West divide

   (B) Creation of World Association of Nuclear Power Generators

   (C) Increasing collaboration between scientists and personnel from the East and the West

   (D) The establishment of a one billion dollar fund for nuclear safety

   (E) Having engineers review safety standards

7. According to the passage, the purpose of the initial test of the nuclear reactor was to measure:

   (A) The reliability of the automatic shutdown mechanism

   (B) The manual expertise of Chernobyl-4's nuclear engineers

   (C) The momentum of turbines without main power

   (D) The effects of unpredictable circumstances on low power

   (E) The instability of the reactor operating at low power

8. The passage places the blame for letting the reactor become dangerously unstable on:

   (A) Soviet nuclear policy

   (B) Soviet design flaws

   (C) The engineers who began the test

   (D) The plate that contained fissile material

   (E) Insufficient communication between the East and West

Passage 37

The relationship between technology and productivity is considered an engine of the New Economy, an economy heavily influenced by information technology. The growth of an economy is always related to an improvement in the ability of people to produce things for consumption or trade. As the amount of production of an economy begins to level off in relation to the amount of time, resources and people that can be committed to output, growth can only be maintained by somehow managing scarcity using the
5   same resources, time and people more efficiently, or devising ways to augment these inputs. It is here that technology becomes a force in productivity. Technology facilitates using scarce resources to increase production or decrease the amount of energy and time that will be needed to make the same things. But, technology itself is a tool. That is to say, technology, in itself, does not drive the economy, and the agencies that control the economy do not produce for production's sake or innovate for technology's sake, but for some qualitative gain. Thus, individuals, firms, institutions and nations all create and direct wealth by managing and rearranging
10   social order, political rules and influencing the actors who innovate. They choose the way in which technology can advance, and the way in which it will be used in economic reform. These decisions are made without a dedicated eye towards technological advancement, but for economic reasons.

In effect, economies do not move along a one-way course, with the rate of technological development being the only variable which dictates how quickly they prosper. Technology is not, all things being equal, the only factor that determines which national
15   economies are successful and 'competitive' and which not. Social systems influence economies. It is the participant's needs or perceived objectives for which an economy is crafted. It is the very premise for which an economy and its technological solutions are in service.

Historical examples of the importance of social factors for the economy are demonstrative. The relative positions of Medieval Europe and fourteenth century China are instructive. Although the Chinese were significantly more advanced in key industries
20   (ship building, navigation, chemicals, agriculture and warfare), Europe surpassed China after the fourteenth century as the economic center of world trade. China did not decline simply through technological deficiencies, but from decisions on the part of the Chinese imperial state (and alternatively the haggling European nation states). Indeed, because Imperial China had perceived itself as the center of the world, or more accurately, as the world in total, and had a surplus of money coming in from the West, there was no pressing need to risk the empire's resources on further exploration accompanied by widespread and unregulated technological
25   development from within. China effectively entered into a stage of isolation and stagnation in response to a calculation on the part of its leaders that they had achieved a level of stability that would be excessively threatened by a commitment to additional growth or by the proliferation of certain technological advances, especially in munitions production. Thus, expansion and technology double as a threat and as a bonus for a particular society depending on how the economic elite and power brokers decide how those threats or opportunities should be translated into real industrial production, stability and labor output.

1.   The central topic of the passage is:

    (A)   The development of Medieval Europe

    (B)   The definition of technology

    (C)   The decline of China

    (D)   The overlap of social and economic spheres

    (E)   The reasons for the primacy of political influence

2.   Overcoming stagnation is discussed in the passage as being influenced by:

    (A)   War

    (B)   National character

    (C)   Currency values

    (D)   Factors outside the control of political leaders

    (E)   A movement towards technological improvement

3. It can be inferred from the passage that technological advance:

   (A) Is the only factor influencing economic development

   (B) Is inevitable

   (C) Has no influence on economic growth

   (D) Can be hampered by the motives of economic decision-makers

   (E) Is always sought by political leaders

4. The author presents technology-driven growth as being:

   (A) Able to advance unchallenged for the purposes of economic growth

   (B) A goal which is universally accepted as desirable

   (C) Always ineffectively used by leaders seeking to prosper without the risks of progress

   (D) Usually used to undermine politicians

   (E) Influenced by political factors

5. In halting further technological improvements China's leaders assumed:

   (A) Further technological growth was a long way off

   (B) China was behind other imperial societies

   (C) Technological advances would be difficult to contain

   (D) Technological investment would disturb the inflow western cash

   (E) Technological advance might lead to economic progress

6. Using relative Sino-European positions to support the central argument of the passage would be inappropriate if which of the following were true:

   (A) China's decline came as it turned away from technological advance

   (B) China and Europe used completely different political structures

   (C) Chinese imperial officials made a decision to push for technological growth

   (D) Technology was never the sole factor in Chinese growth

   (E) China's growth was technological, while Europe's was a political accomplishment

7. Which of the following scenarios is in agreement with the Chinese argument?

   (A) A major manufacturer of printer components refusing to lay off employees in lean times

   (B) Farmers unable to sell their crops on the open market because of agrochemical overproduction

   (C) The establishment of free trade zones to allow uninterrupted flow of goods across borders

   (D) The unwillingness of a major corporation to allocate funding for a spin off product which threatens current stocks with obsolescence

   (E) The reinvestment of surplus profits of a major corporation into its research and development department at the expense of dividends

8. In the sentence beginning with 'Technology is not. . .' (line 14), the phrase 'all things being equal' is included to emphasize:

   (A) Technology can be the deciding factor in what allows a nation to resist international influence

   (B) Technology is the deciding factor in the development of competing nations

   (C) The use of resources and organization of society can have a bigger influence than technology does on the development of nations

   (D) That 'all things' are never equal, and thus the dependent conclusion is illogical

   (E) Even comparable nations do not actually compete with each other in an economic sense, thus it is not useful to draw conclusions on the effect of technology on the development of international power

Passage 38

Increasingly, war historians have recognized the importance of military intelligence as a major factor in the outcomes of great power confrontations. Still, it is only recently that the people critical to military intelligence in World War I and World War II are becoming widely known. Clearly, a reason for this has been the sensitive nature of the information contained in historical records. Governments have taken a long time to declassify these records.

5   Universal publication of the case by case undertakings of military intelligence can not be expected to find immediate and international corroboration in an atmosphere in which the ebb of governmental transparency has realpolitik ramifications. However, there were groups that played an undeniable role in the outcome of these war times who deserve more recognition of their service to their countries. Both Britain and the United States have activists of this type. Mathematicians and chess masters in Britain, and Native American tribes in the United States, have clamored for their overdue acknowledgment in contributing to the war effort.

10 In Britain, under Churchill, a top secret camp of code breakers was assembled from far flung reaches of the United Kingdom's intelligence community to help defeat the German enigma code, initially weakened by Polish cryptographers during the inter-war period. This group of mathematicians, linguists, chess masters, crossword puzzlers and philologists saved thousands of lives by deciphering German U-boat transmissions to keep the Allied supply lines open between America and its European coalition. However, after camp was broken at the end of the war, the group was disbanded with orders to never reveal the nature of their
15 relationship to one another or to his Majesty's government.

In America, a great deal of fanfare has erupted around the existence of Native American 'wind talkers' who have also kept their silence, under military orders not to reveal their contribution to the winning of the Pacific War by the United States during World War II, or to the capturing of the beaches of Normandy. These Indian tribes (Navajo, Choctaw, and Comanche to name a few) made it possible to compete with the highly-sophisticated German enigma machine and the crack analysis of Japanese code-breakers by
20 creating a method of transmitting battlefield information that proved extremely secure, and ultimately unbreakable by enemy probes. The use of Native American languages could also be rapidly employed for a message in the field of battle, at least ninety times faster than the mechanical means advanced by the Germans. Both groups of code-makers and code-breakers have been demonstrated by historians to have shortened the length of the war by at least as many as three years. Those years would have meant countless lives lost. Instead, countless lives were saved on account of the British camp and the Native American radiomen.

25 Thus, while it is important for nation-states to conceal their military secrets, and not risk providing a budding enemy with information on the logic informing each nation's strategy of defense, the governments of these states must remain appreciative of the struggle of all those who acted on behalf of their fellow citizens in a time of crisis. In time, it will become clear that the danger posed by releasing this information for broadcast is minimal. Once that is the case, states should not pass up an opportunity to recognize those people to whom so many lives are owed. They ought not just admit to these contributions when pressured by the descendents or
30 advocates of these groups, but be anxious for an opportunity to announce these accomplishments publicly, turning these heroes into household names.

1. The primary impediment to awarding credit to deserving members of sensitive war projects discussed in the passage was:

   (A)   the difficulty in crediting individual members for group projects

   (B)   lack of historical evidence of the contributions of possible participants

   (C)   the understanding that the war effort was a joint contribution by all members of society

   (D)   the threat to national security posed by the disclosed information

   (E)   the discomfort of members towards being identified

2. The main achievement of the British code-breakers and the Native American radiomen is presented in the passage as:

   (A)   The number of ships saved

   (B)   The effort to keep military secrets

   (C)   The number of lives saved

   (D)   The penetration of German codes and the defeat of Japanese cryptographers

   (E)   The unrealized threat to national security

3. It can be inferred from the passage that the author believes government transparency

    (A)   is the right of the people whom the government serves

    (B)   is dependent on the expectations of a country's citizens

    (C)   is not an issue during a time of war

    (D)   is contingent on the lack of any threat to the government's stability

    (E)   is the job of civic-minded individuals to ensure

4. Based on the passage, what statement can be construed about governments?

    (A)   governments do not have to consider the interests of the majority of their citizens as their primary concern

    (B)   governments should recognize those who have served them because individual rewards should be proportionate to their efforts

    (C)   governments should recognize those who have served them because individual rewards should be egalitarian

    (D)   governments should recognize individuals because it encourages other citizens to be patriotic

    (E)   governments should not reveal information to compensate a minority of people

5. The political system supporting the observations made in the passage is:

    (A)   Autarky

    (B)   Counter-culture

    (C)   Meritocracy

    (D)   Bureaucracy

    (E)   Monopoly

6. The passage regards the American and British decisions in the past to keep their war programs secret as:

    (A)   Unreasonable

    (B)   Unpatriotic

    (C)   Acceptable

    (D)   Capricious

    (E)   Historical fluke

7. The change on the part of American and British Governments which would most closely satisfies the writer of the passage would be:

    (A)   A move towards domestic affairs and a move away from foreign policy

    (B)   Introduction of a system of risk analysis for releasing information to the public

    (C)   Increased political asylum for people involved in secretive programs

    (D)   Establishment of a department to publicize declassified material and liaise with the affected parties

    (E)   Continuation of wartime practices of information concealment during peacetime

8. The term 'extremely secure' in line 20 describes which characteristic of Native American language important to Japanese cryptographers:

    (A)   it was very difficult to reproduce a system that was so well-encrypted

    (B)   it was very difficult to approach a Navajo radioman in the field

    (C)   it was very difficult to determine how to decode the Native American cipher

    (D)   it was very difficult to create a machine that could encrypt a message as quickly

    (E)   it was very difficult for the Japanese to use the Navajo cipher

Passage 39

Innovations in network technology have played a part in a current debate regarding the potential of technology to isolate individuals and hollow social bonds normally formed through the type of community affairs that bring together neighbors for town meetings, picnics and civic discourse. Commentators have voiced the contention that the freedom the net brings people to avoid direct interactions previously required for leisure activities and conflict resolution in one's home environment (by transferring both consumption
5 and production economies, as well as social gatherings, from home to the net) will further hamper civic participation. The staple argument in the debate was first composed by Harvard sociologist Robert Putnam, the veritable inventor of the notion of social capital. He cites data that there has been a decline in community gatherings, political party (Democrat and Republican) participation, and religious activity in the late twentieth century. This sociologist considers that this decline in organized participation is a direct result of the rise of television, the suburbs, and a different perspective on professionalism. The straightforward extension of
10 these arguments is that intensive use of the Internet is another component in the decline of 'social capital' which is so vital to the functioning of a responsive democracy.

The Internet seems like a suitable fourth horseman to Putnam's bearers (T.V., suburbanization, and professionalism) of brittle democracy. While the Internet may not yet have the placement rate of television in the U.S., certainly it will grow to be nearly as prolific. Moreover, online time is either adding to or replacing television hours. Certainly, it is not reducing the number of hours spent
15 indoors. While objections to the growing use of the internet concede that people online are more interactive than they are in front of the television, they emphasize that the communities on the internet do not provide a substitution for face to face 'social capital', and the rise of the internet coincides with the decline in political party participation. Yet, all this does not mean that the current spread of the Internet is incompatible with the flourishing of democracy.

Part of the reasoning for departing from the Internet threat argument is that Putnam's initial argument interprets the changes in
20 democracy as the end of democracy. Putnam worries about the decrease in the popularity of his preferred democratic institutions, while not seeing how lower union membership is offset by a rise in other voluntary behavior. This may result in less interest in specifically 'civic' behavior, but is balanced by a rise in support of issue-oriented politics, or a rise in participation in groups.

Democracy in a post-materialist world has moved into an age of conspicuous consumption of social issues such as environmentalism and the fight against racism. This takes participation away from traditional government organizations like the Junior Chamber of
25 Commerce, and hands it to special interest groups like Amnesty International. The loss to democracy is uncertain at best. Likewise the Internet seems to divert people from being passive recipients of information (via television) to becoming active users. Specific content, technologically marketed to statistically targeted individuals, may create much narrower markets, but the loss of a culture-spanning forum is not much of a penalty as the creation of wide-open culture was itself highly artificial, promoted through branding to lower the costs of marketing. Active users of the Internet are simply part of a democratic trend towards post-materialism. Class
30 issues and class mobilization are no longer the most important issues.

1. Which of the following assertions is the author most likely to cite in a rebuttal of Putnam's argument?

   (A)   The internet simply transfers television time to online time

   (B)   People have a constitutional right not to be civic-minded

   (C)   Volunteering is more common, on a project by project basis

   (D)   Democracy has flourished in China regardless of Communist party control

   (E)   Participation rates in interest groups are a poor measure of civic participation

2. From the passage it can be inferred that the author believes

   (A)   Democracy needs to be carefully monitored to regulate change

   (B)   Democracy is changing to accommodate social factors

   (C)   Democracy ought to be discussed in a forum that is inclusive of all citizens

   (D)   Democracy is to be measured issue by issue

   (E)   Democracy traditionally grows out of groups committed to a social cause

3. The perceived danger of marketing content to only those individuals who are interested in it according to the passage is:

    (A)   The expense of such an extensive and precise marketing campaign

    (B)   The perception of social causes in terms of conspicuous consumption

    (C)   The decline in support for the type of projects done by civic groups

    (D)   The creation of an elite, isolated group of knowledgeable power brokers

    (E)   The elimination of confrontation and response as a means of discussion

4. In the sentence beginning with 'Specific content, technologically,' the word 'artificial' in line 28 implies what about the resulting audience:

    (A)   It was not really interested in the culture that was offered

    (B)   It was largely homogeneous as a group

    (C)   It shared a common view on the issues society had to resolve

    (D)   It received a uniform culture

    (E)   It shared a class consciousness

5. The passage uses the word 'preferred' in the sentence beginning with 'Putnam worries' in line 20 to emphasize that:

    (A)   Putnam focused his studies on labor unions

    (B)   Political parties are irrelevant

    (C)   Community gatherings will cease

    (D)   Putnam's credibility is limited because his observation pool is too shallow

    (E)   Putnam's conclusions are logical, but too dated to apply

6. It can be inferred from the passage that the author views party politics to be a version of:

    (A)   Religious activity

    (B)   The caste system

    (C)   Ineffective political activity

    (D)   Class action

    (E)   Internet-based activity

7. The basis for social bonds which Putnam acknowledges are part of his notion of a healthy democracy depends on what?

    (A)   Availability of knowledge

    (B)   Education

    (C)   Volunteer groups

    (D)   Geography

    (E)   Class

8. The passage concludes that the conspicuous consumption of social causes:

    (A)   Does not compensate for social discourse

    (B)   Reduces the level of responsibility people take for civic participation

    (C)   Is compelled by social conventions rather than being an independent choice

    (D)   Is connected to the growth of individualism and interest groups

    (E)   Is ineffective

Passage 40

Koalas are placental mammals of the marsupial genus on the Carolinian chart of taxonomy. Having few natural predators, koalas' success has at times been their undoing. With over-breeding has come over-browsing, and subsequent habitat destruction. Koalas can be vulnerable to a pattern of dramatic growth followed by catastrophic decline.

In koala ecosystems, when the source of koala food, the eucalyptus leaf, is foraged into short supply, all koalas find their range too
5   small to sustain their own good health. As a result, they become vulnerable to disease, and the few predators eager to make short work of them. However, most seriously, they collectively face starvation. Humans have attempted to aid koalas by innovating fitting solutions such as contraceptives. However, koala contraception has proven to be extremely expensive. Over time, it has become an unpopular solution with conservationists, who reason that it is an uneven draw on funds needed by a variety of other species, each with its own obstacles. However, human intervention does not have the last word on the koala's unlikely paradox. Nature
10 has given koalas natural processes that help correct their population dilemma without man-made solutions that, so far, have been disappointing.

One such natural check on koala breeding has been the spread of diseases that are linked to their habits of aggressive reproduction. Chlamydia is a disease-causing bacterium found in many mammals. This bacterium plays an important role in facilitating population caps. In fact, Chlamydia is observed to be the primary pathogen affecting koalas today. Chlamydia gives its name to a sexually
15 transmitted disease that can cause respiratory ailments, infertility, blindness and death. It has also been known to cause conjunctivitis and a urinary tract infection known as 'dirty tail'. Since Chlamydia can be transmitted sexually or connately, it has achieved near universal penetration of the koala community, and is found in most species of the animal. With over-breeding and an overburdened ecosystem, the presence of a sexually transmitted disease which thins koala populations might be regarded as a sign of the species' own long term vigor.

20 Without such pathogens, it is possible that, at its apex, the koala population would reach sufficient numbers to wipe out all the edible vegetation in their habitat. This would result in huge numbers of the "Australian bear", all being equally vulnerable to starvation. The result would be sharp, periodic spikes and troughs in koala numbers. Koalas would reach enormous numbers in terms of population, and then find themselves simultaneously too much for their ecosystem. Almost all would die, leaving just the few koalas capable of being supported by what little overlooked eucalyptus vegetation remained. These koalas may continue to reproduce,
25 prosper, and ultimately even repeat the cycle. However, most importantly, first the surviving koalas would represent more limited genetic diversity, a sure deterrent to their species' potential for natural adaptations. On the contrary, reality has it that the bacterium Chlamydia has a role in regulating this process. Since it exists as a chronic infection in most koalas, and as the koala ecosystem is nibbled to its stem, many of the weakest koalas find their slow decline in nutrition accompanied by an increased likelihood of Chlamydia related diseases. As disease takes hold of these animals, it limits their ability to compete for the remaining food, leaving
30 sufficient supplies for the healthy koalas to consume, grow and reproduce. This process effectively prunes the species' growth resulting in a long-term homeostasis, without forcing the population to travel to distant extremes of genetic diversity.

1. The most serious danger of habitat destruction to the koala species is:

   (A)   It causes starvation

   (B)   It results in spikes and troughs in the size of the koala population

   (C)   It decreases the species' genetic variety

   (D)   It makes weak koalas and healthy koalas equally at risk

   (E)   It has brought the surviving koalas close to extinction

2. Which statement conveys a conclusion most similar to that of the passage?

   (A) As long as we plant enough trees to offset its green house emissions, we do not have to be concerned about the environmental impact of jet carbon.

   (B) The space program will be an invaluable asset to the future of the human race if the planet remains polluted.

   (C) The repopulation of the American condor could never have taken place if the U.S. government had not regulated pesticides.

   (D) Though the American cougar has been displaced by man, small animals will be only a minor threat to western crop sustainability if these animals continue to undergo stress induced thyroid problems leading to dispersal and inactivity.

   (E) Man has made great strides to accommodate the fish of Oregon's industrialized Snake River, but can only come close to returning fish stocks to pre-industrial replacement levels.

3. From the passage it can be inferred that a conservationist would most likely agree with which of the following?

   (A) Japanese village brigades are wrong to lure monkeys away from habitats experiencing human incursion.

   (B) Spending hundreds of millions extra on the accuracy of a missile launch device to protect one more life is narrow in scope

   (C) Planting many new carbon-absorbing saplings can be defeatist if it convinces people that logging slow-growth forests is acceptable

   (D) A species should be preserved at whatever cost

   (E) Deforestation can be acceptable

4. The main theme of the passage is:

   (A) Man's failure to solve the problems of koala reproduction

   (B) Natural systems maintain balance for koalas

   (C) Chlamydia is important to the survival of koalas

   (D) Characteristics of Koalas

   (E) The loss of genetic diversity is what may eventually bring koalas to the point of extinction

5. The main benefit of Chlamydia to koala adaptability and survival is:

   (A) It incapacitates all koalas

   (B) It is transmitted by the same processes that contribute to the over-breeding of koalas

   (C) It exists in nearly all koalas at the same time, so it incapacitates without hurting genetic diversity

   (D) It is contracted only during times of stress, allowing koalas to remain healthy in times of plenty

   (E) Its ability to cause infertility

6. This passage is likely to be taken from a piece titled:

   (A) Where Man Falls Short: Nature Takes Care of its Own

   (B) Symbiosis of the Koala-Chlamydia Populations

   (C) Incidence of Natural Processes Leading to Homeostasis

   (D) Pathogen Contributions

   (E) Smarter than the Average Bear: How Koalas and their Hangers-on can Consistently Outperform Predictions of the Population Cap

7. From the passage, it may be inferred that one possible contribution to koalas' unusual rate of growth is:

   (A)   The lack of population restricting diseases

   (B)   The unintended consequence of human intervention to protect koalas

   (C)   Their position at the top of their geographic food web

   (D)   The lack of sufficient predators who focus on koala protein

   (E)   The high cost of koala contraception outside of captivity

8. The word "connately" used in line 16 can be read here as:

   (A)   The same time or process

   (B)   Asexual

   (C)   From birth

   (D)   The coupling of same sex partners

   (E)   Any variety of non-sexual fluid exchanges

Chapter 4

Verbal Training Set IV - Analytical Writing Assessment

Essay I - Analysis of an Issue

Question:

"Manufacturers should be responsible for the quality of their own products and making sure that their products are safe. If their product injures someone, no matter what the reason is, the manufacturer should be legally and financially accountable for the injury."

Discuss the extent to which you agree or disagree with the opinion expressed above. Support your point of view with reasons and/or examples from your own experiences, observations, or reading.

Essay II - Analysis of an Argument

Question:

The following is an excerpt of an annual business review from the business manager of a department store.

"Clothing stores in the local area reported that their profits decreased, on average, for the third fiscal quarter which started on August 1 and ended on October 31. Stores that sell home products reported that their profits, on average, increased during this same period. Apparently, consumers have a preference of purchasing products for their homes instead of clothing. To leverage on this trend, we should reduce the size of our clothing departments and expand our home furnishings and household products departments."

Discuss how well reasoned you find this argument. In your discussion be sure to analyze the line of reasoning and the use of evidence in the argument. For example, you may need to consider what questionable assumptions underlie the thinking and what alternative explanations or counterexamples might weaken the conclusion. You can also discuss what sort of evidence would also strengthen or refute the argument, what changes in the argument would make it more logically sound, and what, if anything, would help you better evaluate its conclusion.

Essay III - Analysis of an Issue

Question:

"The presence of competition is always beneficial to a company as the company is forced to improve its practices."

Discuss the extent to which you agree or disagree with the opinion stated above. Support your views with reasons and/or examples from your own experience, observations, or reading.

Essay IV - Analysis of an Issue

Question:

The following is an excerpt of a memorandum from the director of Advax, a large pharmaceutical corporation.

"The proposal to increase our employees' health and retirement benefits should not be implemented at this time. An increase in these benefits is not only financially unjustified, as our last year's profits were down from the year before, but also unnecessary, as our chief competitor, Baieer, offers lower health and retirement benefits to its employees than what we currently offer to our employees. We can assume that our employees are reasonably satisfied with their existing health and retirement benefits since two-thirds of the respondents in a recent survey expressed their favorable views."

Discuss how well reasoned you find this argument. In your discussion be sure to analyze the line of reasoning and the use of evidence in the argument. For example, you may need to consider what questionable assumptions underlie the thinking and what alternative explanations or counterexamples might weaken the conclusion. You can also discuss what sort of evidence would also strengthen or refute the argument, what changes in the argument would make it more logically sound, and what, if anything, would help you better evaluate its conclusion.

Chapter 5

Verbal Training Set I Solutions - Sentence Correction

1. To answer this question, you first have to realize that the basic structure of this sentence is fairly simple. The main verb of the sentence is "grown". What is grown? A flower is grown, not its derivative. Choices A, B, C and D all imply that it is a derivative or a powder which is grown out West and not the flower. This is a clear flaw in logic. The only answer choice that has the correct subject is Choice E.

2. This question is quite tricky. It involves parallel structure. You have to look carefully to figure out what form the comparison takes. The comparison is not one of similarity, it is one of equality. Saying x is y is quite different from saying x is like y or x is similar to y. Choices B, C and E all change the fundamental underlying concept of the sentence. Choice D disrupts the parallel structure. The parallel structure is "trying to mimic" and "attempting to sing". Choice A is the correct answer.

3. This question has to do with parallel structure. Something causes officials to plan, build and offer. Choices A and C disrupt parallel structure by using an "ing" form inconsistently. Choices D and E are incorrect as you cannot cause someone to evacuation route planning or to a planning. Cause should be followed by the infinitive. Choice B is the correct answer.

4. This is a very easy question because the only mistakes you have to correct are mistakes in subject/verb agreement and subject/pronoun agreement. The subject is the sting. So you want the correct verb form to go with the singular, sting. That leaves you with C, D and E as possible choices because they say the sting É is rarely dangerous. Another mistake you have to correct is a subject/pronoun agreement mistake. The venom belongs to the sting. Therefore, you would use 'its' before venom because sting is singular. That leaves you with choices D and E. Choice E makes another mistake by saying they cause red welts to appear. The scorpions don't cause the red welts to appear, the sting of the scorpions does. Therefore the singular 'it' needs to be used. Choice D is the correct answer.

5. This sentence involves parallel structure. What did the earthquake do? It destroyed and led. These are actives verbs rather than the passive constructions in A and B. C also does not provide parallel structure. D is wordy and uses the wrong tense. The past perfect should be used as the city had become a disaster zone before people came to believe this. "The belief of the city as if it were" is also non-idiomatic. Choice E is the correct answer.

6. This question has to do with dangling modifiers. There is no subject in the first phrase, the part before the first comma. Therefore the subject of the verb in that phrase must come directly after the comma. What is the verb in the phrase? Offering is the verb. Who or what does the offering? Karate offers. Therefore karate is the subject and must come directly after the first comma. The only choice which offers this is A.

7. The first issue you need to be aware of is pronoun reference. It should be employees' legal right, not employers'. Therefore, you can eliminate A and D. The singular "an employee" does not go together with the plural "their". Option B does not have agreement between the plural "employees" and the singular "he". Option E has an unclear pronoun, "they", at the end of the option. It is not clear whether this word refers to the employees or the employers. Only option C is correct.

8. This question has to do with ambiguity arising from a lack of pronouns and improper word order. Choices C, D and E all imply that tourists are the ones who were riddled with bullets, shattered by bombs and hidden in alleys. This is a case of dangling modifiers. Choice A implies that the buildings may have been the ones traveling to more well-known memorial museums. Choice B uses the pronoun "who". This correctly connects all the parts of the sentence. Choice B is the correct answer.

9. Option A is incorrect as it is unclear to what "which" is referring. It should refer to organizing rallies but the placement means it is referring to the democratic principles. B is incorrect as the subject "Rallies" does not agree with the verb "is". Option C states that organizing rallies is beginning to take shape. The democratic principles are beginning to take shape. Choice D has an ambiguity resulting from the pronoun 'they'. It is unclear to whom 'they' is referring. Choice E is the correct answer.

10. This question has to do with parallel structure. You have to have a continuity of verb tenses and structures. Because you say 'five x had', then you have to follow it by saying, 'but only one y had'. The only two choices that even have a verb in them are D and E. Choice D uses a different verb tense, the simple past. Choice E is the correct answer.

11. Eliminate A and B on the grounds of a dangling modifier. New Jersey must come after the first comma in options A and B but it does not. "No such one" in option C is non-idiomatic. There is a lack of agreement in Option E between "taxes" and "has". D is correct.

12. This question has to do with efficiency of language. What follows the comma is going to give you some peripheral information about the work. You don't need to precede it by any unnecessary words or phrases such as 'for' or 'as'. D changes the meaning by its use of 'a paradigm' rather then 'the paradigm'. 'A paradigm' implies that there were others. The other options are wordier than B. Choice B is the correct answer.

13. Choice C has an incorrect idiom: while as. Choices A, C, D & E have passive constructions in the last part of the options. A also unnecessarily has 'the' before 'energy costs'. E eliminates 'energy'. This word is needed or the meaning of the sentence would be altered. Choice B is the correct answer.

14. The word 'interval' is critical in this sentence. You might want to ask yourself why use the word 'between' at all? You need the word because of the word 'interval'. 'Interval' implies that something is happening. That something has two parts to it. 'Interval between' is the correct idiomatic expression. A is incorrect because it uses the verb form 'recessing', which is not connected to a recession in the economy. This type of recession is what the sentence is discussing. Choice C is the best answer.

15. The part of the sentence you cannot change includes the fact that someone ordered another person or group of people. The correct following structure in this type of sentence is the infinitive. Only E provides this.

16. This is a very straightforward question of singular or plural and of usage of the words 'each' and 'every'. When you use the word each, you always use the singular, even if you are referring to multiple elements. You would say, for example: each boy in the class is wearing a sweater. Despite the fact that you are referring to multiple boys, you still use the singular. Therefore choices D and E are incorrect. Choice B could be correct if it were: 'all the paintings tiny etched landscapes'. Choice C uses 'all' with the singular 'its'. This is also wrong. Choice A is the correct answer.

17. The main thing you have to determine in this sentence is whether to use 'like' or 'as'. Use 'like' to compare nouns or pronouns. Use 'as' to introduce either a clause, which is a group of words with a verb, or a phrase starting with a preposition. The sentence compares hummingbirds to insects. Nouns are being compared so you need 'like'. The word 'do' in option D is unnecessary. B is more economical than D. 'From one flower to another' is also the correct expression rather then 'from one flower to others'. B is correct.

18. Choices B, C and E are ambiguous as it is not clear who or what has been branded. D is wordy and the phrase 'for those of them branded' is not idiomatically correct in this sentence. Choice B is the correct answer.

19. The correct noun to use is 'consumption' rather than the word 'consuming'. Choice D has a mistake in grammar. You need to use the plural instead of 'that was required'. Choice E is the correct answer.

20. Parallel structure demands agreement in verb tenses. The only option using the same tense throughout is C.

21. Here the first thing you have to ask yourself is: what did the judge rule? Did he rule on two ping-pong ball manufacturers or on restitution? No, the judge ruled that they owed something. That means that A, B and C are the only possible answer choices. You have to also maintain an agreement in tenses. The judge ruled that somebody owed something, not owes. That eliminates choice C. One difference between choices A and B is the use of different idioms. The manufacturers owed restitution for something, not because of something. This is the correct idiomatic expression. The use of 'their' is B is also ambiguous. Choice A is the correct answer.

22. A, C and E are wordy. B maintains parallel structure in that you have a subject, 'revenue', and a verb, 'decreased', followed by the pronoun 'it', standing for revenue and another verb 'might have been expected'. D has a subject, 'revenue' and then another subject 'its rise' Because of the two different subjects this option does not have parallel structure. Choice B is the correct answer.

23. You can have an equivalent number but not equivalent people. A and B incorrectly apply 'equivalent' directly to the several million Chinese men. In the same way C incorrectly applies 'equal' to the men, not to the number of men. It implies that soldiers are equal to something. The correct comparison here is between the number of soldiers and the number of students. Choice D also makes a mistake in reference in that it compares soldiers to the noun 'enrollment'. Choice E is the correct answer. It compares Chinese soldiers to Indian students.

24. This sentence is comparative. X does more of A than Y does of B. What is the X? The United States. What is the Y? North Korea. The simplest structure of an English sentence is to start with the subject and the verb. D & E start in this fashion. A and C are passive. The use of 'they' in B is incorrect as it is unclear to what 'they' refers. Choice D has a mistake in parallel structure. It uses spends/spending. Choice E is the correct answer.

25. Choices A, B and E all imply that humans should be struck by vehicles, not that they are or will be. Should implies a sense of moral purpose, which is clearly not the right thing to say here. It is tantamount to saying that if too few people are hit by vehicles, then extra humans will be hit. That leaves us with choices C and D. Choice C disrupts the parallel structure necessary to make the rest of the sentence fit. D has the correct parallel structure: Every three minutes something happens and each minute something else happens. C also implies that it is the same human being that is struck every three minutes. Only choice D doesn't use the word should and maintains correct parallel structure. Choice D is the correct answer.

26. The sentence as written is incorrect as it places 'both' too far from the parts of the sentence to which it refers. B corrects this error. C unnecessarily repeats the subject using the pronoun 'it'. It also does not have parallel structure in that it uses 'work' and 'working'. D and E repeat the problem with the placement of 'both'. D is not parallel in that it uses 'working' and 'are working'. E implies that there are only two adult entertainers. B is correct.

27. When used as an intensifier 'so' is applied to adjectives while the intensifier 'such' is applied to an adjective and a noun. For example, you can say 'such a hot day' or 'the day was so hot'. B is therefore incorrect as it does not fit this pattern. The correct adjective is addictive not addicting as used in C. D is not a complete sentence. E changes the meaning. The correct option, A, emphasizes that coffee is so addictive. E loses this emphasis.

28. The first thing you want to look at in this sentence is parallel structure. Because you say in the beginning 'raised in a family', you have to maintain the singular form of family. That eliminates choices C and E as possible answers. Also, the parallel structure carries over to prepositions. In the beginning, it says 'raised in a family of x than in a family of y'. You have to maintain that structure of 'in a family'. That leaves you with two possible choices: A and D. A uses the word 'where', which is incorrect. 'Where' refers to locations. The placement of 'only' in A and E is incorrect. It implies that the only thing this parent does is to care for a child. Choice D is the correct answer.

29. There are two possible constructions after 'require' One is 'someone requires someone else to do something'. The other

uses the subjunctive. For example, 'I require that you be on time'. The subjunctive is always introduced by 'that'. Choice A does not fit the correct subjunctive pattern as it uses 'should', instead of just the infinitive of the verb without 'to'. B is grammatically correct but it is passive. C is passive and uses 'retaining' instead of 'retention'. D incorrectly implies that there is only one employee. E is also grammatically correct and is shorter and simpler than B and is therefore the correct answer. It is active rather than the passive B.

30. This sentence clearly has to do with tense agreement. You can reduce the sentence down to the simple form: A woman was guided in x and y. Choice E uses different tenses. The use of 'by' in the part of the sentence which cannot be changed means that the verb before 'by' will be in the passive. E is active and changes the meaning by saying that she guided herself, rather then being guided by a sense of courage. 'And' in options A and C is more economical than 'as well as' in the other options. The use of 'also' in B is unnecessary. C is wordy. You could eliminate 'and that she was'. D repeats this error. A is correct.

31. Because 'values' is plural, you need the plural form of the verb 'to be'. Eliminate A, B and C. The placement of the preposition 'against' in E is better than in D. Prepositions should not come at the end of phrases. Choice E is the correct answer.

32. The sentence excludes a subset or an event from a larger group. You can eliminate B, D an E because they convey the opposite meaning as they say the subset and the group have the same characteristics. A is wrong because 'Except for' should be followed by a phrase, not a sentence. Choice C is the only possible answer.

33. 'Demanding' is incorrect as it sounds as if the action is taking place now rather then during WW1. C changes the meaning and introduces an unclear pronoun, 'their'. E also has an unclear pronoun, 'them'. If the pronoun refers to the Russian state, it should be singular. Only D is correct.

34. The first thing you should consider here is whether to use rather or instead. Instead does not have an element of choice in it, merely an element of replacement. You would say, for example: I went instead of Jack. You would also say: He is a weak man rather than a timid man. Because this is not a case of replacement, you need the word 'rather'. That leaves us with choices A, B and C as possible answers. A correct comparison is required. The planets are a 'phenomenon... rather then a type'. You are correctly comparing two nouns so A can be eliminated. 'Incidental of' is an incorrect structure. 'Incidental to' is correct. Therefore only B is eliminates all these errors and is the correct answer.

35. The first thing you have to determine in this sentence is whether the verb 'to have' should be in the singular or plural form. To what does the verb 'has' refer? It refers to the attempts. You can shorten this sentence and isolate the core: the attempts (x) have done something (y). That means that only D and E can be possible answers. Choice E is too wordy. Choice D is the correct answer.

36. The first thing you should ask yourself is whether the programs have something or do something? They do something. They mandate something of somebody else. That means that choices D and E are incorrect. Now you have to determine which tense is correct. Do you mandate that someone do something, or that someone to do something? Clearly not to do something. That means choice B can be eliminated. Choice C has the wrong tense, the future. The subjunctive is required after the construction 'mandate that'. Choice A is the correct answer.

37. 'Convince about' and 'convince for' are idiomatically incorrect. Eliminate C and D. The other issue in this sentence is parallel structure. The parallel structure is 'join' and 'attempt'. A and E violate parallel structure. Choice B is the correct answer.

38. Choice E does not demonstrate the contrast in the original sentence because it does not use 'although' or a similar conjunction. Choice D is an incomplete comparison as it eliminates the necessary first 'as' from the phrase 'as brilliant as'. However,

choices A, B and C don't particularly have errors of grammar or efficiency. However, stating that something will not be finished or that it is remaining unfinished does not make the necessary logical connection that he and he alone is responsible for the unfinished state of his thesis. Remember that active voice is preferred in the GMAT over the passive voice. C is the correct answer as it uses the active voice.

39. The pronouns 'their' and 'them' in A, B and E are ambiguous. In choice D there is a grammatical mistake: The verb does not refer to 'drugs', it refers to 'abuse' and therefore should be singular. Choice C is the correct answer.

40. This question has to do with tense agreement. Choice A uses the wrong tense. Because you have the word ended (past), you would have to say might have been, not may be. Choice B uses the wrong word, 'able'. Choice C implies that the singers were decreasing their tips. Choice D also implies that the singers were actively decreasing something. The audience is responsible for the tips, even though it is never directly mentioned here. Choice E is the correct answer.

41. Group is a collective noun and therefore requires a singular verb. Consequently, choices B, D and E can be eliminated right away. Using the word should is incorrect. The subjunctive, as seen in option A, is necessary after the construction 'it is important that...'. Choice A is the right answer.

42. This question is all about parallel structure. The basic structure is this: Someone was advised of x, told y, and given z. The only answer choice that has this parallel structure is B. Every other choice introduces different verb forms among x, y and z. B is the correct answer.

43. The first thing you have to do is figure out what the basic structure of this sentence is. X is Y. Something is estimated. That is critical verb in this sentence. Therefore, you need to find an answer choice that has a matching order of words. Despite the fact that it appears to be fairly complex, there is only one answer that even comes close to that core structure. Choice E is the correct answer. Once you realize what the core is, eliminating the rest of the choices should be fairly simple.

44. There is a simple grammatical question. What thing/things is/are common? Praise is common. Praise is singular, so we say 'is common'. That leaves us with choices D and E. It is correct to say that we associate x with y, not to y. 'To' often implies movement. As a plural noun 'statistics' requires the third person plural verb 'show'. Choice D is the correct answer.

45. This question has to do with parallel structure. The correct structure is 'grow', 'become' and 'threaten'. Only B has this combination.

46. Because he sees her in a dream at a given period of in time in the past, he sees her as she was, not as she had been. The simple past is correct. There is no need to use the past perfect. Choice C is not idiomatically correct. 'Appear' is the wrong word to use: it changes the meaning of the sentence by implying that she may only momentarily appear. Choice A is the correct answer.

47. This sentence is a simple comparison. All you have to do is determine what is being compared. The colonies are being compared. Only choices C and E directly compare the colonies. Choice E is more complicated than choice C. Choice C is the correct answer; it directly compares a to b, or colonies to colonies.

48. X has happened, but y has also happened. Choices A, B and D eliminate the necessary verb. D does not provide for tense agreement as it uses the past tense. Choice C is the correct answer.

49. Does someone think of something to be something else or as something else? Do you think of movies as a form of entertainment or to be entertainment? 'As a form' is the correct idiomatic expression. Someone thinks of x as y. That leaves us with

choices D and E. Choice E uses the passive. Choice D is the correct answer.

50.   This is a question of order of relevance. Who or what is the subject here? Seven households. Knowing the subject makes this question very easy. Actor/agent usually comes first and that is the case here. B and D incorrectly use the singular verb form 'owns' with the plural subject 'households'. C and E are passive. A, the correct answer, is active.

51.   You have to determine whether to use seeming or seemingly. Because you are modifying the comparative adjective 'less healthy' you need an adverb. Seemingly is the adverb. 'Seeming' is therefore incorrect and we are left with B and D. Parallel structure, 'permits' and 'forbids', leads us to B as the correct answer. In addition, the use of 'such...as' in B is far more efficient than the wordy construction in D.

52.   Is someone is doing x doing y, for doing y or to do y? What would you normally say? If you say doing x doing y or doing x for doing y, it implies a sequence, and lacks the element of causation that is necessary for this sentence. You want to use the infinitive form because it expresses causation. Someone is doing x (because) to do y. The inspectors are reviewing the weapons to do something. Choice E is the correct answer.

53.   B implies all experiences in 30 percent of the men were homosexual. C implies more than 30 percent of men may have had homosexual experiences. That leaves A, D and E. D is the shortest, simplest and clearest and is therefore correct.

54.   The verb needs to cover the period of time from the operation to now. Therefore the present perfect is necessary, not the simple past. Eliminate A and B. 'Since' is the correct accompaniment to the present perfect, rather than 'after' or 'subsequently to'. C is correct.

55.   A is simplest, shortest and clearest. It is correct. B and D are not complete sentences. C is too wordy. 'It' in E does not refer to anything.

56.   This is a very simple question of a dangling modifier. Who is the student devoted to modern art? Fanny. Therefore, the part of the sentence after the first comma must begin with the word Fanny, who happens to do something. The only choice that does that is A, the correct answer.

57.   This is a comparison. When you use 'more' you must use 'than'. Eliminate A and B. You must compare like with like, songs with songs. Songs is a plural word. 'That' in C is singular. Eliminate C. E does not compare songs with songs. It either compares songs with people or implies that the songs are singing. D is the correct answer.

58.   Choices B and E change the meaning. Choice C has a wrong order of words. It should read 'how one can...'. Choice D implies that the problem lies in how to feed the cake to the family rather than in how to bake the cake. A is correct.

59.   The idiom 'from...to' should be used here. That leaves A and D. There is no need to use the pronoun 'it' to repeat the subject. A is correct.

60.   The first thing you have to realize in this sentence is that only the senior citizens are more likely to do or have something. Choice A implies that the senior citizens and their families are likely to die sooner. In C the verb form 'runs' is incorrect. That leaves B, D and E. B is simplest, shortest and clearest and is therefore the correct answer.

61.   Mary does things to make something more inconvenient. D and E change the meaning in that they represent her husband as doing something inconveniently. C changes the meaning and implies the inconvenience is necessary for him to have a good time. A is grammatically correct and is simpler and clearer than B. A is the correct answer.

62. You have to spot the grammatical error. The subject is plural in A, B, C and D, therefore you have to use the plural verb form. Not 'it makes', but 'they make'. That means choices A, B and C are wrong. Choice E has a singular subject, his love of basketball, so the verb form would have to be the singular 'makes'. Only D is correct.

63. This question has to do with time agreement. Because the university gave the award in the past, it must further refer to a performance that had happened before that. Therefore the past perfect tense is required to refer to the performance. Only A has this tense. E also changes the meaning. A is correct.

64. Is it 'five times more likely' or 'five times as likely'. The correct expression is 'five times more likely'. When you use 'more' you must use 'than'. Eliminate A, B and E. C is shorter, clearer and simpler than D. C is correct.

65. D and E change the meaning. 'Significantly affecting' is different from 'significant in affecting'. B is shorter and clearer than A and C. B is correct.

66. C is wordy and uses the incorrect expression 'effects in'. It should be 'effects on'. D changes the meaning. B is shorter and clearer than A and E. B is correct.

67. The first thing you have to figure out is do you use with or that first. The intention of the sentence is not to state what will happen, but what may/can happen. The point is that she does not have a chest cold with a persistent cough, but that her chest cold, if it were to have a persistent cough, could produce some other result. Consequently, choices B, C, D and E are incorrect. Therefore, choice A is the correct answer.

68. This question has to do with differentiating whether you are comparing two actions or two things. You would say, for example, the frenzied man is like the raging bull. But you would have to say: the man can be whipped into frenzy just as a rampaging bull can be whipped into a further state of rage. When you compare two actions, you need to use as, not like. That leaves two possible choices: D and E. Choice D is incorrect, however, because it implies that the bull is piercing itself with swords. Choice E is the correct answer.

69. B incorrectly associates 'more rapidly' with dreaming rather than with eye movement. A, C and E incorrectly refer to the process of waking rather than the period of time of being awake. Choice D is the correct answer.

70. The first verb in the sentence is in the past. The past perfect in B is incorrect as the moving did not take place before the losing. The verb form 'having been forced to' in D is incorrect. The placement of 'from their apartment' in C is much better than in A. C is shorter and simpler than E. C is correct.

71. The first thing you should look at here is subject/verb agreement. Is the subject in this sentence singular or plural? The word 'disagreements' is plural, so you should use the verb "have". Note how the GMAT tries to trick you by putting the word 'child', which is singular, next to a verb that should be plural. That eliminates choices A, B and C. Choice E is wordy and inefficient. Choice D is the correct answer.

72. 'Likely most' is incorrect idiomatically. Eliminate A and B. 'To so talk' in C is also incorrect idiomatically. 'Due to' in C is also incorrect. 'Due to' can only be used as a replacement for 'attributable to'. For example, 'the low level of the lakes is due to the lack of rain'. 'Would likely appreciate' in C and E is also incorrect idiomatically. D is correct.

73. Choices A and E are missing clear noun references. Who or what is making or having the identification? The students. Choice D is wordy. 'Would' in C is not correct. 'Can' in B maintains parallel structure. B is the best answer.

74. This question is straightforward. You simply have to correct mistakes in grammar in the area of subject/verb agreement. The American school is one school, singular, so you would use its, not their. That eliminates choices A and B. Also, because the American school is singular, you need to use has and not have. That eliminates choice C. Choice D uses a pronoun, 'that', that has no clear reference. That what? The adverb of frequency, 'always' should come before the main verb. Choice E is the correct answer.

75. This sentence is causative. 'Because' or 'for' the reason that everyone was not talkative, something happened. The word 'with' is clearly the wrong choice here. It does not imply instrumentation, not causation. Choice B changes the meaning. 'Not everyone knew' has a different meaning from 'everyone did not know'. Last of all, choice A is incorrect because it is too wordy. Choice E is the correct answer.

76. B and C change the meaning. She made copies of more than fifty of the diaries, not merely more than fifty copies. If you accept the latter option it could be that she copied the entire collection fifty times. D is passive. That leaves two possibilities: A and E. Choice E is in the wrong tense, however. The sentence begins in the past tense and must continue in the past tense throughout. Choice A is the correct answer.

77. This question largely has to do with dangling modifiers. Who used the methods? The Chinese generals did. The subject must come after the comma. Eliminate A, B and E. Although there is no comma, D has a similar problem. D is also passive. C is correct.

78. The easiest thing to figure out here is whether or not to use 'of' at then end of the option. Would you say he is as melodramatic of a man as any I have seen, or he is as melodramatic a man as any I have seen? The latter is sufficient. That means you can eliminate choices A, C, D and E. Choice B is the correct answer.

79. If the first part of the sentence is in the past tense, then what happened earlier should be in the past perfect tense. That eliminates A, B, D and E. Choice C is the correct answer.

80. This is a very simple question involving subject/verb agreement. Should it be 'two children enter' or 'two children enters'? They enter (plural). That eliminates choices A, C and E. Choice B implies that one of the children is a wheelchair. Choice D is the correct answer.

81. This question deals with parallel structure. The important thing to realize here is that commas function differently from conjunctions in what they imply about parallel structure. If you say 'to cook, serve', you are not using parallel structure. If you say to cook and serve, you are using parallel structure. The 'and' carries the implied structure over, the comma does not. Choices B, D and E make this mistake. Choice C has a more straightforward mistake in parallel structure: it is missing the 'to' in 'to buy'. D and E also use the wrong tense and therefore change the meaning. Choice A is the correct answer.

82. This question involves dangling modifiers. What burned out eons ago? Thousands of stars did. 'Thousands of stars' and not 'the night sky' must therefore come after the comma. Eliminate A and B. C has an incorrect tense. It should be 'spot' and not 'are spotting'. Choice D also has a mistake in tense. The stars are not burnt out at present, they burned out a long time ago. Choice E is the correct answer.

83. What is the comparison being made in this sentence? It is being made between two sets of children: Maria's and her neighbor's. Choices B, C, D and E all imply that the comparison is being made between Maria's children and her neighbor, not between Maria's children and her neighbor's children. Choice A is the correct answer.

84. The sentence should have a contrast within it. Even though the housewife seems content, she is unhappy. E does not have

this element of contrast. Choices A and B present the pronoun 'she' without any clear reference. It is better to have the pronoun after the noun to which it is related, not before. Choice C has a dangling modifier. The person who is content must be mentioned directly after the comma. Choice D is therefore the correct answer.

85. The sentence as written implies the students may be unlikely to learn the language in other months of regular teaching. For example, they may be unlikely to learn in January and February. This would imply that they may be able to learn in March and April, for example. This is clearly not the intention of the sentence. Eliminate A, B and D. 'Under' in D is also incorrect. E reverses the meaning by adding 'not'. C is correct.

86. The first thing you should determine is whether to use 'during' or 'at'. 'At' is usually used with a specific time, not with a period of time. You would say, for example, 'at five o'clock', but not 'at this year'. That leaves you with A, B and E as possible answers. The placement of 'by seventy percent' is poor in E. Choice A uses the word 'down'. This is redundant, because you already have the word fell. Choice B is the correct answer.

87. You have to ask yourself what word should follow 'active'. The committee itself is not a drawing together. Eliminate B. You also would not say someone is active to do something, rather you would say someone is active in something. Choice A is the correct answer.

88. The word 'actors' is plural. Therefore, the actors have become known as prime examples. That means choices A and B are incorrect. 'Being' is unnecessary in Choice C. Choice D would be correct if it said between x and y, not between x with y. Choice E is the correct answer.

89. This question is about parallel structure. The parallel structure is 'report' and 'release'. Only D has this.

90. This sentence compares two actions. The part of the sentence that cannot be changed says 'other drugs should also be covered'. The earlier part of this comparative sentence should maintain this structure. Choice B incorrectly compares a noun, 'alcohol' to this action. C also compares 'alcohol' to the action. E incorrectly compares another noun, 'the discussion' of alcohol' to the action. D uses 'while', a word which introduces a contrast, not a comparison. For example you would say, 'while paper is available, cardboard is not'. Choice A correctly compares two actions, 'alcohol is discussed' and 'other drugs should also be covered'.

91. There is an ambiguity that arises without the use of an appropriate pronoun in this sentence. Choice A compares the adults to the formation. In choice D it is not clear to what the 'they' refers. D also changes the meaning. Choice C does not maintain parallel structure as it has 'among', which is not parallel to the earlier 'of' in the sentence. Choice E is not as efficient as choice B. B, by using the word that, refers to the correct comparison: the formation of social groups by two different age groups. Choice B is the correct answer.

92. Do you use the word economic or economical? Economical means thrifty. Economic is correct. 'The shipping of raw materials being improved' in D is idiomatically incorrect. Choice E is the correct answer.

93. The first thing you have to look at is whether to use the singular or plural pronoun. 'The puffin' is singular. So you will need to use the singular. That eliminates choices A and B. In E there is no clear connection between the items listed and the puffin. Ms. Kardon could very well be studying social organization in general. Therefore eliminate E as it changes the meaning. Now you have to pick between choices C and D. Choice D unnecessarily adds a second 'about'. Choice C is the correct answer.

94. D and E incorrectly use the past and past perfect tenses, implying that the increase has occurred and is finished. The sentence

as written implies that an increase may continue to occur. Choices A and C imply a degree of conscious agency which is inappropriate for the sentence. They imply that someone or something may quite deliberately increase fatal accidents. Choice B is the correct answer.

95.   Choices A and B use the singular pronoun 'that' with the plural verb form 'remain'. 'Almost as much in value' in C and D is idiomatically incorrect. Choice E is the correct answer.

96.   Choice A has the wrong tense. It is incorrect to say that she will be forced to do something now. She will be forced to do something in the future or she has to do something now. B and D have the same problem. Choice E separates 'is' and 'forced' by placing several words in between to make a very clumsy construction. Choice C is the correct answer.

97.   What is the comparison being made here? It is between the Americans and the French. Choice A does not compare the Americans and the French because it incorrectly adds the word 'that'. 'Unlike' is simpler and shorter than 'dissimilar to' and 'lacking similarity to'. Eliminate D and E. The simple present is necessary to describe a habitual action. 'Lingering' in option C implies the French are lingering now. Choice B is the correct answer.

98.   The first thing you have to determine is whether to use the simple past or the present perfect. Because you are talking about a period of time which started in the past and continues in the present you need the present perfect. If you were talking about a specific point in the past you could use the simple past. Eliminate A and E. B also has the wrong tense. C unnecessarily splits the verb 'has been'. Choice D is the correct answer.

99.   'Equally high or more so' is idiomatically incorrect. B is also idiomatically incorrect. The incidence of something somewhere could be equal to the incidence of something somewhere else, but not just equal to somewhere else. In choice C, or more what? Choice D is also incomplete. Equal to what? The only answer choices which is clear is choice E, the correct answer.

100. The easiest way for you to deal with this sentence is to look for any glaring grammatical errors that might eliminate several choices. In fact, choices B, C and D all make the same mistake in tense agreement. The caregivers enjoy. This is present tense. Hence 'recover' is correct, not 'recovered'. That leaves choices A and E. A is shorter and simpler than E. Choice A is the correct answer.

101. This question has to do with the words that we use in combination with countable and non-countable nouns. Do you say a quantity, amount or number of people? Quantity and amount are used with non-countable nouns. In other words, you can only have a number of people (i.e. 1, 2, 3, 4, etc.) but not a quantity such as 9 and a half people. This makes the correct answer, C, quite obvious. It is also unnecessary to use both 'both' and 'alike' in options B and D. D changes the meaning by using the active voice. Please note that 'great numbers of' is equivalent to 'a great number of'.

102. If you use words such as combine and mix, you should use the preposition 'with'. In other words, you don't mix x to y, you mix x with y. The only choice that uses 'with' is D.

103. To answer this question it helps to simplify the situation. Ask yourself, would you say: this is a competition where two people fight, when two people fight or in which two people fight? If you say where, it implies a physical location, not a characteristic of the competition. When implies a period of time, also not a characteristic of the competition as a competition. Eliminate A and B. C changes the meaning by using 'pitched' as a verb instead of as an adjective. C also has an incorrect order of words. D could mean that there are only two competitors who engage in fencing. In reality, while only two competitors are involved in each bout, there are many people who practice the sport. The end of option D, 'that has', is also not as precise as 'with' in the correct option, E. 'That has' implies that the battle, rather than the competitor, has the swords. Choice E is the correct answer.

104. This question deals with parallel structure. Scientists have determined that people have been found to have (present perfect tense throughout). That leaves us with choices B and E. Should it be 'increasing' or 'increased'? 'Increasing' implies that the difficulties are increasing over a period of time. This would change the meaning of the original sentence. Choice B is the correct answer.

105. The sentence introduces a contrast. Although x is not certain, Montreal does y. This contrast is not as easy to see if the phrase 'even if' is used. Eliminate A, B and C. The use of the future in B changes the meaning. E is not idiomatically correct. Choice D is the correct answer.

106. Do you pick 'which may limit' or 'an effect that may limit'? The relative pronoun 'which' must refer to the word immediately before it. In this sentence it is meant to refer to the fact that the drugs are addictive. However, it is incorrectly placed next to patients. Eliminate A, B and C. That leaves us with choices D and E. Now another ambiguity arises. In choice D, it is unclear what the 'their' refers to. Choice E is the best answer.

107. 'Up to three times of' in C is idiomatically incorrect. The use of the past tense in D and E is incorrect. The sentence is referring to the present. Do not be confused by the use of the word 'consumed' in option A. This is not a use of the past tense. Rather it is a reduced relative clause. You could say 'that which is consumed'. In this way option A can be seen to be using the passive voice, present tense. That only leaves us with choices A and B. Now it is simply an issue of parallel structure. The sentence as written refers to food consumed in America, so you will also say 'consumed in Japan'. Choice A is the correct answer.

108. The second 'not' in option B is unnecessary and incorrect. The 'no' in E is similarly unnecessary and incorrect. Option D is not parallel. Option C is more efficient than option A. C is correct.

109. 'Have insisted' in B is the incorrect tense. It implies an action which has occurred up to the present time. However, the sentence as written implies that the civil libertarians still insist something. The sentence can be simplified to a choice among 'the way is to reduce', 'the way is the reduction' or 'the way is reducing'. Only the first is correct. Eliminate C and D. A is more efficient than E. A is correct.

110. The first thing you have to determine is who or what was unchallenged? The Native Americans or the white man? The white man was unchallenged. Therefore that phrase should go first after the word 'firearms'. That leaves choices C, D and E. The second thing you have to determine is who or what feared the thunder sticks? The Native Americans. So you need a pronoun which refers correctly to the Native Americans. Choice C is the correct answer.

111. The sentence is not complete as it is written. There would have to be an 'and' between taught and imparted for it to be correct. B is incorrect as it unnecessarily repeats the subject by using 'he'. Therefore you must use 'imparting'. The final clause should have parallel structure within it. Therefore E is correct, not C or D. 'Imparting' and 'encouraging' are parallel.

112. Once again you have to figure out whether to use the simple past or the present perfect. The action has a consequence in the present so the present perfect should be used. Eliminate B, C and E. In addition, did the smoking damage her lungs only once or over a period of time? Clearly over a period of time. That eliminates choices B, C and E right away. Now you have to determine whether serious modifies an adjective or noun. It refers to damage, so it should be left as an adjective. Choice D is the correct answer.

113. The sentence is not correct as written. The damage has occurred but the second part of the sentence talks of preventing the damage. Eliminate A. What can be prevented? Is it the damage or the fact that deer cause damage. It is the damage that can be prevented. Eliminate C. D has the same problem as A. The word 'which' is misplaced in E. As it is written 'which' refers incorrectly to the plants. B is the correct answer.

114.   This is clearly a question of a dangling modifier. Who or what was upset by the litter? Jane. Therefore, Jane should go immediately after the comma, otherwise the sentence implies that something or someone else was upset by the litter. That leaves us with choices C and D. Choice D changes the meaning and sounds like detention is favored. The word 'as' in D is also incorrect. The correct expression is 'substituted for'. Choice C is the correct answer.

115.   The only correct idiom offered among the options is to distinguish x from y. Choice A is the correct answer.

116.   This question looks complicated, but it is largely a question of sorting out very simple grammatical mistakes. If you say child, then everything has to be singular. If you say children, it has to be plural. All you are looking for is consistency of singular or plural forms. A doesn't have it. It uses the singular 'child' and the plural 'themselves' and 'their'. C also has a lack of agreement, this time between 'child' and 'themselves'. D and E incorrectly use 'families where'. 'Where' is used for locations. Therefore, choice B is the correct answer.

117.   If you are not a native speaker of English, you might have some problems with this one. It is simply a language and style check, involving the usage of the idiom, no less an x than y. It is common to say in English media, for example, no less a superstar than Mrs. Jones. The correct answer choice here is A.

118.   This is a question of parallel structure. Because you have 'but because' not underlined, you need a parallel form using the word because. The correct idiom not because x, but because y appears in two answers: D and E. Now you have to go to the second mistake in parallel structure. Not because they are x, but because they are y. Choice E does not have this structure. Choice D is the correct answer.

119.   This is a question of parallel structure. You already have the non-underlined form: as much by wearing. Now you need to find match to that structure. The idiom in English is as much by x as by y. That leaves you with choices D and E. Choice D violates parallel structure by using the word disregard instead of disregarding, to match wearing. Choice E is the correct answer.

120.   The first thing you have to untangle is a simple grammatical mistake. What does the excess or exceeding refer to? It refers to the number, not the tourists. Number is singular, so you would not say 'the number were' in excess, nor would you say 'number numbered'. That means choices A and D are wrong. What else does number refer to? Does the number of tourists exceed local customers or the number of customers? Remember, you can't compare apples and oranges. Choice C refers to the wrong thing. Also, the numbers didn't have anything, per se, so choice B is incorrect. Choice E is the correct answer.

121.   This question involves determining whether words are modifying adjectives or nouns. What does wretched describe? The mendicants. The word 'mendicants' is a noun, so wretched stays as an adjective. That eliminates choices D and E. What does increasing refer to? It refers to the word 'prevalent', an adjective. Therefore you need an adverb to modify the adjective. Eliminate A and B. Choice C is the correct answer. In addition, the relative pronoun 'that' is correctly placed in C, next to the word to which it refers, 'money'.

122.   C and D unnecessarily add 'the person'. It is unclear to whom 'the person' refers. A incorrectly adds 'though'. B is shorter and simpler than E. Choice B is the correct answer.

123.   This is a question of parallel structure. It can resize documents, lighten documents, collate documents and copy (or copying) documents. The form copy needs to be used, because this form is consistent with the rest of the sentence. That eliminates choices A, B and C. Choice D is incorrect as it changes the subject of the sentence to the functions of the machine, rather than the machine itself. The word 'simply' is in the wrong place in the sentence. The tense is also incorrect. Choice E is the correct answer.

124. This question once again deals with idioms. In this case, the idiom you want is 'not only x but also y'. The 'not only' adds a degree of emphasis that the simple conjunction 'and' cannot transmit. That leaves us with choices B and D as possible answers. D is shorter and simpler than B. 'Was' rather than 'were' should be used. Choice D is clearly the correct answer.

125. This question involves a dangling modifier. Who or what is obedient? The cat or the Smiths? The cat. Therefore the word 'cat' should come after the word 'the'. That leaves us with choices C, D and E. The clause containing 'dogs respond' uses the simple present tense. Therefore we want a similar form for the cat. Dogs respond, and the cat follows. Choice C is the correct answer.

126. Choices B, C, D and E incorrectly use the singular 'dancer'. Choices D and E also incorrectly uses the singular 'a singer' to refer to the plural 'actors'. Choice A is the correct answer.

127. 'And have', 'and to have' and 'and they have' in B, C, D, and E are unnecessary. Choice A is, therefore, the correct answer.

128. This question involves parallel structure. The attorney weakened something and the jury doubted something. A has this structure. B uses the wrong tense. C is too wordy. D and E are not parallel. Choice A can be the only possible answer.

129. The first thing you have to determine is whether you have less people or fewer people. People are countable. Fewer is correct. The next thing you have to examine is whether to use 'as' or 'than'. This sentence is comparative. Fewer people did this than did that. As implies similarity. Choice E is the correct answer.

130. This question involves a dangling modifier. Were the policies Germany's most infamous leader? No. Then they should not go first in the second part of the sentence. That eliminates choices A, B and C. Choice E is not as efficient as D. Choice D is the correct answer.

131. You forbid something or someone to do something. 'Forbid from' and 'forbid that' are idiomatically incorrect. Choices D and E use the passive voice and are wordy. Choice B is the correct answer.

132. Should it be 'eventual' or 'eventually'? The word modifies a noun, 'salary increases'. Therefore you need an adjective. Eliminate A and B. D changes the meaning and implies that there was a commitment. The 'one' in E is not correct. It implies that a commitment would also be a publicity stunt. 'Was' in E is incorrect as the subject of the verb is plural. 'A commitment' would therefore also have to be changed to 'commitments'. Choice C is the correct answer.

133. The first thing you have to look at is subject/verb agreement. To what does the verb 'to be' refer? It refers to the effect, which is singular. That means you have to say is regarded. That leaves you with choices C, D and E. Choice C disrupts the as/as idiomatic phrase that you so often see on the GMAT. Choice D uses a passive construction. Choice E is the correct answer.

134. The structure of this sentence is that someone suggested that someone else do something. This structure requires the subjunctive. This is formed with the infinitive of the verb, without 'to'. Eliminate B, C and E. B also does not have parallel structure in terms of the tenses. It uses 'suggested' and 'encourages' Choice C implies that the teenagers are already protected. This would change the meaning. It also incorrectly uses the present continuous 'are having'. E does not have parallel structure in terms of the tenses. D is more efficient than A. Choice D is the correct answer.

135. If you use the phrase 'the means', that implies that there is no other possible way of organizing such information. This would change the meaning of the sentence. If the sentence said, for example, SAS is the only database-forming language, then you would use the phrase 'the means'. That eliminates choices C, D and E. Now you have to determine whether you have an

amount of facts or a number of facts. Facts are countable. So you have to use the word 'number', not the word 'amount'. Choice B is the correct answer.

136.   If you use the word 'neither' you must also have the word 'nor'. In Choices C, D and E, you have 'neither' without 'nor', so they are incorrect. Choice B implies a contrast which is not present in this sentence. Choice A is the correct answer.

137.   The first thing you have to ask yourself is whether the procedure is inherent in the third trimester, or whether it merely happens in the third trimester. Because it merely happens, you have to say it is used in the third trimester first. That leaves choices A, B and C as possible answers. 'Involving' in options A and B refers to the procedure of partial-birth abortion. 'Involving' is too far from its reference. As the options are written 'involving' could refer to the pregnancy. The use of commas in option C make it clear that 'involves' refers to 'partial-birth abortion'. 'Of involving' at the end of B is less clear than 'it involves'. Choice C is the correct answer.

138.   Is 'where' or 'while' correct? 'Where' is used for locations. While is used for contrasts. This sentence introduces a contrast. Eliminate A and B. 'Agreement' in C is not correct. 'Agreeing' in D is correct. D is also more efficient than C and E. Choice D is the correct answer.

139.   This question deals with parallel structure. Mothers want a resolution, something available, and a decreased prominence or a decrease. This is the parallel structure. Eliminate A and B. The original sentence has the phrase 'abundant and often casual violence'. D repeats that wording. C and E change that wording and so change the meaning of the original sentence. Choice D is the correct answer.

140.   The correct expression is 'known to be' rather than 'known for being'. Eliminate B. There is no need to use the future tense in C and E. Its use makes these options wordy. D is also wordy. Choice A is the correct answer.

141.   The phrase 'over the past decade' is repetitive, as the beginning of the sentence refers to the last ten years. Eliminate A, D and E. The population has increased over a period of time in the past. That period started in the past and continues up to the present. Therefore the present perfect tense should be used. Eliminate B. Choice C is the correct answer.

142.   This question has to do with concordance of grammar. Choices A, B and C all use a human with one's or oneself. The proper idiom in this case would be itself, or him/herself. Choice D, however, makes the mistake of being unclear as to what the 'them' refers. Does it refer to the organs, the pigs or the humans? Choice E is the correct answer.

143.   The first thing you must decide is whether to use the simple past or the past perfect. The expectations of the meteorologists occurred before the hurricane affected the metropolitan area. Therefore the past perfect should be used. Eliminate C, D and E. B is shorter and simpler than A. Therefore B is the correct answer.

144.   Because you have the word 'emphasized', you also need to use the word 'that'. That leaves choices D and E as possible answers. D has a better order of words than E has. You are not so much emphasizing a fact shown in the records as emphasizing the fact that it was the hottest day on record. Choice D is the correct answer.

145.   This question deals with parallel structure. The parallel elements herein are: tries to find and tries to return. Even if the entire phrase is not repeated, parallel structure is still maintained by preserving the form. The only choices which use 'return' are B, C and D. Choice C, however, does not make it clear that it is the organization itself which returns the lost pets. In this way there is a slight change in the meaning of the original sentence. D uses the incorrect idiomatic expression 'tries at finding', instead of 'tries to find'. Choice B is the correct answer.

146. The question involves efficiency of language. Only C provides efficiency. Choice C is the correct answer.

147. This question deals with the past simple or the present perfect tenses. Because of the critical phrase 'not since' you have to use the present perfect. The word since demands a perfect tense, as in, since then this has been happening. It began and continues to this day. That leaves us with choices A, C and E. Choice E uses the word 'whether' but has no other alternative. 'Whether' needs two possibilities. It is also inefficient. Choice E is wrong. Choice A uses the wrong word after citizens. It is not 'a right that they could do x', it is a right 'to do x'. Choice C is the correct answer.

148. This question also involves usage of the present perfect tense. Because it is 'in recent years', you need a form that can cover those years. Neither the simple past tense nor the present tense can do this. You need a tense that goes back into the past and covers the period up to the present. That means choices A and B are incorrect. C is not a complete sentence. E unnecessarily adds the word 'since'. Choice D is the correct answer.

149. When two alternatives are presented it is better to use 'whether' rather than 'if'. C, D and E change the meaning. Choice B is the correct answer.

150. Choices A, C and D have incorrect comparisons. They imply that the industry is larger than any other Canadian City, whereas, in fact, the tourist industry in Montreal is larger than the tourist industry in any other Canadian city. C uses the wrong tense. B removes the word 'any' inappropriately. It is necessary to emphasize that the tourist industry in Montreal is larger than the tourist industry of any other Canadian city. Choice E is the correct answer.

151. This question is primarily concerned with countable and non-countable nouns. Sources are countable, so you must use 'fewer' before 'sources'. Eliminate B and D. Would you have less than ten dollars in your pocket or fewer than ten dollars? Fewer would refer to the actual bills. You are referring to an amount of money. You do not say 'a fewer amount'. Eliminate E. The correct idiomatic expression is 'less than', not 'lesser than'. Eliminate C. Choice A is the correct answer.

152. This is a very simple question of parallel structure. If you say first of all, then you should say, second of all. If the phrase is not complete, then the appropriate structure must be inserted anyway to imply the completed phrase. Choices D and E are the only choices that have the correct parallel structure of first and second. Choices A, B, C and D make the same grammatical mistake. The 'they' and 'their' refer to 'family', which is singular. A and B also unnecessarily repeat 'for'. C changes the meaning. Choice E is the correct answer.

153. 'Notice being given' in A is idiomatically incorrect. 'Notice of the upcoming execution to give' in C is also idiomatically incorrect. D and E omit reference to the convicted murderers. Choice B is the correct answer.

154. A has an incorrect word order. To be correct the option would have to read 'More Manolo Blahniks than ever...'. B unnecessarily adds the phrase 'than previously'. C omits the words 'number of' before 'Manolo Blahniks'. Manolo Blahniks are countable. Therefore use 'number' and not 'amount'. E is correct.

155. This first question you should ask yourself is: who or what is distressed? The PTA. So the PTA should go immediately after the comma. The only answer choices that reflect this are D and E. D is passive. Choice E is the best answer.

156. There are two possible structures. You require someone to do something, or you require that somebody do something. The latter is a use of the subjunctive. E does not have either of these possible structures. Options A, B and D incorrectly use 'a professor' with 'their'. Choice C is the correct answer.

157. There are several common idioms that the GMAT tests you on that involve the word as. For example, just as...so too, as many as, as much by x as by y, etc. Also, this sentence wants to emphasize, not merely state, a similarity. Using the words 'like' and 'similar' does not convey the same sense of emphasis as the words 'just as..., so too...'. So that eliminates choices B, C, D and E. Choice A is the best answer.

158. Once again, this question involves a dangling modifier. The first question you should ask yourself is: who are the immigrants? The answer should come after the comma. Only choices B and E are possible. Choice E has an incorrect order of words. 'Opened' is too far from 'Schwartz's deli'. Choice B is the correct answer.

159. This sentence involves another common idiom: not only, but also. The idea here is not only to convey comparison, but also to emphasize. Choice C is the correct answer.

160. This question has to do with word order. The attempt was begun fifteen years ago. Options A and D could imply that the United States was begun fifteen years ago. C has poor word order by splitting 'begun' and 'fifteen years ago'. It also incorrectly uses 'for electing'. E uses the wrong tense. Choice B is the correct answer.

161. The first thing you must do is to decide whether to use the word 'whether' or the word 'if'. The word 'if' can be used if you have a single possibility. You can say, for example, "If you go to the store, I will come with you." There is no second possibility mentioned in the sentence. There are two possibilities in the sentence you are considering here. Consequently, you know you have to use the word 'whether' here. That leaves choice A and C. Choice C is not efficient. Choice A is the correct answer.

162. Choices A, B and D are all repetitive as they use 'he', which is not needed because it is clear that Albert and only Albert is being referenced. Choice E does not have the correct parallel structure. It also incorrectly uses 'it' to refer to Albert. Choice C is the correct answer.

163. The early part of the sentence, the part which we cannot change, does not use a gerund. Parallel structure dictates that gerunds not be used in the latter part of the sentence either. Eliminate A and B. 'A protesting' in C is incorrect. D could imply that the current government makes the protest. E is correct.

164. This question has to do with a dangling modifier and a comparison. What is being compared in this sentence? The old play and the new play. Therefore, the order of words should reflect that comparison. Only choices D and E are possible answers. Choice E has an incorrect structure, 'has an inspiration of'. Choice D is the correct answer.

165. This is clearly a question of parallel structure. Choices B and C are incorrect because they have 'to compare' and 'comparing'. Choice E is not parallel. It has 'the brilliance of Beethoven' and 'diamonds' value', rather then 'the value of diamonds'. Choice D uses the word like, which is distinctly different from saying something is something else. That is the main point of this question: to see if you can differentiate a comparison from a statement of equality. Choice A is the correct answer, not only because it has the correct parallel structure, but also because it adheres strictly to the sense of sameness: that to do a is to do b, not merely 'like' it. D also has an incorrect comparison by comparing the value of diamonds with plastic baubles, rather then with the value of plastic baubles.

166. This question has to do with parallel structure. The correct structure is 'to use' and 'to try'. A and D have 'using' and 'to try'. Choices C and E do not have parallel structure either. They compare 'a walker' with 'to try'. Choice B is the correct answer.

167. This question involves parallel structure and agreement between subject and verb. Because we have the word 'steps', we need to use the plural. That means that choices A, B and E are wrong. Choice C is incorrect as it is missing a word between

'molding' and 'smoothing'. The best answer is D.

168. 'Which' does not refer to 'divorce'. Eliminate A and E. Choice C has a pronoun with no clear reference. Who is the 'they' who had sued the men? B is closer in meaning to the original sentence than D is. The men had been sued rather than just experiencing suits. The correct answer is B.

169. The correct expression is 'not only...but also...'. Eliminate A. B changes the meaning by eliminating 'she believed'. Choice C is inefficient as it uses the word 'themselves'. Choice E uses the wrong tense, the present. Choice D is the correct answer.

170. The first thing you have to determine in this sentence is what is being compared. Time is being compared, as in today x is more effective than x was ten years ago. You are not comparing the vaccine to ten years ago. That eliminates choices A, B and D. Choice E has an unnecessary preposition, 'in'. Choice C is the correct answer.

171. This sentence is testing your ability to spot improper or ambiguous usage of pronouns. To whom does the 'they' in 'because they usually' refer? This is not clear. Choices A, B and C are therefore incorrect. In fact, choice B implies that the disciplinary decisions cause less trouble and are more repentant. Choice D has an incorrect comparison: it compares decisions to boys, not girls to boys. Choice E is the correct answer.

172. This is simply a question of ambiguity. Choices A, B and C all imply that the suburbs have some degree of independence, and not the teenagers. The teenagers are the ones who have the independence. Choice D has an incorrect verb, 'are'. Choice E is the correct answer.

173. The neighborhoods have been changed, have become gentrified. B, D and E incorrectly use active verbs. A is more efficient than C. The sentence is correct as written.

174. The first thing you have to do in this question is distinguish whether to use the simple past or the past perfect. The first part of the sentence uses the simple past. To maintain [parallel structure the second part should also. Eliminate A, C and E. can be eliminated. You have a right to something, rather than a right that. Choice D is the correct answer.

175. 'When' refers to times and 'where' refers to locations. Both are inappropriate here. 'While' introduces a contrast. There is a contrast present in this sentence. Choice E is the correct answer.

176. You must decide whether this sentence requires the simple past or the present perfect. What the president's spokesman did at a conference occurred at one particular point in time, not over a period of time. Therefore it warrants the simple past tense. That leaves choices B and D. B is more efficient than D. Choice B is the correct answer.

177. This question concerns a dangling modifier. What is thought to emanate? The pheromone trails are. Therefore 'pheromone trails' must come directly after the comma. Eliminate A and D. The 'this' at the end of option B refers to the trails. You cannot have a singular pronoun referring to a plural noun. Eliminate B. E implies it is the ants, rather then the trails, that can be used. Choice C is the best answer.

178. This question deals with efficiency of language and parallel structure. Choice A would have to say 'the rich' and 'the poor'. Choice B is not parallel. Choices C and E are not as efficient as choice D. Choice D is the correct answer.

179. This question involves parallel structure. Once you pick a pronoun form, you must use it consistently throughout the sentence. Because the sentence says 'your new purchase', you and its derivatives are the correct pronouns. That leaves us with choices B and E. Choices E is passive. Choice B is the correct answer.

180. B changes the meaning in saying that Brad was suggested by his counselor. C and D imply that Brad is the suggestion. A is more efficient than E. Choice A is the correct answer.

181. This question has to do with subject/verb agreement. If you say 'quirks that' or 'quirks which' you have to say 'illustrate' (plural). Eliminate A and B. D is not parallel. It would have to be 'illustrated'. 'Who' is inappropriate to use with 'quirks'. 'Who' is applied to people, not to things. Choice C is the correct answer.

182. Choices A is not efficient. The use of 'he was' is not necessary, nor can 'he was' be used without first mentioning a noun. D does not have parallel structure in terms of the tenses. Choices C and E are inefficient. Choice B is the most efficient option and is therefore the correct answer.

183. The correct relevant idiomatic expressions are 'regard as' and 'consider to be'. Eliminate B, C and E. D has the wrong tense. Choice A is the correct answer.

184. This sentence compares the CIA to the KGB. The plural pronouns 'their' and 'them', are inappropriate as they refer to the CIA, a singular entity. Eliminate A, B and C. That leaves you with choices D and E. Choice E uses the incorrect preposition 'of'. It is a similarity between two things, not of one with another. Choice D is the correct answer.

185. DO you make a 'conclusion that', or 'a conclusion of'? 'Conclusion that' is correct. Eliminate A, B and D. The tense is wrong in E. The simple past, as in C, is correct, rather than the past conditional, as in E. Choice C is the correct answer.

186. Choice D has the most efficient use of language. It is the shortest, simplest and clearest option. It is the correct answer.

187. The first thing you have to consider in this question is whether to use 'based on' or 'on the basis of'. This is a question of a dangling modifier. The historians are not based on the customs. Eliminate A, C and E. That leaves us with choices B and D. B is shorter and more efficient than D. Choice B is the correct answer.

188. The correct tense for the verb 'seem' is the past. Choice A uses the past tense and is the shortest and most efficient of the options. Choice A is the correct answer.

189. The correct preposition to use with 'substitute' is 'for'. Eliminate A, C and E. B is shorter and more efficient than D. Choice B is the correct answer.

190. Should you use 'whether' or 'if'? There are two alternatives. Either the company was as responsible as the newspaper, or it was not. When there two alternatives it is better to use 'whether'. Eliminate A, B and C. E is shorter and more efficient than D. Choice E is the correct answer.

191. There is a misplaced modifier in this sentence. As it stands it implies that the employees were the ones who were added to the increase in monthly wages. That means choices A and B are incorrect. Choice C has an obvious grammatical mistake in it. 'Increase' is singular so it should be 'the increase in wages was discussed'. Choice D has the same error. Choice E is the correct answer.

192. The correct idiomatic expression is not 'so much by x as by y'. The correct answer choice is D.

193. Is it better to say 'the percentage of students is ten' or 'ten percent of students'. The latter is better. Eliminate D and E.

Choice A disrupts parallel structure: it says 'ten percent of... students', then 'it is five percent'. Choice B makes the same mistake. Choice C is the correct answer.

194.   This question attempts to disguise a very simple grammatical mistake: is 'contrast' singular or plural? It is singular, therefore you have to use the word 'has', not 'have'. The contrast has done something. That leaves choices D and E as possible answers. However, use of the word 'favors' in choice D slightly changes the meaning of the sentence. It should be a contrast between one thing and another. Choice D does not use the use the word 'and' and is therefore also incorrect for this reason. Choice E is the correct answer.

195.   Unanimous opposition is necessary 'to improve', 'for improving' or 'in improving'. 'To improve' is correct. Eliminate A and D. B is passive. It is not 'the prejudice', a specific example of prejudice which is to be opposed. Rather 'prejudice' in general is to be opposed. Eliminate E. Choice C is the correct answer.

196.   It is not 'the undersized models', specific examples of undersized models, that the sentence is considering. Rather it is undersized models in general. Eliminate B and D. The 'they' in B, D and E is incorrect. Although it seems the pronoun should refer to the plus-sized woman, grammatically it could refer to the undersized models. In any case, if it refers to the plus-sizes woman the sentence mentions it should be singular. This can also be seen from the use or 'her' later in the sentence. The word order in C is incorrect. The phrases 'fashion failure will result' and 'to the plus-size woman' are divided by too many words. The pronoun 'for' is more appropriate than 'to'. Choice A is the correct answer.

197.   The major issue that you have to consider in this sentence is parallel structure. Only C has parallel structure. Choice C is the correct answer.

198.   You protect something for someone, not to someone. Eliminate B and D. 'More than' is the correct comparative expression. Eliminate C. E lacks the necessary auxiliary verb 'does'. Choice A is the correct answer.

199.   This sentence has the following structure: x and y are to z what a and b are to c. You don't want to use the words 'like', 'as' or 'just'. That leaves choices C and D as possible answers. The Victorian era occurred in the past, therefore you must use a verb in the past tense. Choice C is the correct answer.

200.   'Because' is more efficient than 'for the reason that', 'for the reason' and 'in that'. Eliminate A, B and C. Misbehavior is singular. The verb must be 'affects'. The correct idiomatic expression is 'on the part of' not 'on the parts of'. Eliminate E. Choice D is the correct answer.

201.   There must be tense agreement in sentences. Both events are in the past, so you must use the past tense of 'embody', 'embodied'. That leaves choices A and B. Choice A is shorter and simpler than B. Choice A is the correct answer.

202.   'Hopefully' is an adverb. It can be used in a sentence such as: The skier looked hopefully at the sky in search of snow. It cannot be used as a replacement for 'I hope', 'we hope' or 'it is hoped'. Eliminate A, C and D. It is not correct to say 'pollute such as aerosol cans do'. Eliminate E. The correct answer choice is B.

203.   The sentence has to do with the idiomatic usage of words for countable and non-countable nouns. Do you say: there are 'less than five people here' or 'lower than five people here', or fewer than five people here? Because you are referring to a number, five thousand in this sentence, you would use less. This is because you are essentially saying that something is less than a number. 'Lesser than' is incorrect. That leaves you with choice A. Note that soldiers are countable so you must use 'fewer' to refer to the soldiers, not 'less'. Choice A is the correct answer.

204.   You need to have appropriate tense agreement. 'Can' is incorrect because it is in the present tense. That leaves you with choices B and E as possible answers. You rely on something, not for something. Choice B is the correct answer.

205.   B changes the meaning. The sentence as written refers to the practice being favored, not the song being favored. Eliminate B. C incorrectly implies that a song is a practice favored by stations. D has the same mistake. E incorrectly has the word 'and'. The subject of this option is therefore plural, but the verb 'increases' is singular. The correct choice is A.

206.   The 'they' in the sentence as written is a pronoun without a clear reference. Does it refer to the treaties or to the Americans? Although logically it refers to the treaties, grammatically it could refer to the Americans. Therefore A is incorrect. B, C and D repeat the same mistake. E is the correct answer.

207.   Do you use the past or present tense here? It is thought now that hunters extracted oil. Therefore you must use the present tense to describe that thinking. Eliminate B, C and E. Choice D is incorrect because it places the things the hunters did in the present tense, whereas what they did is a past action. Choice A is the correct answer.

208.   The relevant correct expressions are 'neither...nor' and 'either...or'. Eliminate A, B and C. D is missing something between 'better times for investing' and 'more of a relaxed sense of national security'. The phrase at the end of option E 'nor is it' is also more efficient than the phrase in D 'and it is not'. Choice E is the correct answer.

209.   B suggests that humans practice a particular type of cloning, rather than cloning in general. In C 'reflect' should be 'reflects' to agree with its subject 'practice'. D changes the meaning by eliminating the phrase 'to the Raelians'. It implies the human life did come from the aliens' cloning practices. The sentence as written says that this is just the Raelians' view. E also changes the meaning by saying that humans should return to practicing cloning. There is no suggestion in the original sentence that humans practiced cloning. Choice A, then, is the best answer.

210.   Amounts do not expand, they increase. Eliminate A and B. The 'it' at the start of C is a pronoun without a clear reference. E has the same problem. Choice D is the correct answer.

211.   The rekindling referred to in this sentence occurred in the past. Eliminate A. The phrase 'there are many known people' in C is incorrect. D has the same problem. The use of the present tense in E is incorrect. The clause 'rekindling ...is known for many people' is also idiomatically incorrect. Choice B is the correct answer.

212.   This sentence is quite difficult. What is it that causes errors in judgment? Is it working overtime? No. It is working an excessive amount of overtime. This is a practice. Eliminate A, B and C. The phrase in D 'the potential for causing' is idiomatically incorrect. Choice E is the correct answer.

213.   You have seen many questions like this, that involve usage of as idioms. If you say: X happens not so much because of y, what follows the not so much idiom? The word 'as'. For example, he is not so much witty as he is talkative. Eliminate A, D and E. B is not parallel. Choice C is the correct answer.

214.   The verb 'was' in A and B refers to 'cities'. Therefore you should use 'were' not 'was'. Eliminate A and B. Efficiency of language leads you to eliminate the 'which were' present in C. Although the word 'were' is not present in the sentence we have merely left it out to increase the efficiency of the language. "Being" in D connotes a continuous tense and is unnecesary in this sentence. E is therefore the correct answer.

215.   Choices A, B and E all imply that it is the librarians that have been damaged. You need to insert a pronoun to correct the ambiguity which otherwise arises. The pronoun 'it', in the singular, correctly identifies the cover of the aging tome as being the thing that had been damaged. The cover had been damaged before the librarians read it. The use of the past perfect twice in D is therefore incorrect. The action which happened second, the reading, should be expressed using the simple past tense. C is the correct answer.

216. 'As a result from' in B is incorrect. 'Costing reconstructions' in C is also incorrect. D implies that the reconstruction would be done with European governments. According to the original sentence, it was the negotiations which were conducted with European governments. Eliminate D. E implies that the costs came more directly from negotiating. The costs came from the reconstruction. Eliminate E. Choice A is the correct answer.

217. As you can see a contrasts within the sentence, you want to find the phrase that best stresses that contrast. The contrast is absent in B. C, D and E completely change the meaning of the sentence. Choice A is the correct answer.

218. Did the monk occur or did his immolation occur? Clearly the immolation occurred. Eliminate A, B and E. The phrase 'occurred by some detectives' in C is incorrect. Choice D is the correct answer.

219. The correct idiomatic expression is not 'desire for plus gerund'. The correct expression is 'desire to do something'. Eliminate C. Among the other options, B is shortest and simplest. Choice B is the correct answer.

220. Choices A and B both have a mistake in agreement. Scores are plural, so you need 'those' not 'that'. Choice C is incorrect because it implies that the comparison is between scores and white students. The pronoun 'their' in E has no clear reference. Choice D is the correct answer.

221. The idiomatic expressions using 'as' come up again and again on the GMAT. Even if you did not want to make the sentence more efficient and have correct as/as parallel structure, you could immediately eliminate choice A. It uses the word 'was' which should be plural were because it refers to victories. Choices B, D and E are clearly wrong as well. The correct expression is 'not so much by....as by'. Choice C is the correct answer. It has parallel structure and is efficient.

222. This question has to do with usage of the preposition 'between'. If you use 'between' you need to use 'and'. Eliminate A and B. 'Which' in C and D refers to the interchange. However, it is placed next to 'neutrons', meaning that grammatically it refers to 'neutrons'. This is incorrect. The tense in C and D is also incorrect. The earlier part of the sentence is in the simple present tense and the latter part should be also. Choice E is the correct answer.

223. Option A does not provide a complete sentence. The expression is 'it is common that.' E has the same problem. The noun 'desires' is plural so the verb referring to desires must also be plural. Eliminate B. It should be 'as have the desires' not 'as has the desires'. That leaves C and D. It is necessary to say 'as it is' rather than 'as is' at the start of the option. D is also incorrect because it says 'the opinion...have'. The correct answer is C.

224. Choices A, B and E do not make it clear who does the collaborating to overthrow the foreign governments. D changes the meaning. Choice C has parallel structure and is the correct answer.

225. The expression 'developed after when' is incorrect. 'Developed after' is sufficient. Eliminate A. Choice C unnecessarily repeats 'foreign speculators'. Choice D has the wrong tense. The sentence is in past tense, not present. 'Developed after there being' in E is also incorrect. Choice B is the correct answer.

226. This sentence has to do with another common idiomatic phrase: not only, but also. Eliminate A, B and C. It also has to do with parallel structure. Choice E does not complete the sentence by using a structure parallel to the earlier part of the sentence. 'Gather' is not parallel to 'causing damage and destroying'. Choice D is the correct answer.

227. The key to answering this question is determining what preposition to use at the end. Is it surveillance by someone against/to/of something? All the choices here are passive, so you cannot rewrite this sentence using the active voice. The correct expression is 'surveillance of'. Only choice B is correct.

228. You are comparing more than two cultures, so you are not going to use the word between. Therefore you can eliminate choices D and E. In choices A and B the singular pronoun 'that' incorrectly refers to the plural noun 'misunderstandings'. Choice A also uses the incorrect expression 'greater as'. Choice C is the correct answer.

229. The correct expression is that the farmers were required to do something, not to have done something nor to have had done something. Eliminate A, B and C. 'Either' in E is incorrect. As E is written it implies the farmers were required to do one of two things: either destroy animals with mad cow disease or perform a second action. The second action is missing. Choice D is the correct answer.

230. The first thing you have to determine is whether to use 'such' or 'so'. You use the word 'so' in connection with adjectives. For example, you would say that 'The purchase of the necklace is so extravagant that it must be returned.' The word 'such' is used in connection with nouns. For example, 'the restaurant offers such exquisitely prepared cheeses that they melt in your mouth.' The latter formula clearly applies here. That means that choices A, B and E are incorrect. The present tense, not the present perfect, is necessary to describe habitual actions. Eliminate D. C is also more efficient than D. Choice C is the correct answer.

231. You should first decide whether to use the word 'frequent' or 'common'. 'Common' is correct here. The use of 'should' in C is incorrect. The phrase 'couples in which' in E is incorrect. 'Earning' in E is also incorrect. E also incorrectly implies that the couples become more common. Choice D is the correct answer.

232. As it stands the sentence implies that the comparison is between wines and wineries. This is not the case. You can compare wine with wine or wineries with wineries. Choices A and D have misplaced modifiers. The placement of 'which' next to 'Germany's' in C is incorrect. 'Which' refers to Germany not Germany's wines. It is not clear to what the 'those' in E refers. Grammatically it could refer to the wines or the wineries. Choice B is the correct answer.

233. Choice A uses 'since' and the present tense. The present perfect is necessary. For example, 'since 1990 there have been many cases...'. The correct subject of the sentence is 'the number of diagnoses', not 'the diagnosis of cases'. Eliminate B and C. 'Tripling' in D is incorrect. Again the present perfect would have to be used to describe an action which started in the past and has continued up to the present. Choice E, the correct answer, shows this use of the present perfect. 'The number...has tripled.'

234. Choices D and E both imply that the glasses or middle age are the things that have been damaged, not the eyes. 'A consequence from' in B is incorrect. Choice C uses the wrong verb tense, the simple past. The present should be used to form parallel structure with 'discover'. Choice A is the correct answer.

235. Parallel structure should be flashing before your eyes. The structure here is: as a result of x, y and z. 'As well as' is not as efficient as 'and'. Eliminate A and E. C is not parallel. D is shorter and more efficient than B. Choice D is the correct answer.

236. Choices E and D are clearly wrong because there is no noun preceding the 'it' that can be referenced. This question involves a dangling modifier. What is touching? The novel. The novel should therefore come after the comma. Eliminate C. 'Shall' is not usually used in the third person. It is usually used in the first person. It is used to make suggestions or to give offers of help. For example, 'shall we go the beach' and 'shall I help you with those bags'. The sentence is correct as written. Choice A is the correct answer.

237.   'Having bought on rumor' in A is incorrect. Similarly 'having had to sell' in B is incorrect. 'Those who had bought on rumor' in D is incorrect. Option E does not provide a complete sentence. There is no verb for the subject 'investors'. The phrases 'having bought on rumor and having to sell' merely describe the investors. Choice C is the correct answer.

238.   Choices A and E are ambiguous. It is not clear to whom the 'their' and 'they' are referring. Choice D is equally ambiguous because you do not know who or what is absorbing information. Choice B is missing the necessary auxiliary verb 'do'. Choice C is the correct answer.

239.   Choices B, C and E change the meaning by adding the words 'alone', 'solely' and 'if only'. These choices imply that the Senator supports the legislation for only one reason. It is possible that there are other reasons for the Senator's support. 'While' introduces a contrast. There is no contrast between the Senator's belief and the basis for that belief. Choice A is the correct answer.

240.   One thing you have to consider in this sentence is parallel structure. Because you say 'people exercising daily', you have to maintain the same form later. That eliminates choices C, D and E. Choice B uses the inefficient expression 'not any healthier'. Choice A is the correct answer.

241.   The correct expression is 'to try to do something', not 'to try and do something'. Eliminate B. It is 'retrieve from', not 'retrieve out of'. Eliminate C, D and E. Choice A is the correct answer.

242.   D and E change the meaning 'Which' in B is incorrect. This question also concerns parallel structure. Directors that create are similar to conductors who direct. Choices A and E use the wrong form of the verb direct. Choice C is the correct answer. It has parallel structure.

243.   This sentence simply has to have its parallel structure corrected. It begins in the present tense, 'are usually reliable', so the sentence should continue in the present. Choice A is not in the present tense. 'They' in A, C, D and E is a pronoun without a reference. Choice B is the correct answer.

244.   The issue being raised in this sentence is one of parallel structure. The basic structure of this sentence is: to do x is to do y. The only choice that fits that pattern is choice A, which is the correct answer.

245.   Choices A and B incorrectly imply that the degree in music depends on the talent of the musician. The modifier 'depending on his talent' is misplaced. C and E are incorrect as they imply the talent graduates from college. D is the correct answer.

246.   This question deals primarily with parallel structure. You can say something has resulted not from x but from y. The only answer choice that maintains parallel structure is B. B is the correct answer.

247.   The use of 'seeming' in A is incorrect. 'Thought' later in the sentence places the sentence in the past tense. 'Seemed' is necessary. Eliminate A. The use of 'was' in B and D changes the meaning. The use of 'in that' in C is not as good as the use of 'because' in E. 'Because' establishes the reason something happened. Choice E is correct answer.

248.   You distinguish a from b, or distinguish between a and b. The only option which follows either of these patterns is B. B is the correct answer.

249.   The singular verb 'knows' in B incorrectly refers to the plural subject 'her new listeners and her old fans'. The use of the past 'knew' in C is incorrect. Choice D incorrectly uses 'would have to be posted'. 'Must be posted' is more efficient. It also

incorrectly uses the past 'what was going on'. E incorrectly uses the past perfect 'what had been'. Choice A is the correct answer.

250.   A and E are passive. This question also has to do with order of relevance. What is the most important thing the fencer did? She defeated her opponents. That should be mentioned before the fact that she capitalized on their slowness. Eliminate C. B may not appear to be parallel but it is more efficient than D. It describes how she defeated her opponents. This is the intention of the sentence rather than listing a series of activities the fencer did. A list would require parallel structure. Choice B is the correct answer.

Chapter 6

Verbal Training Set II Solutions - Critical Reasoning

1. The best way to approach these types of questions is to draw your own conclusion first, without looking at the answers. The bio-chemists realize that the bee has to be present for the flower to cause an allergy. Therefore, the flower is not the only cause of the allergy. The research suggests that the presence of the bee is a necessary condition leading to the presence of the new allergy. A is the best choice.

2. This question deals with biased population samples. People who read 'Hook, Line & Sinker' will tend to be more likely to buy or want a new fishing boat during the summer. Your job in this question is to isolate the biased population and demonstrate that readers of this magazine are different from the rest of the consumers in the market. Choice D best demonstrates that bias.

3. What is the investment advice? It is that investing in fishing boats would be profitable, based on the assumption of greater demand than supply. Something that demonstrates that the demand for fishing boats is not as high as the magazine claims will undermine the soundness of the advice. Choice E satisfies that condition, by showing that only half of those who claim they want a fishing boat end up buying one.

4. What is the basic assumption made by the study? That both groups are starting out at the same point. If psychologists want to determine whether a certain situation creates a certain pattern in people, they need to test two groups of people with the same pre-existing conditions. Choice E suggests that there may be another cause for the different rate of insomnia in the two groups. This consequently undermines the psychologist's conclusion.

5. Choice B is the best answer since the purpose of expanding inventory is to increase the number of mobile phones sold. However, if the top nine mobile phones already account for almost all the mobile phones in the market, increasing inventory to include the top 12 mobile phones will not significantly increase sales.

6. While it may be true that non-party members who work in businesses employing many party members make similar wages, if their wages are dependent on the higher wages of party members, as choice D suggests, then the association with the party determines income.

7. The deferral of payment on salaries does not eliminate the earnings shortfall problems but transfers the associated costs to the employees. This allows the company to collect interest on the employees' salaries as they incur interest payments. Choice C is the correct answer.

8. The first thing you have to do is identify what the conclusion is. The conclusion is the last sentence, which starts with 'In order for Andovia'. The argument states that Andovia should close its borders and not issue visas. What most weakens the argument will be something that demonstrates that the problem may occur anyway. Only one answer choice demonstrates that tightening border controls and restricting visas will not affect the import of drug X - and that is choice E, as it, if true, demonstrates a condition whereby such restrictions would prove ineffective.

9. The goal of the Flerenchian government import restrictions is to increase chocolate sales by decreasing competition that is hurting the local chocolate industry. However, if there are already significant stockpiles of foreign-made chocolate in Flerenchia, then the import restrictions will have little effect. If D is true then Flerenchian produced chocolate will continue to face competition from foreign-made chocolate until the stockpiles are depleted. Choice D is the best answer.

10. What is the problem with the bus company's logic? They kept cutting out bus stops to decrease transit time until they had virtually no customer base left. The only way to have a bus route that makes money is to have it pick up people at enough stops to make a profit. If you have too few stops, how do you correct this? By adding more stops. Choice B adds more stops.

11. Since the university takes more money from students with one set of academic qualifications and less money from students with a different set of academic qualifications, it can be said that the university puts different financial demands on different students in order to equalize access to the university. Choice B is the best answer.

12. The conclusion being made is that Pokia will become the low priced alternative to existing models, not that Pokia will result in huge revenues and replace future models. Answer C suggests that the Pokia camera may become either more expensive or associated with something more expensive. Answer B talks about future models from competitors, not existing models. Therefore, both B and C are not relevant. A and D focus on the potential sales of the new Pokia digital camera. Only E directly challenges the underlying assumption in the argument.

13. The passage draws the correlation between the race car and the outcome of the race. Since the outcome of a race tends to be dependent on the quality of the car, a new car is more likely to improve the driver's performance. Choice B is the best answer.

14. What is the city's fear? That pre-existing railroad tracks offer an unfair advantage. What would ease the city's fear would be something that demonstrates a problem the cargo railway company may have. The best choice is A.

15. This question is a time waster. You simply have to go through all of the choices and see which facts are available in the text. The text says nothing about efficiency, so choice A is out. Choice B is never addressed in the text - as the opinion of Southern Haul on bus transport is never mentioned. Choice D relates to legal questions that are never addressed and choice E is based on future projections that are never made. Only choice C is answered by the text - in that the city states that Southern Haul makes a profit on cargo transport.

16. Since total sales increased, the reduction in profits would have to come from increased costs, or a reduction in prices. None of the choices notes a reduction in price in America Mart's walk-in stores, which, we assume, made steady sales, if sales increased. Thus, the cost of the internet site could account for lower profits the year the site was introduced if the cost of setting up the site cut into profits. Choice E is the best answer.

17. Aristotle is better than 90% of his class, thus in the top 10%, while the article says Alexander is not in the top 10% of his class. Choice C is the best answer.

18. If for some reason it was not possible to install carbon tubing in cars in a way that was comparable to plastic, then the option of carbon tubing would not be a substitute for plastic as a source of light, stable material. Choice D says carbon tubing has quality control problems which may make it less economical, less safe, or less reliable than plastic.

19. The automobile manufacturer's claim is that they are not motivated solely by profit motives. Choice B states that automobile companies choose not to use carbon tubing for reasons that have to do with their reluctance to invest in its production, rather than with the suitability of carbon tubing as an alternative material in automobiles.

20. Only professional pianists are the accepted judges of pianos, and these pianists will not accept that any sound is better than existing pianos. Since it is impossible to create a sound that is better than existing pianos, choice D is the best answer.

21. What is the plan of the company? It is to continue its profit making trend. In other words, whatever changes the company implements, the changes will be ones that will tend to increase their profits. Therefore, the choice you are looking for is the one that is oppositely related to profit making as a determinant. This is choice D, which involves a decrease in profits.

22.   Increased security would lead to increased revenue, if it addressed a concern that caused people not to fly when they otherwise would have. Clearly, choice A is the best answer.

23.   The statement assumes that the students were correct for some portion of the time and incorrect for some portion of the time. That assumption requires the teacher to be able to distinguish between a right answer and a wrong answer. Thus, choice E is the best answer.

24.   The claim of the other theorists could be true if making a symbolic step is connected with successful completion of negotiations but does not cause the parties to complete negotiations successfully. Choice D suggests that this may be the case, and so is the best choice.

25.   The emergency response officials claim that more fires don't happen, more are just reported. Something that weakens their claim will be something that demonstrates that, in fact, more fires actually do happen. Choice B is the correct answer because it identifies a situation in which more fires do happen during certain intervals.

26.   What is the farmer doing? He is setting a limit on what are to be considered good apples. For every 9 apples he will get rid of 2 to ensure quality. (This is the ratio of 45:10 reduced). What is wrong with this sort of calculating? How can you be sure that the seven apples that remain will all be of the same quality? What if, in one week, there are four bad apples for every 9 and he still only throws out 2. 2 bad apples are left. The answer you want should precisely demonstrate that the percentage of apples remaining will not ensure quality. That is choice E.

27.   What is Save-a-Tot's claim? It is that the new safety seats are indeed safer. Something that challenges that claim will demonstrate that the seats are, in fact, not safe. Choice A demonstrates that the plastic in the seat turns brittle, which renders them unsafe. It is the best answer.

28.   This question is relatively easy for the GMAT. You are given two conditions: those who want to leave have no money, and know many foreign languages. You are asked to find the opposite of these conditions. All you have to do is go down the list of answers and select which choice matches at least one, if not both of the following conditions: someone who has money and someone who knows no foreign languages. Choice D matches both of the conditions. It is the right answer.

29.   In order for the comparison of mechanics to imply something about the importance of technical education, the subject group being compared needs to be relatively homogenous in terms of factors which will affect their income as auto mechanics, otherwise the results we see do not clearly reflect how the course increases the ability of auto mechanics to earn a better income. Choice B is the best answer.

30.   A, C, D, and E do not strengthen the conclusion that the IT sector is growing. Choice B is the best answer.

31.   Although there is no evidence that high-voltage transmission lines are linked to cancer rates, the incidence of headaches and other ailments conflicts with the claim that legislation cannot be implemented on health grounds. Choice A is the best answer.

32.   Since the argument made in the passage is concerned with the effects, or non-effects, of high voltage transmission lines on people's health, the legislation could be justified for protection of age groups other than children. Choice B is the best answer.

33.   Politician A seeks to make a moral statement against Qarnak and eliminate its form of government. Politician B wants to retain the Qarnak government while changing its policies and making it more open. They have different goals. One method of goal attainment is to use military force. This contrasts with the second method of attaining goals through economic measures. Choice C is the best answer.

34. Choices B and D are the possible answers. Though choice B is a plausible choice, it is still not known if other companies need to incur great costs when relocating their factories out of Qarnak. Choice D confirms a negligible impact of the boycott on the economy. Therefore, choice D is the correct answer.

35. There is a logical link missing in the argument of the management. What most weakens their claim is that link. The management says water sources are polluted. The first thing you should ask yourself is 'why are the water sources polluted?' If it is possible that the plant is somehow polluting water sources, then that would substantially challenge the management's argument. Choice C is the best instance of linkage whereby the pollution source can be connected to the plant.

36. What is the basic assumption being made about the rice cakes? That they are made from the rice that is grown in Hunan, where there was a flood. It is necessary to find something that significantly weakens the argument that the price of rice cakes must inevitably rise because of the flood - one needs to demonstrate that there are sources of rice that were not affected by the flood. Choice B demonstrates that other regions can also supply rice for rice cakes. It is the best answer.

37. You are given a statement: when x happens, y happens. Then comes a counter-statement which says that even though y should happen, something else is happening. Clearly, another factor is affecting the x-y relationship. Choice E demonstrates that there may be another factor. It is the proper conclusion to draw.

38. Acme University seeks to maintain constant standards. If it is difficult to judge the quality of applicants by their personal statements, using personal statements alone would not be a helpful way to evaluate the quality of applicants. Choice E is the best answer.

39. If people tend to join organizations that serve their interests, then the fact that many large women's rights groups consist almost entirely of white middle class women indicates that these groups do not serve the interests of people with other ethnic backgrounds or economic positions. Choice E is the best answer because it supports the conclusion.

40. The conclusion of the article is that actually women's suffrage took its first steps in the West. Choice B would then explain why the West was more progressive on women's suffrage.

41. Since the intent of building the cable by the Terra Now Mining Corporation is to increase cost competitiveness, choice B would negate the gain Terra Now Mining Corporation is seeking by building the space elevator. Choice B is the best option.

42. This question deals with biased population samples. People who read magazines about guns will tend to be more likely to buy or want a second gun than those who don't read such magazines. Your job in this question is to isolate the biased population and demonstrate that readers of this magazine are different from the rest of the population. Choice D best demonstrates that bias.

43. What is the investment advice? It is that investing in Jones & Weston would increase the value of one's stock portfolio. What does this mean about the company? The company anticipates making a large profit. It can do this by selling more of its product, namely guns. Something that undermines the validity of this advice will be something that demonstrates that the demand for guns is not as high as the magazine claims it is. Choice E satisfies that condition, by showing that only 25% of those who claim they want a second gun end up buying one.

44.   The question is asking you to determine the validity of the claim that falling asleep with the light on reduces the incidence of nightmares in children. One way of determining whether having the light bulb on is the actual factor responsible for dealing with nightmares is to see whether or not this works with other control groups as well - such as teenagers. Choice D correctly links a successful instance of a decrease in nightmares among teenagers with keeping the light on.

45.   The best way to find the solution to this question is to draw a chart for yourself depicting the information in a visual form. Bear in mind that if someone is in the top three and someone else is in the top ten, you have no way of knowing, for sure, who is higher than the other. That is the trick in this question. The only statement you can be sure of is choice C, because the passage says Jake is in the top three and Tom is not in the top three.

46.   The justification provided by advocates of child abuse in the article is that children must be beaten because they are not able to make logical conclusions leading to the ability to respond appropriately to their surroundings. Choice C directly contests that assertion, weakening the argument.

47.   Since the group-date system is designed to allow people to better assess interpersonal skills of their dates, the creation of unnatural stress interfering with participants' normal interpersonal attributes would diminish the purpose of this arrangement. Choice E is the best answer.

48.   We can reduce this statement to the following format: x does y assuming z, in the first instance. In the second, x does something else also assuming y. In other words, because both redesigns are for upscale customers, they are assuming in both cases that an upscale clientele would be interested in both products–pick-up trucks and compact cars. Choice B is the only choice that identifies this correlation.

49.   What is the argument? That the courses are unnecessary. What would challenge this argument? You have to look for a biased population sample, or something that explains why students who do not take these courses have higher scores - as the teachers claim. The only answer choice that demonstrates an incidence of population bias is choice A.

50.   If an increase in the number of violators is reported using a more effective method of catching violators, then the cameras are not causing traffic violations. Cameras are merely recording violations more accurately and thus making it seem as if more violations occurred after the installation of cameras. Choice C is the best answer. Choice D weakens the city's claim as well, however, marginally. A, B and E are not relevant.

51.   While driver error is not stated as passage an unimportant contributing factor to accidents, the passage notes that improvements may be made by knowing the conditions under which accidents take place. Thus, the passage would presume that if the conditions that lead to accidents, and even driver error, can be known, then they should contribute to a reduction in accidents. Choice D is the best answer.

52.   Since the threat to Sepharia by the embargo is related to the fact that there may be a 20 fold increase in the cost of the derivative, the ability of Sepharia to purchase the derivative for only 1/4 more would weaken the premise of that threat. Choice E is the best answer. C addresses the issue of reserve and future supply within Sepharia, but not the price. A, B and D are less relevant.

53.   All the choices pertain to whether residents of Delta City are happier or economically better off as a result of the parks and greenways construction except for choice B.

54.   Because the percentage of the garbage produced by people between the ages of 13 and 55 has increased, the percentage of the garbage produced by those older than 55 and younger than 13 must have decreased. Choice D is the best answer.

55. Prices reflect the relationship between supply and demand. Higher unemployment and taxes may decrease demand. A decrease in supply may maintain or increase the ratio of demand to supply, maintaining or increasing prices. Choice A is not relevant since it talks about used apartments. Choice B doesn't address unemployment rate and whether or not moderate and low income families are the primary buyers of new apartments. Choice C implies no change in the new apartment price level. Choice D leads to an opposite result. Choice E is the best answer.

56. 25 days out of 1825 days, or 5 years, is a small percentage. Therefore, it is choice D "these 25 days are not representative of normal temperature measurements" that is the proper conclusion to draw.

57. If more rabbits became sick in the cage where they were exposed to colder temperature, as opposed to the warmer cage where fewer rabbits became sick, after being injected with the same toxins, it can be assumed that the combination of cold temperature and the toxin makes more rabbits sick. Choice A is the best answer. All other choices can be true on a stand-alone basis. However, they do not support the technicians' conclusion.

58. The assumption in the passage is that opium companies are unable to reduce other expenses in order to keep the price of opium unchanged. Choice A is the best answer. Choices B, D and E are not relevant to the argument. Choice C weakens the argument.

Chapter 7

Verbal Training Set III Solutions - Reading Comprehension

7.1   Standard Reading

Passage 1

1. Choice D is the right answer because the passage affirms that malpractice suits from patients have been shown to have only a minor impact on health care costs.

2. Choice B is the right answer because one of the main purposes of the passage is to state that the number of people who die from medical malpractice is very high.

3. Choice C is correct because the passage suggests that though most penalties are given out for fraud and drug abuse, more penalties need to be given in addition to these penalties.

4. Choice A is the correct answer because the passage states that a congressional report found that malpractice claims account for only a minor portion of health care costs.

5. Choice E is most in tune with the argument of the passage since the passages speaks directly about the role of doctors in inflating the costs of health care through malpractice and patients having unequal recourse to recoup those costs

6. Choice D is the correct answer because the sentence addresses the contradiction between the policy making of Congress in aiming to lower health care costs by restricting patient awards and the research of the Congressional Budget Office that says malpractice suits account for a minor part of health care costs.

7. Choice C is the best answer because if policing is to work it must be possible to improve the performance of doctors.

8. Choice A is the most appropriate because the idea that jury awards should be reduced is connected to the idea that patients are claiming too much in the way of compensation. Please read this sentence "It is the hope of lawmakers in capping jury awards to plaintiffs that it may be possible to reverse the tide of rising health care costs."

Passage 2

1. Choice E is the best answer. It is supported by the sentence "...an employee who decides to report illegal or unreasonable behavior to the authorities regularly finds himself to be the subject of intense scrutiny, or even fabricated accusations, if he continues to stay at his place of employment, it is necessary to make the act of bringing unethical performance to light appealing enough to outweigh the disincentives posed by angry coworkers, punitive bosses..." Choices A and B are the opposite of what is said in the passage. Choice C is not correct as it is not realistic to expect new laws to uncover all corrupt practices. Choice D is not correct as it is not stated in the passage that the direct aim of the new laws is to save money.

2. Choice A is the best answer, emphasized by the sentence: "These incentives were meant to make whistleblower laws both a progressive reform, and effective legislation."

3. Choice D is supported by the sentence: "Government bureaucracy and state-financed corporations can at times appear to operate above the law, outlasting administrations, evading the discipline of elective review, and oiling their machinery while largely hiding from the public eye."

4. Choice E is explained by the sentence "incentives were meant to make whistleblower laws both a progressive reform, and effective legislation, so much so that the lucrative prospects of being a whistleblower has not only brought many reluctant employees forward, but also has encouraged some to go into the business of poaching through phonebooks for dubious employers with an eye towards reporting them to government investigators and collecting their prize."

5. Choice A is the best answer since the passage makes a distinction between legal reforms and effective whistleblower legislation to which lawmakers seek to attach financial inducements. The existence of ineffective legislation would imply that laws were not followed.

6. Choice E is the correct answer since 'oiling their machinery' typically means keeping the day-to-day means of the business functioning.

7. Choice B is the correct answer since all the other options designate a negative connotation to the author's attitude towards whistleblower laws. This negative connotation is not supported by the passage. In addition, choice B is supported by the sentences: "Government bureaucracy and state-financed corporations can at times.... Therefore, it is especially important to make it possible for courageous employees...." and "These incentives were meant.... but also has encouraged some to go into the business of poaching .... once a decision is reached."

8. Choice C is the best answer since plaintiff in this case refers to the person suing the business or government to obtain compensation or to correct a practice that he asserts is wrong.

Passage 3

1. Choice C is the best answer since the first sentence seeks to introduce one of the most important economic powers worldwide in the passage. Choice B is incorrect because the passage does not need to clarify the number of parties in trans-Atlantic trade since it is clear in the passage that there are only two parties being discussed. Choice D is not necessarily true. Choice E is unrelated to the sentence.

2. Choice C is the correct answer because it is the only answer out of the five choices relevant to increased benefits to corporations at the expense of other parties, including those interest groups who may advocate for corporate taxes to address social issues. Choice A is what peripheral groups advocate for, not one of their concerns.

3. Choice B is the best answer since the exchange between the U.S. and the E.U. is a persistent disagreement over a certain topic. Choice A is incorrect because it suggests no progress can be made. Choice C is incorrect because it refers to an explicit political process which is not identified in the passage. Choice D is incorrect because there is not evidence of it in the passage. Choice E is incorrect because the dispute between the actors is more important than a dispute involving banter.

4. Choice C is the best possible answer, supported by "While bringing standards of production into alignment is a goal that ought to raise the quality of production and the level of cooperation across the continent, it also creates an opportunity to establish a standard contra to European expectations of international regulation."

5. Choice E is the correct answer because lower environmental standards, for example, could make doing business cheaper for US companies than for other companies. The passage mentioned "the United States is noncommittal on E.U. proposals calling for the alignment of labor regulations, the opening of consumer forums and the offer of an audience to environmental groups". Choice A is incorrect because it addresses the opposite concern. Choices B, C and D are not mentioned in the passage.

6. Choice A is the best answer since 'callous' refers to a lack of care, and the passage notes that interests groups in Europe express concern about liberalization based only on corporate advantage.

7. Choice C is the correct answer since the last sentence states: "The route to economic expansion is a prominent issue in both the U.S. and the European Union, and some with a say in the matter repeat these protests as a screen for their own plans to tip the balance of economic advantage towards their own region at the expense of all other involved parties in the process of exploring for parity."

8. Choice D is the correct answer since the United States has hesitated on, but not rejected, TAFTA.

Passage 4

 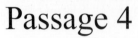

1. Choice D is the correct answer because the theme of the passage deals with rebellion as a corrective. Indian rule was predictable rather than random. Britain could not be described as an absentee governor of India. British bayonets maintained the local despots in power. The resemblance between folklore and history is not dealt with in any detail in the passage. Indian rule was not completely interrupted by the British as they made use of what was already the declared law.

2. Choice E is the best answer because the passage speaks of the British in the following way: "Their methods took advantage of existing "doctrines of lapse", and made use of what was already the declared law in cases of heredity.".

3. Choice E is the best answer as the final sentence in the passage places the blame on "British bayonets" for insulating cruel and indulgent princes from the discipline of a resistant populace.

4. Choice A is the best answer because though the author laments the constant decline of Kings into "feeble inheritors", he notes that rebellion and deposition are the correctives of despotism, securing for the people able and vigorous princes at fixed intervals.

5. Choice C is the best option made clear by the last four sentences.

6. Choice E is the best option as it is exemplified by the British policy of coordinating with princes in need of support.

7. Choice A is the correct answer because the British aided princes who were vulnerable and were competing with another prince. This action required little up front British influence in order to determine the outcome of the dispute, while making Britain the effective "kingmaker" in the region and allowing the British a great deal of influence later. Choice B is not correct because the British did not take over the leadership role. Choice C is incorrect because the British were not helping the princes to discuss their dispute. Choice D is incorrect because the British influence in the area was not impartial, but self-interested. Choice E is incorrect because there were local candidates for leadership.

8. Choice C is the correct answer as Choice C is demonstrated by the British decision to seek to advance their own interests in India when it was possible to do so during times of disorder.

Passage 5

1. Choice B is the correct answer. The passage states that the two interpretations of the functioning of congress are the expert review by a specialized elite of committees and the pork barrel politics of committees seeking to bring back largesse to voters in their states.

2. Choice C is the correct answer since the passage states that media corporations and local groups battle for control.

3. Choice A is the correct answer. Choice A is supported by the statement that the 'act was a technical reformatting of the law.'

4. Choice B is the correct answer. 'advances' refers to the act of ensuring legislation flows smoothly through Congress.

5. Choice C is the correct answer. Choice C is supported by the statement: " The legislation will inevitably determine, one way or the other, the type of national telecommunications market and the nature of the relationships among participants such as business groups, local groups and the public sector".

6. Choice B is the correct answer as stated by the sentence: " Innovators in these fields had long been looking for an opportunity to enfranchise the public, at last, with electronic and spectrum commons".

7. Choice C is the best answer because the last sentence states: "It can be said that the 1996 Act provides very strong backing for both interpretations of how Congress works. Yet, realistically, it seeks to extend a fundamental public resource, the spectrum, while considering the upcoming role media will play in the formation of the civic attitudes of people". This suggests the author has an interest in the 1996 Telecommunications Act as a way of extending the public good, which the passage asserts is the interest of 'innovators' in the field.

8. Choice B is the correct answer. Choice B is backed up by the statement that there is 'a great deal at stake' for large media corporations and local broadcasters and thus, while the law needs to be rewritten for technical reasons, these groups are 'battling' one another which implies that there is conflict. Since there is no mention of their contention over the best design of the law for technical purposes, it can be assumed that these 'constituencies' are in conflict over the opportunity to influence legislation to advance their own interests.

Passage 6

1. Choice A is incorrect because the passage is not about Flanders but the Belgium economy. Choice B is correct because the passage discusses the Belgium economy under structural readjustment. Choice C is incorrect because the passage is not about Flanders. Choice D is incorrect because the passage only mentions P.M. Martens as influencing economic restructuring. Choice E is incorrect because the topic of the passage is not only the damage done by the government.

2. Choice A is incorrect because the passage is not about Flanders. Choice B is incorrect because the passage does not demonstrate how all of Belgium could have followed Flanders's example in order to prevent economic hardship. Choice C is correct because the success of Flanders in some sectors and the decline of Wallonia in other sectors exemplify the change in the economy as a whole. Choice D is incorrect because it is not demonstrated that Belgium was in a position to experience "runaway" economic growth. Choice E is incorrect because there is no one factor which drove away growth in the Belgium economy.

3. Choice A is incorrect because the oil price hikes were not a structural problem with the Belgium economy, but rather an outside event. Choice B is incorrect because policymaking did not immediately change in response to the oil price hikes. Choice C is correct because the oil price hikes revealed the inherent weakness in Belgian economic organization. Choice D is incorrect because the precarious Belgian economic condition preceded the oil price hikes. Choice E is incorrect because the passage does not represent the oil price hikes as an opportunity to turn to exports to spur growth.

4. Choice A is incorrect because Martens is not treated in the passage as only a source of mismanagement. Choice B is incorrect because the passage does not consider Martens' efforts to be misspent. Choice C is correct because the passage seeks to show that the progress Martens made was amid genuine economic difficulty. Choice D is incorrect because the passage does credit Martens with improving aspects of the Belgian economy. Choice E is incorrect as things did improve.

5. Choice A is incorrect because it does not seek to apologize or interpret poor actions in a good light. Choice B is correct because it is providing a historical interpretation of the actions taken during a period. Choice C is incorrect because the passage does not seek to assert a political position. Choice D is incorrect because the passage does not seek to argue against an interpretation of the facts. Choice E is incorrect because the passage is better understood as a historical interpretation.

6. Choice A is incorrect because the passage mentions ways in which the government responded advantageously using its power. Choice B is correct because the passage suggests that it is economically inefficient to aid ailing industries. Choice C is correct because the passage does not suggest the market can be ignored. Choice D is incorrect because the passage does not accuse the government of making decisions too slowly. Choice E is incorrect because the passage seeks to demonstrate the need to structure an economy in a way that is appropriate to minimize the effects of market fluctuation.

7. Choice A is incorrect because it is too broad, and unsubstantiated. Choice B is incorrect because the passage does not assert that economists are not pragmatists. Choice C is correct because the piece is an historical interpretation and making assessments of the correct course of action after the fact is different from making decisions in the time of issue. Choice D is incorrect because the piece does assert that correct answers cannot be found Choice E is incorrect because the passage does not mention that the policy decisions were popularly motivated.

8. Choice A is correct because the passage acknowledges the advantages and disadvantages of high rates. Choice B is incorrect because the passage mentions an advantage of high interest rates. Choice C is incorrect because the passage sees some advantages in high interest rates. Choice D may be considered correct except for the concern expressed by the author regarding slowing the Belgium economy. Choice E is incorrect because the passage does not expect failure as the natural consequence of high interest rates, but acknowledges successes and difficulties.

Passage 7

1. Choice A is correct because the passage demonstrates that people can be affected by environmental influences that create a cycle of addiction. Choice B is incorrect because the scientists who see the relationship between decisions and environment note that it is not always possible to control surroundings once decision-making skills have been compromised. Choice C is incorrect because the passage makes a distinction between being vulnerable to a cycle of addiction and having no responsibility over one's own actions. Choice D may be correct but it is not affirmed in the passage. Choice E is incorrect because the passage does not say that overeaters are unable to overcome the difficulties of withdrawal.

2. Choices A and D is incorrect because there is a relationship between these two factors, but other things could influence dopamine levels, so those levels are not necessarily dependent on whether drugs are administered or not. Choice B is incorrect because the relationship is not presented in the passage as being directly correlated. Choice C is correct because there is a relationship between administering drugs and dopamine levels. Choice E is incorrect because they are related.

3. Choice A is incorrect because companies are still responsible for protecting consumers from possible side effects that they may experience. Choice B is incorrect because corporations are expected to provide consumers with a safe product or to warn them of its dangers. Choice C is correct because it eliminates the threat of an addiction caused by the product by establishing that obesity is a result of consumer habits not addiction to products. Choice D is incorrect because corporations are still liable for the unforeseen damage caused by their products. Choice E is incorrect because corporations still have to provide safe food.

4. Choice A is incorrect because, while it may be true, the purpose of the scientists, as presented in the passage, is not to argue about strict diets. Choice B is incorrect because it is not necessarily true. Choice C is incorrect because one does not necessarily have to have a genetic precondition to obesity in order to contract the disease. Choice D is correct because regarding obesity as a disease allows people to understand that obese people suffer from their behavior in a way that people without the disease may not. Choice E is incorrect because it is not true and is not stated by the scientists mentioned in the passage.

5. Choice A is correct because the researchers object to the conclusions reached based on the evidence found by their colleagues. Choice B is incorrect because there is no mention in the passage of finding fault with the controls. Choice C is incorrect because there is no mention of the proponents making assumptions. Choice D is incorrect because there is no mention of the method, or of the opponents' objection to it in the passage. Choice E is incorrect because the researchers do not contest the validity of the data collected.

6. Choice A is incorrect because the dissenting scientists do not object to the way diseases are categorized. Choice B is incorrect because the scientists mentioned in the beginning of the passage acknowledge that there are several factors that contribute to a person's behavior. Choice C is correct because opponents view "qualitative" consumption choices to be primarily behavioral not primarily chemical problems. Choices D and E are incorrect because these assumptions are not made.

7. Choice A is incorrect because dopamine makes rats happier as they pursue consumption and therefore they feel encouraged to eat more. Choice B is incorrect because dopamine does not block opiates. Choice C is incorrect because opiates are not replaced by dopamine. Choice D is incorrect because dopamine is linked to the reward mechanism which activates when rats receive opiates. Thus Choice E is the right answer since rats are encouraged to eat more.

8. Choice A is incorrect because the lawyers do not say the government lacks knowledge. Choice B is correct because the passage states that lawyers argue that there is 'a responsibility to regulate food and educate people about the abuse of "unhealthy foods" in a way that is comparable to society's control of opiates and narcotics. Corporations that target this vulnerability in human beings can then be held liable...' Choice C is incorrect because lawyers are arguing that it is the responsibility of corporations to keep the consumers informed and to account for damage caused by their products. Choice D is incorrect because the lawyers do not assume governmental incompetence. Choice E is incorrect as the passage does not place the responsibility for a good diet on the individual.

Passage 8

1. Choice E is the best possible answer because "singeing the King of Spain's beard" communicates inconveniencing Spain, though without doing irreversible damage to Spain. Choices B and C are incorrect because Drake did not physically strike near either subject. Choice D is incorrect because we can presume from the passage that Drake's mission was risky and had a practical purpose, and was not merely to cause the King of Spain to lose face. Choice A may be true. However, we can not assess its accuracy from the passage.

2. Choice A is the best answer because it is clear that Spain relied heavily on its colonial ties by the reaction of Spain to the plundering of these colonies by Drake.

3. Choice B is the correct answer because the passage notes that both Spain and England attempted to conceal their own military build up by floating arguments for peace.

4. Choice B is the correct answer because it was the most effective measure exercised by the British to derail the Spanish assault.

5. Choice B is the correct answer because the passage states that Spain sought to use England's tactic as a passive shield, thus presenting themselves as passive when in fact they were assembling a military force.

6. Choice A is the best answer because the sentence is signaling the end of peace talks coming as a premature result of the revelation of Spain's intent.

7. Choice D is the best answer because by revealing their intention to the world for the sake of international support, Spain was not able to make use of its previous strategy of arguing peace while preparing to attack England.

8. Choice D can be concluded as correct from the third sentence stating " They had considered themselves fully prepared to invade, whilst England hardly was."

Passage 9

1. Choice A is correct as mentioned in the passage. Choices B through E were not mentioned as causes of the Central Artery project being labor intensive.

2. Choice A is incorrect because the tunnel is not viewed in the passage as aesthetically conservative. Choice B is incorrect because there is no mention in the passage of the unification of Boston with the surrounding suburbs. Choice C is incorrect because the relevance of the bridge as a symbol is not represented as being connected to its capacity to help Boston grow. Choice D is correct because a symbol is a physical expression of an abstract notion. Choice E is incorrect because there is no mention of Boston as a global city.

3. Choices A, B and C are incorrect because they relate physical structures to abstract ideas. Choice D is incorrect because Red Square does not terminate at the Kremlin; it would exist even without the Kremlin. Choice E is correct because the Eiffel tower is joined to its spire, and comes to its highest point at the spire.

4. Choice A is incorrect because the passage does not indicate this was the first time the slurry wall technique was used. Choice B is correct because it was the first step engineers took in shoring up the walls. Choice C is incorrect because slurry walls were not used for the subway tunnel. Choice D is incorrect because there is no mention of slurry walls being the best option for cave-ins. Choice E is incorrect because there is no mention of the theoretical and practical potential of slurry walls for the Central Artery Tunnel.

5. Choices A, B and D are incorrect because they are not mentioned in the passage. Choice E is incorrect because this is not how the city benefits from undertaking the Central Artery Tunnel project. Choice C is correct because it is the benefit mentioned in the passage as a result of the construction of the Central Artery Tunnel.

6. Choice B is best because the passage does not clearly express the author's personal view of the merits of the project.

7. Choice B is correct because the passage speaks most directly about how the underground highway had to pass under the tunnel, thus necessitating the removal of the rock under the tunnel. Choice A is incorrect because the subway tunnel was not weakened. Choice C has nothing to do with undermining the subway tunnel. Choice D is incorrect because the Central Artery does not go through the subway tunnel. Choice E is incorrect because the tunnel is still necessary.

8. Choice A is the correct answer because it is mentioned in the passage. Choices B, C and E are incorrect because the central artery tunnel will not replace them. Choice D is incorrect because the Central Artery Tunnel project will create the tunnel to Logan airport.

Passage 10

1. Choice A is the correct answer because the passage states that "style" can become too recognizable, and thus would presumably be changed, but plot or method continue to allow con games to trick victims.

2. Choice D is the correct answer because the passage notes that a short con seeks to relieve a "mark" of what he has on him, and a long con seeks to send a "mark" for more of something at another place.

3. Choice E is the best answer because the passage mentions that the "mark" would be overwhelmed when considering the possibility of a con

4. Choice B is the best answer because the passage speaks generally about what con games are and how they work

5. Choice B is the best answer because the passage notes how con men must calculate the returns of a con after the costs expended during preparation and also consider the risks of failure.

6. Choice C is the correct answer because the sentence uses the phrase to imply that there is more than one type of con.

7. Choice A is the correct answer because the passage notes that the aim of a con is to make it seem like the odds are in favor of the mark when in fact the outcome is already determined by the conmen.

8. Choice B is the correct answer because it continues the logic of the previous paragraph. The role of the insideman is still being discussed. The other options would be more appropriate later as conclusions to the whole piece or as more general statements.

Passage 11

1. Choice D is the only answer mentioned in the passage distinguishing World War I from World War II.

2. Choice D is the best answer as pointed to in the sentence: "Germany unleashed the lengthiest bombing campaign of the war on the people of London primarily to weaken British morale."

3. Choice C is supported by the last section of the passage. "The popularity of these masks was dependent on internalizing their use in children ...This potentially reduced the element of fear. If the element of fear could be diminished, gas masks might be employed by their owners more quickly in the event of an attack, and also worn without interruption."

4. Choice C is indicated by the sentence "All of this would increase the chances of survival of the youth population, of no small concern to a nation with large numbers of its working age males facing the perils of combat overseas."

5. Choice B is the best answer since the passage primarily discusses the role of civilian terror tactics and the provisions needed to protect children from those tactics.

6. Choice C is the correct answer since an expedient is something prepared to be helpful or useful in a particular situation.

7. Choice E is correct since the passage states: "The popularity of these masks was dependent on internalizing their use in children by making their presence part of a perceived game. This potentially reduced the element of fear that the masks conveyed on their recipients. If the element of fear could be diminished, gas masks might be employed by their owners more quickly in the event of an attack ..."

8. Choice C can be inferred to be the right answer since the point of providing gas masks in familiar form is to allow civilians to make the correct decisions by being prepared to act correctly.

Passage 12

1. Choice C is the best answer because the passage mentions how the Soviet leaders had thought drug use was the just result of decadence, an aspect of the social decay present in western societies.

2. Choice B is the correct answer because the opening line suggests the proliferation of narcotics is assumed by Russian officials to be fundamentally a result of social mismanagement, while the second line and the following paragraph point out that drug proliferation came as regional political instability increased the opportunity for supply points to diversify.

3. Choice C is the best answer because it is the independence of the former republics which allowed them to become sources of drugs.

4. Choice B is the best answer because the passage notes that Russian officials feel that they must underreport their drug abuse statistics and that it is expected of them.

5. Choice C is the best answer because Soviet Union saw drug abuse in the major cities of Moscow and St. Petersburg, while post Soviet Russia experiences narcotic usage in most areas, of which many were previously unsullied.

6. Choice D is the best answer because the passage mentions the problems with widespread drug use in Russia are the "accompanying illnesses of addiction", which the passage notes may lead to a public health crisis that officials must take more seriously than preserving the image of idealized austerity.

7. Choice D is the correct answer because the passage states that "Canvassing of the Russian people seems to demonstrate that psychoactive substances are used in high quantities".

8. Choice A is the best answer because the passage discusses eliminating the perception of officials that they must conceal the drug problem. The accuracy and continuity of information which reaches head officials would thereby be improved.

Passage 13

1. Choice C is the correct answer since it is supported by the section of the passage that states: "If one holds the contention that the passage of the anti-trust law and the emergence of legislation legalizing the holding company made mass production 'politically feasible' and boutique production (heavily reliant on associations of laborers and merchants) illegal, one can make the argument that the large corporation owes something of its success to government..."

2. Choice A is the best answer since the passage expresses no opinion as to the benefits of mass producers.

3. Choice D is the best answer since it is the only choice which raises the greatest chance of taste different from a standard.

4. Choice E is the best answer since the author acknowledges that there may be other versions of history but is presenting the one she or he believes to be correct.

5. Choice C is correct. It is supported by the statement that the perception of government's role in the development of industry determines whether corporations owe their success to government.

6. Choice D is the best answer since the passage discusses the fact that government had a role in the rise of big business.

7. Choice D is the correct answer since the passage notes that government enabled the rise of the large corporation by hampering small businesses by making it impossible for them to form cartels. D enabled A to happen and was thus the turning point for the economy.

8. Choice D is the correct answer since it is the only choice mentioned in the passage.

Passage 14

1. Choice A is the correct answer and is demonstrated by the description in the passage of perceived injustice which opponents saw in the new Indian post system.

2. Choice A is affirmed in the statement saying that the half-penny post system was more responsible for reducing isolation in India than the telegraph

3. Choice C is the correct answer because the passage observes that benefits provided by uniform postage were the elimination of wrangling with the local postman and the creation of reliability. If the result of these changes in the system was increased postage, then the disorganization caused by the previous system may have been more costly than shipping a letter across India at a set rate irrespective of cost.

4. Choice A can be deduced from the experience of Dalhousie in different roles in the administration and internal development of the region as well as his willingness to disregard the criticism of traditional financiers, whom we might assume were using traditional methods of problem resolution.

5. Choice C is the correct answer because "reduction ad absurdum" literally means to reduce something to an absurd degree, or to extend something to an absurd degree

6. Choice B is the correct answer as indicated in the sentence stating "The system was more reliable for the person mailing the letter, and encouraged increased patronage."

7. Choice D can be seen as the correct answer from the sentence stating "The proof of his success was the renewal of the postal system as a self-sustaining organization rather than its continuance as a chronic drain on British colonial finances."

8. Choice E is the right answer because wrangling with the local postman appeared costly because it limited the reliability of the system. This unreliability decreased patronage and raised costs.

Passage 15

1. Choice D is the correct answer as shown by the statement 'quickly removing a manufacturing sector in order to encourage the growth of an information and service sector can unnecessarily remove jobs'.

2. Choice C is the correct answer since the passage mentions that the comparison 'overlooks the fact that, as economist Paul Krugman favors saying, countries are not direct competitors with one another'.

3. Choice D is the correct answer since the passage states that states can not really be considered rivals because they must continue to trade with one another.

4. Choice D is the best answer since the passage 'does not assume that an information economy does not give a nation certain political, military and status advantages over other nations'.

5. Choice B is the best answer since the passage notes the importance of institutional actors in guiding economies.

6. Choice D is the best answer since Choices A, B, D and E are not supported by the passage. Choice C is supported by the passage since the passage notes that even in post-industrial economies removing manufacturing jobs can be detrimental.

7. Choice C is the best answer since the passage discusses using the resources a country has to improve its economy according to a plan which relates to its characteristics rather than adopting a pattern of change used by foreign economies with different characteristics and types of organization.

8. Choice D is the best answer since the passage seeks to criticize the common assumption that economies must eliminate manufacturing jobs in order to advance in a global world of post-industrial nations.

Passage 16

1. Choice D is supported by the statement that "the laws of physics contain elements of randomness."

2. Choice E is supported by the sentence: "The clearest demonstration that the laws of physics contain elements of randomness is the behavior of radioactive atoms."

3. Choice E is stated in the sentence "In reality, each atom chooses a random moment at which to release its energy".

4. Choice D is the correct answer because the passage states that everything preceding the age of "quantum physics" is in the deterministic tradition.

5. Choice C is the correct answer: "But there would be an even worse consequence if radioactivity were deterministic: after a few billion years of peace, all the uranium 238 atoms in our planet would presumably pick the same moment to decay...blowing our whole planet to kingdom come."

6. Choice E is the best answer because the passage deals with moving into a new era of physics by seeing how the old tenets of physics needed to be understood in terms of new principles. Choice A is too specific to supernovas and the rise of life in the world. Choice B would be for a broad review of the principles of classical physics in general. Choice C is incorrect because the passage does not say that Quantum physics is the most basic principle in physics. Choice D is incorrect because the passage is not debating the merits of the Classic and Quantum models of physics, merely asserting the relevance of quantum physics to all previous models of physics.

7. Choice E is the correct answer. Choice A is inappropriate because the piece does not conform to the impartial, formal style of journalistic news reporting. Choice B is incorrect because the piece is a prepared argument. Choice C is incorrect because the piece does not urge a response or action. Choice D is incorrect because the passage is not trying to cover objectively a broad range of detailed knowledge in a formal style. Choice E is the best answer because the passage does present a considered argument.

8. Choice C is the correct answer because the passage presents quantum physics as a new version of physics which interprets the world in a completely different way than the previous analytical tools allowed. Choices A, D and E are incorrect because they are not addressed in the passage. Choice B is incorrect because quantum physics is not presented by the passage as a supplement to Newtonian physics.

Passage 17

1. Choice C is the best choice because synergetics is described in the first line of the passage as an epistemology and an epistemology is an interpretation of knowledge.

2. Choice B is the best answer because the word "heuristic" refers to a system of education under which the pupil is trained to find out things for himself or herself.

3. Choice A is the correct answer because a "morphology" refers to the study of the form of animals and plants or the study of the form of words and the system of forms in a language.

4. Choice C is the correct answer because the passage describes a "system" as the first division of the universe, thus a "system" is a "subgroup".

5. Choice D is the correct answer because the passage states that Fuller used geometry as his heuristic model, and the most basic unit of that model was the "tetrahedron".

6. Choice C is the most appropriate answer because the passage notes that Fuller used synergetics "as a method for describing the behavior of whole systems whose behavior cannot be predicted."

7. Choice E is the best answer because the passage describes "carafes" as intended 'to carry and relay the derived logic of empirical knowledge'.

8. Choice E is the best answer because all of the other choices are examples of unpredictable systems with many inter-related systemic components.

Passage 18

1. Choice D is the best option since the passage indicates that though Charles II's financial policy needed to mitigate the British financial situation created by support for the military expenditures of Cromwell preceding Charles II's coronation.

2. Choice D is said to be the unique change from previous debts to the modern version of national debt. Please note that at the end of the passage, it says: 'But what was novel was the intervention of Parliament to try to reform government expenditures though careful review of the exchequer's books... by reordering the King's revenue.'

3. Choice C is explained by the sentence: 'The financial disorders of the reign of the English King Charles II are believed to have been the source of his unpatriotic aberrations in foreign policy.'

4. Choice E is supported by the sentence: 'But a correct estimation of the financial difficulties of Charles' government will almost inevitably lead posterity to reconsider its adverse verdict on Charles, and to transfer some part of the blame from him to the House of Commons.' Since the House of Commons was reacting to the world political climate influenced by Cromwell's strong military policy, the author would agree that many of Charles' problems were sowed by the military policy of Cromwell and the House of Commons.

5. Choice E is correct because the passage notes that the House of Commons reacted to Charles' 'aberrations in foreign policy' which were financially driven by creating the Treasury System.

6. Choice C is correct as noted by the sentence: 'From the moment of his accession Charles II was compelled to adopt the system of financing the government through private bankers. This system was not a novelty.'

7. Choice B is the correct answer because the passage indicates that the role of Charles II in the debt crisis will probably be reconsidered as the Parliament is blamed for its military spending.

8. Choice B is correct since it was Charles' relationship with France which moved Parliament to action.

Passage 19

1. Choice C is the best answer since the passage states that the Moravians considered themselves Anglican and had no intention of leaving the Anglican Church.

2. Choice B is the best answer. The passage states that the Moravian teaching style became the order of the day though the society considered itself Anglican.

3. Choice E is the best answer as indicated by the first sentence in the passage.

4. Choice C is the best answer as the passage details all the stages that the Moravian Church went through as its founding members moved from being Anglican to the Moravian Brethren, formerly of the Anglican Communion

5. Choice D is the correct answer, since the passage notes that there was not actually a Moravian church in England.

6. Choice D is the correct answer because the passage covers a known historical period with an interest in reviewing that history and retelling it to provide a different emphasis.

7. Choice C is the best answer since the mob disturbances indicate that the Crown was unwilling to recognize the Moravian society until compelled to do so by social unrest.

8. Choice A is the order of progression followed by the Moravians in the passage.

Passage 20

1. Choice D is the correct answer supported by the sentences: "It can be said the most rudimentary measure of the success of the species is its position near the top of the aggregate biomass scale... For human beings, it is a reflection of their claim on territory, and their consumption of resources as a species."

2. Choice C is the correct answer supported by: "However, the ability to adapt one's habitat to the largest ecosystem, while still retaining the flexibility to deal with local demands on the population may be considered high art in the annals of successful adaptation...It is the fact that human beings have remained in a generally undifferentiated form that allows them to rank highly as a single successful species."

3. Choice D is the correct answer supported by: "Still, human beings have been able to adjust their behavior sufficiently to avoid having nature make such extensive piecemeal adjustments to them that entirely distinct workable alternatives of the same model occupy the new space."

4. Choice C is the best answer since the passage notes that it is the "widespread population of different habitats while being able to exchange genetic material with others from their group " which the passage notes as 'distinct' in terms of success over other species. Choice A is incorrect because it is not mentioned in the passage. Choice B is not correct because it is not mentioned in the passage. Choice D is incorrect because the passage mentions that genetic code is dispersed around the world for any given species, but it is the ability of that species to retain its genetic code that is the criterion for success. Choice E is incorrect as shown by the sentences "It might be short-sighted to belittle the success of an emerging species or breed for being small in number if it is evident that the members of the species are elegant and well-adjusted. However, the ability to adapt one's habitat to the largest ecosystem, while still retaining the flexibility to deal with local demands on the population may be considered high art in the annals of successful adaptation."

5. Choice A is correct answer since the passage discusses the effect of ecological change driving species into different habitats which is related to geographic dispersion.

6. Choice D is the best answer since the passage discusses the fact that some species had to co-exist alongside their predecessors.

7. Choice D is the correct answer because the passage discusses the movement of human genetic material as human beings migrated across the earth.

8. Choice C is the correct answer since the passage is a detailed, impartial discussion of a topic.

7.2   Supplementary Reading

Passage 21

1. Choice B is the best answer since the passage seeks to introduce a more refined interpretation of the development of fitness in a species while using the same source as its basis for the surrounding science. Choice A is incorrect because exponents of Punctuated Equilibriums do not say fitness was not an issue. Choice C is incorrect because it is not mentioned in the passage. Choice D is incorrect because the passage does not present the material as putting a model back together that is broken, but refining the model with a different approach. Choice E is incorrect because the passage does not portray the inaccuracies in Darwin's Theory as being the result of dishonesty.

2. Choice E is the best answer as it is supported by "P.E. updates Darwin by noting that the sudden emergence of a differentiation, endowing an organism with more fitness than the rest of its species, would not usually give that organism or its descendants a significant degree of independence in the absence of disastrous conditions. For the evolution reformers, this comparative advantage only leads to speciation if the conditions in which it occurs are cataclysmic for the species as a whole, including massive geographic reformations (like the flooding of the Mediterranean basin) or unexpected ecological devastation."

3. Choice A is incorrect because there is no mention in the passage of the fossil record. Choice B is incorrect because the passage does not say that Darwinists do not consider the role of ecological disasters. Choice C is incorrect because it does not bear on the difference between Darwinists and Punctuated Equilibriumists. Choice D is correct because Punctuated Equilibriumists observe that Darwinist principles function based on drastic changes in nature, but not "by seeping growth and petty attrition." Choice E is incorrect because it is not mentioned in the passage.

4. Choice C is the best answer since the passage asserts, 'P.E. updates Darwin...' Choice A is incorrect since the passage does not present Punctuated Equilibrium as an extension of Darwin, but as an adjustment to Darwin. Choice B is incorrect because Punctuated Equilibrium is not a concise version of Darwinism. Choice D is incorrect because Punctuated Equilibrium incorporates aspects of Darwinism. Choice E is incorrect because Punctuated Equilibrium does not seek to be an extension of Darwinism but a correction of it.

5. Choice D is the best answer since the passage notes that Darwinism is correct but only in a small environment under controlled conditions. The passage asserts that Punctuated Equilibrium asks 'specific questions' regarding evolution that Darwinism does not ask, and thus would regard Darwinism as less detailed or more simplistic.

6. Choice A is the best answer since the passage asserts that speciation happens under 'cataclysmic' conditions or conditions of 'unexpected ecological devastation' which may be understood to be turbulent and something for which a species could not prepare.

7. Choice C is the correct answer since the other choices all represent sudden changes in ecological conditions which would drive species wide change.

8. Choice D is the best answer since the passage seeks to communicate the inability of a species to prepare for an event.

Passage 22

1. Choice D is the best option since the passage claims the difficulty lawmakers have with contending with the abortion debate problem relates to their inability to see past ideologies, while the benefit offered by the researchers is information on the practical results of abortion for society.

2. Choice A is the correct answer since the passage seeks to put forth a position based on information it provides.

3. Choice C is the best answer since reduced crime at an earlier stage in states which first legalized abortion could show that the birth of unwanted babies in other areas is correlated with higher crime in those areas for the length of time that abortion was illegal in those states.

4. Choice D is the best answer since the passage claims that anti-abortion legislation results in higher crime because mothers are unable to care for babies they are legally compelled to have. It is suggested that mothers do not want babies they are not ready to raise in part because they are incapable of raising them.

5. Choice E is the correct answer, as the passage notes that the abortion debate has ideological contentions that do not abate, and a simpler method of resolving the problem may be useful.

6. Choice E is the correct answer, as it is supported in the sentence "As the ideological arguments over abortion refuse to abate, it may be time for hamstrung legislators to consider new sources of information to simplify their decision about reopening the question of abortion reform and government aid."

7. Choice B is the correct answer. Choice A is not necessarily true, since it is only abortions of unwanted babies that researchers assert can be reasonably correlated with lower crime. Choice C is incorrect because population growth is not equated with crime or the birth of unwanted babies. Choice D is incorrect because the passage does not mention the role of non-violent females as a practical consideration in the abortion debate. Choice E is incorrect because it is the opposite of the researchers' conclusion.

8. Choice A is the best answer since the passage communicates a condition in which children are not being provided a sufficient standard of living to assure quality of life and are poorly prepared to decline illicit opportunities for gain.

Passage 23

1. Choice E is the best answer as affirmed by the sentence: "Amid the many potential models, a history of the development of Israel must still contend with the nineteenth and twentieth century phenomenon of nationalism."

2. Choice D is the best answer since it is supported by "History may choose to see the Israeli-Arab conflict as a situation of ethnic strife, as a confrontation of nationalist sentiments, as the learning process of self-determination, or even as an apartheid government in violation of human rights. Producing a work which chronicles the events that have led to present-day Israel may necessitate considering the difficulty of modeling changes using new and old theories of international relations and balancing the concerns of multilateral non-governmental agencies over human rights with traditional concerns of nation states such as imperialism, state building and the formation of military coalitions. "

3. Choice E is the best answer since the passage discusses uniting Jews for nationalist reasons and a softened emphasis on religion.

4. Choice C is the correct answer since the other choices are not mentioned as creating problems in the creation of Israel. Choice A is mentioned but is not characterized as necessarily problematic by the passage. Choice B is not correct as international law is not presented as being ambiguous. Choice D is not correct as there is no mention of incompatible agreements. Choice E is not correct, as financial difficulties are not mentioned. The difficulties which come from a minority seizing power are mentioned.

5. Choice E is provided by "However, the difficulties that have persisted in securing Israel as a Jewish National Home may seem, at times, not to be the problems that would arise from a nationalist cause, but rather the difficulties which come from a minority seizing power, or more simply put, as the trials of colonialism."

6. Choice D is the best answer since the passage states that 'the credibility of each side in the modern negotiations in the Middle East between Israel, Palestine and their Arab neighbors, is heavily linked to understanding what rules applied in international law and warfare.'

7. Choice A is the best answer since the passage observes that "Usurping the land of a native people was thought of by some not as an infringement of sovereignty, but as the establishment of a protectorate."

8. Choice A is the correct answer, and the passage states that compliance with international law is important in establishing the legitimacy of land occupation.

Passage 24

1. Choice C is the best answer since the piece seeks to air and justify an opinion on a contemporary chain of events.

2. Choice D is supported by the sentence " All this threatens stagnation and decline, with tax dollars wasted and educated, opportunistic youngsters chasing foreign advantage."

3. Choice A is the best option because the passage notes that Indian tax payers have invested in the education of the technology students so that the students would make an investment in India. Choice B is incorrect because the Indian government and the students do not actually have a written contract or an agreement with one another regarding working in India once they have met the requirements of their education. Choice C is incorrect as the opposite would be true and the pledge would be to work in India. Choice D is incorrect because 'redeem their pledge' is the opposite of refusing a request. Choice E is peripheral to the use of the phrase 'redeem their pledge'.

4. Choice D is the best answer since the passage seeks to communicate the second look emigrated Indians are taking toward their country, after becoming wealthy abroad, in order to understand what the best policy for India is and if the path they have taken is good for the future of India.

5. Choice D is the best answer since 'crisis' is a word that refers to a severe consequence of an action or a number of actions.

6. Choice B is the best answer since the passage refers to the gains achieved by first world countries without having to pay for the costs of educating the labor. Choice A is incorrect because it has nothing to do with the usage of the term. Choice C is incorrect because the passage does not discuss the predictability of the success resulting from attracting labor. Choice D is incorrect because the sentence is unrelated to the migration of currencies. Choice E is incorrect.

7. Choice A is correct. This is supported by the sentences: "These provisions have created a crisis in technology policy in countries such as India, where taxpayers in the country regularly finance the education of many young people at elite institutions for math and science so that these students can play a crucial role in supporting or creating national industries. However, the highly technical nature of their training is said to leave them lacking in allegiance to their native country, and willing to trade insularity for higher salaries abroad."

8. Choice E is the correct answer. This can be seen from the last line of the passage.

Passage 25

1. Choice E is the best answer since the unwillingness to enforce air quality standards in one developing nation would compel other developing nations to reduce air quality standards in order to be on equal economic and environmental footing. A shared, socially beneficial resource depends on the collective action of all the participants to be used wisely. If one participant dissents, the resource may become unavailable to the cooperating participants, and the benefits of not cooperating will be gained by the uncooperative party at the expense of others. Choice A is not the best answer because the shareholders in a corporation in this case are not protecting their shares as a non-renewable resource. Choice B or D would be a possible answer, but it is less convincing to compare an evolving market with a non-renewable resource. Choice C is incorrect because the prior dropouts did not necessarily make failing the course easier for the student.

2. Choice A is the correct answer. Choice A can be assumed from the sentence: "However, while this attitude may seem to maximize the benefits for any single participant, collectively these participants are disadvantaged by their overlapping actions."

3. Choice D is the correct answer. Choice A is incorrect because the passage states that the rule of capture has been called the 'Rule of the biggest pump' so farmers had already accepted that some people would taking more advantage of the resource than others. There is nothing in the passage to support choices B, C and E. Choice D is correct and exemplified in the sentences: "In East Texas, groundwater conservation districts have emerged as one solution to appease these locals. However, government still finds it difficult to prevent groundwater ranchers from legally exporting the local supply to other regions for private profit."

4. Choice A is the correct answer, and it is provided in the sentence and phrasing ". . . in places like East Texas, where scarcity is an issue, tempers have flared not in response to the competition between scores of similarly sized farms vying for the output of one water source. Rather, current conflict is the result of very different types of users emerging as competitors in the exploitation of local aquifers."

5. Choice A is the best answer which is demonstrated by the sentences: "In East Texas, groundwater conservation districts have emerged as one solution to appease these locals. However, government still finds it difficult to prevent groundwater ranchers from legally exporting the local supply to other regions for private profit." While providing a solution to appease the locals, the government attempts to acknowledge that it is unable to solve the problem.

6. Choice D is the best answer since the passage asserts 'as a result of the concern about the sustainability of groundwater' farmers are seeking to change the 'rule of capture' now that different types of competitors are seeking access to common water.

7. Choice D can be interpreted to be correct as the passage states that the government seeks to 'appease' locals as it struggles to contend with the problem.

8. Choice B is the correct answer since the passage states that the problems with groundwater conservation come from the fact that local interests must often succumb to the desires of water ranchers.

Passage 26

1. Choice C is the correct answer since the passage notes that the biggest danger posed by the government regarding defendants is its ability to aid the prosecution in ways which are outside the realm of legal review.

2. Choice D is the best answer since it is supported by the statement that people are unaware of all aspects of the policy of government surveillance. The other choices are not stated in the passage.

3. Choice B is the correct answer since the passage notes that the power of the government in the area of prosecution lies in its ability to work around safeguards and to manipulate bureaucracy against a suspect's legal rights.

4. Choice C is the correct answer. Choice C is supported in the passage by the statement that 'the state achieves an advantage by having so many more 'leads' on the individual with which to use bullying tactics, and by engaging in non-judicial activities.'

5. Choice B is the correct answer. Choice B is supported by the statement that the state improves its ability to 'operate extra-judicially' and act in ways that are without redress.

6. Choice C is the correct answer. The passage mentions the murder case as an example of the 'perception' of the public in regard to the benefits of surveillance in contrast to the reality of the state being able to improve its ability to prosecute the defendants it has caught.

7. Choice D is the correct answer. It is supported by the statement that the ability of the government to change the direction of the prosecution or to improve the prosecution reiterates the need for safeguards protecting suspects from abuses in the process of investigation and trial.

8. Choice C is the correct answer. Choice C is mentioned in the passage where it shows the relationship between the monopoly over prosecution and investigation and the ability that this monopoly gives to authorities to disregard official rules and manipulate the defendant.

Passage 27

1. Choice C is the best answer because the passage notes that German engineering programs are a good choice for the passage because they operate according to a logic which says that they do not need to pay heed to external conditions. Thus, a discipline, such as sociology, which studies a range of social conditions, would be less useful as an example.

2. Choice E is the best answer because the passage states that a major problem with the lack of instruction in English in engineering courses is that it makes it harder for students from abroad to take courses in German universities.

3. Choice E is the best answer because it duplicates the adjectival nature of the phrase which relays a notion of observation enacted through diligent examination by many interested parties.

4. Choice B is the best answer because a paucity is a smallness of number or quantity.

5. Choice C is the best answer since the passage asserts that the vocational flexibility provided by the German education system is what is in doubt because of the difficulty in German students being mobile within the system.

6. Choice A is the correct answer because the Bologna Declaration establishes standards.

7. Choice A is the best answer because the passage suggests students should have choices rather than being stuck in one program.

8. Choice E is the best answer because some of the main actors with an interest in reevaluating the German education system are large corporations in need of having access to a wide labor pool, and students who seek to increase their options in the workforce.

Passage 28

1. Choice C is the correct answer because the passage mentions that the AEC sought to "bowdlerize" the contemporary discussion on nuclear weapons. The implication is that they wanted to increase the positive comments regarding nuclear weapons.

2. Choice B is the best answer because the sentence refers to the development of Alaska's coast.

3. Choice C is the best answer since the passage discusses the AEC conducting a "reconnaissance" of the area, a physical scan by reconnaissance personnel on location.

4. Choice A is the correct answer because if individuals interested in Sputnik's successful launching wanted to engage in "one-upmanship", it can be assumed that the statement being made by the Sputnik accomplishment is the thing which these actors consider important.

5. Choice A is the best answer because the AEC was seeking to improve the reputation of nuclear weapons. This assumes that the American public had a negative perception of nuclear weapons.

6. Choice B is the correct answer because the passage notes that the AEC shut down the program because they had reconsidered the reaction their project would earn them, thus implying that they would not be able to curry pro-nuclear favor from continuing their program and thus should not continue "Operation Plowshare" by pursuing Project Chariot.

7. Choice B is the best answer because the term "preferred" refers to a view of something as being the best option.

8. Choice A is the best answer because the authors of "Operation Plowshare" were politically motivated in "spinning" the perception of nuclear weapons with positive images, and thus were seeking politically savvy methods of influencing the discussion on nuclear weapons.

Passage 29

1. Choice E is the best answer because the passage discusses the pros and cons of strategies of industrialization.

2. Choice D is the best answer because the passage discusses the risk of overproduction in the third paragraph.

3. Choice E is the correct answer because the passage shows that a monetary crisis in eastern markets and overproduction of handkerchiefs caused problems in the industry. These problems were exacerbated when demand fell and preferences changed.

4. Choice D is the correct answer since the section of the passage discussing bonnets, which were produced using standardized mass production techniques, refers to overproduction as a major problem the producers faced.

5. Choice E is the best answer since it is demonstrated by the drop in demand. The producers should have reacted to this change by reducing production of items which were no longer sought after. Instead technological advance gave them the opportunity to increase production.

6. Choice D is the correct answer because it is supported by the statement that "Class disparity and capital rigidity would become ... just the things which kept many European producers from settling around a consistent, reproducible pattern of mechanization."

7. Choice C is the best possible answer since the passage says that technological improvements can create economic difficulties as well.

8. Choice C is the best answer as the passage discusses some of the benefits and pitfalls of industrialization. Choice A focuses more on America while the passage focuses on comparing industrial models. Choice B would be a good title for a passage discussing different examples of industry in detail, rather than comparing the pros and cons of industrial models. Choice D focuses more on America than on industrial models. Choice E would be an appropriate title for a passage discussing the advantages of industrial rationalization, rather than discussing the advantages and disadvantages of standardization for different industries.

Passage 30

1. Choice A is incorrect because the passage discusses rhyming as a characteristic of traditional rap. Choice B is acknowledged in the passage but rap aficionados were only a portion of the music's ultimate audience. Choice C is correct because Gangsta rap became successful by integrating both these factors into its music. Choice D is incorrect because it is not mentioned in the passage. Choice E is incorrect because the passage does not discuss the work done by vocalists in post-production.

2. Choice A is incorrect because the passage does not mention that audiences were confused by gangsta rap. Choice B is incorrect because the passage does not mention a disconnect between critical and commercial success for gangsta rap. Choice C is incorrect because the passage does not talk of gangsta rap as only black art. Choice D is correct because the passage mentions that the imagery of violence "enabled West Coast rap to distinguish itself within Hip Hop music". Choice E is incorrect because it was the coupling of indulgence and social activism which resulted in the "gangsta rap" moniker.

3. Choice A is incorrect because gangsta rap was a part of Hip Hop. Choice B is incorrect because the passage does not discuss the alienation of audiences. Choice D is incorrect because gangsta rap appealed to a more heterogeneous audience. Choice E is incorrect because the street credibility of gangsta rap was maintained despite its use of slick production techniques.

4. Choice A is incorrect because the author does not argue for or against gangsta rap. Choice B is incorrect because the author does not view the hedonism and misogyny of gangsta rap merely as tools to achieve the purpose of gangsta rap. Choice C is incorrect because though the author questions whether or not these aspects of gangsta rap have a real basis, he or she does not question the sincerity of their use in the songs. Choice D is correct because the author acknowledges a relationship between these aspects of gangsta rap and its rise. Choice E is incorrect because it is too general a statement.

5. Choices A and B are incorrect because they are not supported by the passage. Choice C is correct because the passage indicates that the music industry in L.A. was long established and made use of such methods, thus it can be concluded that this style had been popularly received and was useful in establishing "Gangsta Rap" as a popular medium. Choice D is incorrect because it makes a connection between synthesized beats and corporate oversight that is not supported by the passage. Choice E is incorrect because it is not mentioned in the passage.

Passage 31

1. Choice E is the correct answer since the passage states it is important "to prevent the symbolism of the message from being misused" and to relay "a decisive message and clear intent".

2. Choice E is the best answer since the passage discusses misuse of the term "Sustainable Development" and explains how it is misused by noting how its use differs from proper use.

3. Choice E is the best answer since the passage discusses "Sustainable Development" from the historical perspective of its original use, and thus may be a call to note the change in the use of that term, as could be read in an editorial.

4. Choice E is the best answer since corporations sought to use the term in describing their publicity-seeking environmental projects by taking advantage of the difficulty in defining "renewable energy".

5. Choice D is the correct answer since the passage faults the U.N. for the fact that its definition led to too general a usage of the term.

6. Choice C is the correct answer since this section of the passage discusses how corporations have influenced the usage of the term by ensuring that non-sustainable activities are associated with sustainable development.

7. Choice B is the best answer since it is the example which is most likely to conserve the present resources of the environment by reducing their exploitation.

8. Choice B is the correct answer since it is supported by the idea that there are many interpretations of what is considered "sustainable", and the fact that some companies which both protect the environment and cause damage to it are objectionable to some environmentalists because the use of the term "sustainable" by such companies misuses the term.

Passage 32

1. Choice E is the best answer since the passage notes that while loss leaders are valuable for branding though they lose money, corporations are wary of profitable products that have negative effects.

2. Choice A is the correct answer, as can be seen from the phrase "the unwillingness of corporations to supply female consumers with their products of choice". Choice B is incorrect because it is contradicted by the fact that it is women's "products of choice" of which they are being deprived. Choices C and E are incorrect because they are not mentioned in the passage. Choice D is incorrect because it assumes more than what is written in the passage.

3. Choice E is correct because it is supported by the sentence: "Based on this, it is evident that conservative pharmaceutical corporations are laden with fear over the reaction of extremist pro-life groups, religious organizations and prominent members of the Republican Party to increased research and even successful marketing of contraceptive alternatives."

4. Choice D is the correct answer since the passage states that "women are afforded a cornucopia of alternatives which suit their lifestyles, sexual appetites, and personal habits." Men have only one method so choice A is not correct. Choice B is not mentioned in the passage. Corporations are not discussed as consumers in the passage so women are not being compared to them. Choice E is incorrect for including wrong answers.

5. Choice D is the correct answer because it can be derived from the sentences "women are afforded a cornucopia of alternatives which suit their lifestyles, sexual appetites, and personal habits. However, for women's sake, this patchwork of options should never be viewed as too varied or as colorful enough."

6. Choice D is correct since it can be accounted for by the sentence "The enormous market of consumers who would welcome convenient alternatives to the daily "pill", such as a patch, monthly hormone injections, or intrauterine devices, continue to wait much longer than necessary for such products on account of the intimidating presence of a minority of well organized non-consumer groups". Choices A, C and E are not mentioned in the passage. Choice B is the opposite view of the author as can be seen from the sentence which supports Choice D.

7. Choice A is the correct option since the passage is concerned with the inability of Americans to discuss sex. This allows anti-contraceptive groups to seem to have a more vocal and organized presence. Choice B is incorrect because increased purchasing of current products may not encourage corporations to diversify. Choice C is incorrect because if men took more responsibility for sex it would presumably be less risky for women to be sexually active, given that the passage indicates that one reason women need an array of contraceptive options is because it is unsafe to rely on their partners for contraceptive availability. Choices D and E are incorrect because they would discourage companies from offering more products.

8. Choice A is the best answer since the phrase refers to the possibility that the man has a contraception alternative. Choices B, D are incorrect because the phrase intends to convey uncertainty, but not a particular degree of uncertainty. Choice C is incorrect because it is completely out of place. Choice E is incorrect because reliability refers to the quality of the contraceptive, and not just whether it is available or not.

Passage 33

1. Choice A is incorrect because the passage does not discuss outgrowing rule-making bodies. Choice C is incorrect because it is not clear that the government intends to increase growth rates. Choice D is the most plausible wrong answer. However, the passage stipulates that only some groups' property rights will be strengthened while others will be sacrificed. Choice E is incorrect because it was not mentioned that the software industry was perceived as a problem. Choice B is the right answer because it is stipulated that previous changes in laws made it possible for lawmakers to engage in economic decision-making.

2. Choice A is incorrect because the property rights of some were limited for the property rights of others. Choice B is incorrect because it is not clear that the administration preferred corporate or individual producers, as some from both groups benefited from changes by the government. Choice C is incorrect because it is not mentioned that lawmakers saw explicit property laws as a better way to benefit the industry than communal property. Choice D is incorrect because the passage merely states that these programs were considered antiquated but not that they were without justification at the time they were enacted. Choice E is correct because businesses were thought to be able to operate without government assistance.

3. Choice C is the most significant reason presented by the passage as being advanced by detractors of the Copyright Act of 1976 was they were interested in protecting the "established" benefits of free and open exchange between the reigning industry actors. Choice A is partially correct, though not all programmers would lose the right to their property. Choices B, D and E are not mentioned in the passage.

4. If the central theme of the passage is how government attempted to redirect the work standards of the software industry, Choice C is the best answer since it discusses the policy making of government influencing the behavior of industry. Choice A is incorrect because it does not deal with the role of government in the consideration of software as a commodity and because the central theme of the passage does not have to do only with the consideration of software as a commodity. Choice B is incorrect because the central theme of the passage has more to do with the influence of government on institutions than just on government's contribution to consideration of software as a commodity, Choice D is incorrect because it is not clear that government sponsored incentive programs prevented businesses from succeeding on their own. Choice E is incorrect because it is not expressed in the passage.

5. Choices A and B are not supported by the passage. Choice C does not apply because while many peripheral contributors to the software were disenfranchised, corporations and primary producers had their rights to intellectual property strengthened. Choice D is incorrect because the opponents of the Copyright Act of 1976 would not consider it either a microeconomic or macroeconomic solution. Choice E applies because of the threat of a "chilling effect" on innovation though there was initially a move towards filing patents and creating software for profit

6. Choice B is correct because chilling generally refers to a slowdown or reduction in the rate of something.

7. Choice A is incorrect because programmers had not perceived the previous practices as theft. Choice B is incorrect because the new efforts programmers took to protect their work were not necessarily related only to a fear of it being copied. Choice C is incorrect because there is no mention that the previous norms of programming were considered to be inadequate by most programmers. Choice D is technically a correct statement, but is stated in the passage, and does not need to be inferred. Choice E is the best answer, since the most distinct change in industry was the type of projects programmers began to take an interest in once it was possible for a few programmers to begin hoarding their work, making it rational for others to do the same and select projects for which that hoarding was beneficial

8. Choice A is incorrect because proponents do not believe software is fundamentally a private effort. Choice C is incorrect because the passage does not mention that professional programmers felt they were being exploited. Choice D is incorrect because the passage does not mention that opponents believe government subsidies are their entitlement for quality output. Choice E is incorrect because there is no mention in the passage of eliminating weaker programmers for the sake of a stronger software industry. Choice B is the correct answer because the difference of opinion between proponents and opponents is the value of fee-simple versus collaborative credit as a practical system of reward.

Passage 34

1. Choice C is the correct answer because it is the only option which attempts to make practical improvements to social norms without grassroots input. The community can be said to rely heavily on its form of social order for indirectly associated purposes.

2. Choice D is the best option since the passage presents technological or social improvements as advancements in society, while observing that those innovations may seem like improvements at first, only to prove to be burdens later on.

3. Choice E is the best answer since it emphasizes the importance of local interests while the scenario posed places large scale objectives over local interests. Choices A and B do not provide a parallel with the dam scenario. Choice C notes the value of redesign, but is not applicable to the posited situation in the question because the flooding of a large river is unlikely to have an 'easy alternative' in its redesign in the event of an unintended consequence. Choice D again mentions redesign, which is not appropriate to the posited scenario.

4. Choice C is the best answer since Choices A, B, D and E assume information not provided in the passage. Choice C can be concluded from the need to redesign the American toilet after it was introduced into Germany, suggested in the phrase "the original American model of the flush toilet was not considered a wholly practical improvement on German customs."

5. Choice E is the best answer since the passage views the difficulty with intervening in a foreign environment to be the effect on social conditions which may provide better elements than are proposed by foreign adjustment of that system. Choice A, B and C deal with too narrow an aspect of the passage. The passage agrees with Choice D, however Choice E covers the wider theme which is presented in the passage.

6. Choice D is the correct answer, based on the sentence: "While the flush toilet is originally an American innovation, German flush toilets have a visibly unique construction style, leaving many unprepared inductees...wondering what to do first."

7. Choice C is the correct answer since the passage seeks to inform the reader that changes in cultural practices must be undertaken with care. Rather than trying to persuade the reader of something, the writer presents a wide range of information. This allows the reader to be influenced not just by the writer's opinion. It is not an argumentative piece in which two sides of issue are discussed and one side rejected. While at times humorous, the passage is not specifically written to be funny. The passage is not biased as it does present information in a balanced way.

8. Choice E is the best option since it emphasizes the relationship between entering foreign markets and having difficulty with one's acceptance later on.

Passage 35

1. Choice E is the best answer since it is supported by the statement that a new wellspring of assenting technicians may support change.

2. Choice B is the best answer since the passage here discusses the adoption of changes.

3. Choice B is the correct answer since the passage states that 'methodologies within the field then change as new advances in techniques or technology are coordinated with the new views of thinkers. This is accomplished as the changes preferred by the dissenters achieve dominance using the tools being developed in the workplace.'

4. Choice E is the correct answer as the passage states that 'computer users, who attempted to apply a less formal logic in developing code, were not only benefited by the proliferation of computers, but by the increased ability of users to reach one another.'

5. Choice A is the best answer given that the passages discusses the fact that 'methodologies within the field then change as new advances in techniques or technology are coordinated with the new views of thinkers.'

6. Choice B is the best answer since the sentence refers to changes in accepted views.

7. Choice E is the best answer since if rules are malleable they can be changed.

8. Choice D is the correct answer, since it is supported by the inclusion in the passage of the phrasing "the need for their input to be the product of numerous individuals or departments had required that code be highly readable, and thus follow a prefabricated style of construction".

Passage 36

1. Choice A is the best answer, proven by the sentence: "Yet, in truth, those dangers had more to do with the isolation of the Soviet Union and the resulting inadequate emphasis on safety than on nuclear instability."

2. Choice E is the best answer since it is alluded to in the sentence stating "However, it was well known that this reactor became extremely unstable when operated on low power..."

3. Choice B is the best answer because the passage attributes the accident 'more to Soviet isolation' which can be deduced as a product of the Cold War.

4. Choice E is the correct answer as it is proven by "the Chernobyl disaster provided a real opportunity to assess all Soviet reactors, and to improve their safety protocols manifold. Improvements were innovated in a process of increased collaboration between design teams and nuclear operators ...through ... the establishment of East-West twinning arrangements."

5. Choice D is the correct answer since the message of the passage is that it is how human beings make use of their tools, which determines whether they are problematic or unproductive. Choice D is the only answer which presents the drawbacks of a technology only in terms of its design, and not in how the user assigns it a purpose.

6. Choice C is the best answer since the passage notes that the most important factor in the Chernobyl meltdown was Soviet isolation, thus collaboration between international scientists on safety as a result of the incident would be the most valuable adjustment to nuclear safety. Choices A and B are not directly attributed to the effects of the nuclear meltdown in the passage. Choice D is provided as proof of the collaboration of scientists, but is not the most important improvement. Choice E is an improvement which resulted from the Chernobyl accident, however it does not explain the international nature of engineers reviewing safety standards, which is the most important step associated with the Chernobyl disaster in overcoming the danger of Soviet isolation for the Soviet nuclear program.

7. Choice C is the correct answer, as demonstrated in the sentence: "At issue was a question of how long the turbines could spin once the main electrical power supply had been cut, always a possibility for a number of unpredictable reasons."

8. Choice C is the correct answer because the passage states that it was well known that the reactor became dangerously unstable on low power, and therefore the operators who began the test, and deactivated the automatic shutdown mechanism were responsible for letting the reactor become unstable.

Passage 37

1. Choice D is the correct answer since the passage discusses the relationship between social factors and economic success.

2. Choice E is the right answer since the passage views technological progress as enabling improvement in the use of resources.

3. Choice D is the best answer since the passage acknowledges that economic development can be influenced by the decisions of leaders.

4. Choice E is supported by the statement in the passage that political factors are weighed in determining how technology will be used.

5. Choice C is the correct answer, and is addressed in the passage in the concern that technological advancements, in such areas as munitions, would proliferate and serve as a source of political instability.

6. Choice C is the best answer, since the passage observes that the decline in Chinese imperial power came as Chinese leaders made decisions to halt the spread of technology and the voyages of exploration.

7. Choice D is the best answer since it parallels the restraining of technological growth.

8. Choice C is the correct answer since the passage observes that economic decision-makers manage and contain the growth of technology by influencing political and social organization.

Passage 38

1. Choice D is the best option, supported by the sentence "Clearly, a reason for this has been the sensitive nature of the information contained in historical records."

2. Choice C is the best option based on the sentence "Both groups of code-makers and code-breakers have been demonstrated by historians to have shortened the length of the war by at least as many as three years. Those years would have meant countless lives lost. Instead, they translate into countless lives lived on account of the British camp and the Native American radiomen."

3. Choice D is the best answer since the author acknowledges the relevance of realpolitik in releasing information during times of crisis, while noting that there comes a time when the Government must release information to the public.

4. Choice B is the best answer based on the phrase "the governments of these states must remain appreciative of the struggle of all those who acted on behalf of their fellow citizens in a time of crisis and credit the contributions of each." Choice A is not stated in the passage. Choice C is incorrect because the passage notes that credit should be assigned relative to contributions made. Choice D is incorrect because patriotism is not mentioned in the passage. Choice E is incorrect because the passage notes that information should be revealed when possible.

5. Choice C is the best answer since the passage supports crediting people according to their contributions, which is a meritocratic principle.

6. Choice C is the correct answer since the passage acknowledges the problems with concealing information about the operations of the war but states that it is necessary under the conditions of war.

7. Choice D is the correct answer because, as the passage states: "[States] ought not just admit to these contributions when pressured by the descendents or advocates of these groups, but be anxious for an opportunity to announce these accomplishments publicly." Choice D deals with publicizing the information and taking the initiative to work with the groups, rather than waiting for the pressure of the groups. Choices A and C are not mentioned in the passage. Choice B is not as appropriate as Choice D since the passage states that it will eventually become clear that the risk posed by divulging information is minimal. Choice E is incorrect as the passage argues against such a continuation.

8. Choice C is the best answer since the sentence addresses the difficulty of decoding the Native American language.

Passage 39

1. Choice C is the correct answer since the passage suggests participating in interest groups and volunteering are replacing participating in political parties. Choice A is incorrect because it concedes part of Putnam's argument. Choice B is incorrect because the author acknowledges the importance of civic action to democracy. Choice D is incorrect because it supports neither Putnam nor a 'volunteer democracy' argument. Choice E is incorrect because it states that participation rates in interest groups are poor measures of democracy but does not claim that democracy continues to resist decline.

2. Choice B is the correct answer. It is supported by the sentence: "Part of the reasoning for departing from the Internet threat argument is that Putnam's initial argument interprets the changes in democracy as the end of democracy." And "this may result in less interest in specifically 'civic' behavior, but is balanced by a rise in support of issue-oriented politics, or a rise in participation in groups. Democracy in a post-materialist world has moved into an age of conspicuous consumption of social issues such as environmentalism and the fight against racism." Choice A is not mentioned in the passage. Choice C is contradicted in the passage by the sentence "Specific content, technologically marketed to statistically targeted individuals, may create much narrower markets, but the loss of a culture-spanning forum is not much of a penalty as the creation of wide-open culture was itself highly artificial, promoted through branding to lower the costs of marketing." Choices D and E are not mentioned in the passage.

3. Choice E is the correct answer as it is supported by the sentences: "Commentators have voiced the contention that the freedom the net brings people to avoid direct interactions previously required for leisure activities and conflict resolution in one's home environment (by transferring both consumption and production economies, as well as social gatherings, from home to the net) will further hamper civic participation." "The straightforward extension of these arguments is that intensive use of the Internet is another component in the decline of 'social capital' which is so vital to the functioning of a responsive democracy."

4. Choice D is the best answer since the passage uses the word 'artificial' together with the words wide-open and culture spanning to indicate a manufactured, marketed culture.

5. Choice D is correct because the passage questions the legitimacy of Putnam's examples by questioning whether they are fully representative of all the groups which are active in democracies today.

6. Choice D is the correct answer since the passage associates the type of democracy that existed before the change into post-materialism with class issues and notes that participation in political parties is on the decline.

7. Choice D is the correct answer since Putnam's benchmarks for democracy have to do with social organizations that relate to physical communities.

8. Choice D is the correct answer since the passage concludes with the statement that the new movements in democracy (consumption politics and individual tastes) are related to democracy moving towards post-materialism, and away from class issues. Choice B is not correct because while the passage notes that it is true that the changes being observed may result in less civic participation, that statement is not the conclusion of the passage, but a consideration which the passage later challenges by mentioning the growth of social organizations. Choices A, C and E are not mentioned in the passage.

Passage 40

1. Choice C is the best answer because the passage mentions the main trouble with widespread death of koalas followed by the regeneration of the koala population would be the reduction in genetic diversity.

2. Choice D is the best answer because, much like the passage, it notes that while man has intervened in the path of natural events, that intervention will not be the deciding factor of the outcome of those events. Nature will achieve homeostasis on its own terms.

3. Choice B is the best answer because the main objection of conservationists in the passage is the need to use resources prudently, rather than invest resources disproportionately for an unnecessarily small number of beneficiaries.

4. Choice B is the best answer because the issues in the passage are relevant because they are the conflicts which pertain to homeostasis in the koala.

5. Choice C is the best answer because the primary concern of the passage is the danger of reducing genetic diversity in koalas. Therefore, chlamydia is beneficial to koalas because it ensures their genetic diversity.

6. Choice C is the best answer because the passage is focused primarily on the process of homeostasis as it exists in a selected animal.

7. Choice D is the correct answer because the passage states that one reason koala population rates may grow out of control is because there are only a few predators willing to kill koalas.

8. Choice C is the correct answer because 'connate' means united from the start of life.

Chapter 8

Verbal Training Set Solutions IV - Analytical Writing Assessment

Essay I - Analysis of an Issue

Question:

"Manufacturers should be responsible for the quality of their own products and making sure that their products are safe. If their product injures someone, no matter what the reason is, the manufacturer should be legally and financially accountable for the injury."

Discuss the extent to which you agree or disagree with the opinion expressed above. Support your point of view with reasons and/or examples from your own experiences, observations, or reading.

Sample Write-up:

I agree manufacturers must be held responsible for the quality of their own products and making sure that their products are safe. They should be legally and financially accountable for injuries caused by faulty products, but they should not be held accountable for injuries caused for whatever reason.

The main reason for my view is that some products, although otherwise safe, may cause injuries simply because of faulty or improper customer use. An injury caused through improper use or outright stupidity, has nothing to do with, and cannot reasonably be blamed on, the manufacturer. For example, if an automobile has a mechanical problem due to manufacturer error, the manufacturer is accountable for any injuries arising from such faulty production, for instance, a fire arising from a fuel line leak. However, no reasonable person would argue that car manufacturers be held accountable for accidents caused by driver error or drunk driving.

Another reason for my view is that manufacturers normally issue detailed instructions on the proper use of their products. This is designed to safeguard them against injuries or damages caused by the improper use of their products. Specifically, over-the-counter medications have detailed warnings regarding child dosages. If a child swallows medication because it is not stored properly, it would be unreasonable to hold the manufacturer accountable.

Some might argue that certain manufacturers, such as tobacco companies or gun makers, sell their products with the full knowledge of the negative results they inflict. They might point to the recent lawsuits in the US between the tobacco companies and some states. Yet, here too people should know that both smoking and guns can kill. Hence blaming the manufacturer for every lung cancer death or gun homicide would be ridiculous.

In conclusion, I disagree with the statement. It would be unreasonable to hold manufacturers responsible for injuries arising "for whatever reason." However, if it is shown that the product was faulty, and that the manufacturer was unaware of this fact, the manufacturer should be held responsible.

Essay II - Analysis of an Argument

Question:

The following is an excerpt of an annual business review from the business manager of a department store.

"Clothing stores in the local area reported that their profits decreased, on average, for the third fiscal quarter which started on August 1 and ended on October 31. Stores that sell home products reported that their profits, on average, increased during this same period. Apparently, consumers have a preference of purchasing products for their homes instead of clothing. To leverage on this trend, we should reduce the size of our clothing departments and expand our home furnishings and household products departments."

Discuss how well reasoned you find this argument. In your discussion be sure to analyze the line of reasoning and the use of evidence in the argument. For example, you may need to consider what questionable assumptions underlie the thinking and what alternative explanations or counterexamples might weaken the conclusion. You can also discuss what sort of evidence would also strengthen or refute the argument, what changes in the argument would make it more logically sound, and what, if anything, would help you better evaluate its conclusion.

Sample Write-up:

In this argument, the business manager of a department store relates that, based on sales in a three-month period, clothing stores reported decreasing profits while stores that sell home furnishings and household products saw increased profits. Based on this observation, he recommends that the size of his store's clothing department should be reduced and the home furnishings and household products departments be increased. His argumentation is flawed in two important respects.

First, his sample size, that is, the three-month period in question, is too small. He does not mention how large the increase in profits was at local furnishings and household stores, or how large the decrease in profits for clothing stores. The data gathered over the August 1 to October 31 period is insufficient to establish the conclusion he draws. After all, the increases/decreases in question may have been marginal, and the three-month period is not necessarily indicative of the entire year's performance at those stores.

Furthermore, the data collected in the three-month period could be prejudiced, or simply reflect seasonal glitches. It is possible that sales figures and trends in one region are not representative of sales figures and trends in other regions, or in different seasons. After all, sales of clothing in the late summer and autumn will likely be higher in colder areas, for example, in New York State, than in warmer regions like Arizona. There is no proof in his report that there is a general movement on the part of consumers away from clothing to furnishing stores.

In conclusion, this argument is unpersuasive. The business manager should provide additional sales figures to make his argument more convincing. These figures should cover the entire sales year and be collected in different locations in order to substantiate his argument.

Essay III - Analysis of an Issue

Question:

"The presence of competition is always beneficial to a company as the company is forced to improve its practices."

Discuss the extent to which you agree or disagree with the opinion stated above. Support your views with reasons and/or examples from your own experience, observations, or reading.

Sample Write-up:

Some people argue that competition is central to the free market system, that it is one of the free market's driving forces. It obliges companies regularly to evaluate their production, marketing and practices. I agree with the opinion stated above.

The main reason for my view is that a company which establishes a monopoly normally feels no need to improve its system of production, its marketing or general practices. For instance, Microsoft has had a virtual monopoly in PC operating systems. The fear of losing customers to the competitor Apple lead Microsoft to re-evaluate its own practices and to develop the Windows operating system, which is more "user friendly" than previous systems, and is based on the Apple/Macintosh operating system.

A second reason for my view is that competition can lead to the beneficial interchange of ideas and resources, which usually leads to better practices. An example of this is the airline industry. Over the last decade, airlines around the world have been forced, largely by the competition they have faced, to streamline their operations and to forge alliances or partnerships. These alliances, such as the Star Alliance, which involves Lufthansa and a half-dozen other international carriers, have solidified the positions of the participating carriers.

Some may argue that competition may not be beneficial for all companies. A firm might well be forced out of business because of competition. Yet, those companies that do not survive have undoubtedly offered a product inferior to that of their competitors. As an example, one might look at the disappearance of Commodore which could not keep up with the superior systems of other vendors.

In conclusion, I would agree with the statement. Companies that do not face competition are usually not forced to improve their practices, simply by virtue of their monopolistic position in the marketplace. As I have shown in the case of Microsoft/Macintosh and the airline industry, competition has forced companies to rethink their practices and to thrive at the same time.

Essay IV - Analysis of an Issue

Question:

The following is an excerpt of a memorandum from the director of Advax, a large pharmaceutical corporation.

"The proposal to increase our employees' health and retirement benefits should not be implemented at this time. An increase in these benefits is not only financially unjustified, as our last year's profits were down from the year before, but also unnecessary, as our chief competitor, Baieer, offers lower health and retirement benefits to its employees than what we currently offer to our employees. We can assume that our employees are reasonably satisfied with their existing health and retirement benefits since two-thirds of the respondents in a recent survey expressed their favorable views."

Discuss how well reasoned you find this argument. In your discussion be sure to analyze the line of reasoning and the use of evidence in the argument. For example, you may need to consider what questionable assumptions underlie the thinking and what alternative explanations or counterexamples might weaken the conclusion. You can also discuss what sort of evidence would also strengthen or refute the argument, what changes in the argument would make it more logically sound, and what, if anything, would help you better evaluate its conclusion.

Sample Write-up:

In this argument, Advax's director argues that the proposal to increase worker health and retirement benefits is both financially unjustified and unnecessary. He reasons that the company's profit shrank last year in relation to the previous year, and that Advax has better benefits than its chief competitor and that most employees are satisfied with their current benefits. His reasoning is not entirely convincing.

First, the director's claim that the proposal is financially unjustified is not persuasive. Although he cites a decrease in profit, the company still is profitable. Profits may have declined, but they could still be very insubstantial. His concern with profits seems reasonable, but he makes no indication that Advax is in financial difficulty. Therefore, the proposal to increase worker benefits does not sound financially unjustified, as he claims.

Second, his assertion that increased worker benefits are unnecessary is also not convincing. To demonstrate his case, he cites the lower benefits provided by Advax's chief competitor, Baieer, and the company's internal worker survey, which allegedly shows that two-thirds of workers are pleased with their current benefits. The problem here is the relative nature of his comment; Baieer's benefits are lower, but may also be not much lower. This is not a good reason in itself to deny Advax workers increased benefits. Workers will likely be happier and more productive with better benefits, and would not bother considering employment elsewhere.

Furthermore, the internal survey he cites does not indicate the number of workers surveyed. The sample size may be very small not allowing for the representative conclusion made.

In conclusion, the argument presented by Advax's director against the proposal to increase benefits is unconvincing. His argument would have been strengthened had he provided evidence that an increase in benefits would hurt Advax's financial stability. Furthermore, he should have provided more detail about the sample size of the company's internal survey, and the way in which it was conducted. Had he done this, we would have a better picture of worker satisfaction or dissatisfaction.

Chapter 9

Verbal Training Sets - Answer Keys

9.1 Sentence Correction

(1) E	(23) E	(45) B
(2) A	(24) E	(46) A
(3) B	(25) D	(47) C
(4) D	(26) B	(48) C
(5) E	(27) A	(49) D
(6) A	(28) D	(50) A
(7) C	(29) E	(51) B
(8) B	(30) A	(52) E
(9) E	(31) E	(53) D
(10) E	(32) C	(54) C
(11) D	(33) D	(55) A
(12) B	(34) B	(56) A
(13) B	(35) D	(57) D
(14) C	(36) A	(58) A
(15) E	(37) B	(59) A
(16) A	(38) C	(60) B
(17) B	(39) C	(61) A
(18) B	(40) E	(62) D
(19) E	(41) A	(63) A
(20) C	(42) B	(64) C
(21) A	(43) E	(65) B
(22) B	(44) D	(66) B
		(67) A

(68) E	(91) B	(114) C
(69) D	(92) E	(115) A
(70) C	(93) C	(116) B
(71) D	(94) B	(117) A
(72) D	(95) E	(118) D
(73) B	(96) C	(119) E
(74) E	(97) B	(120) E
(75) E	(98) D	(121) C
(76) A	(99) E	(122) B
(77) C	(100) A	(123) E
(78) B	(101) C	(124) D
(79) C	(102) D	(125) C
(80) D	(103) E	(126) A
(81) A	(104) B	(127) A
(82) E	(105) D	(128) A
(83) A	(106) E	(129) E
(84) D	(107) A	(130) D
(85) C	(108) C	(131) B
(86) B	(109) A	(132) C
(87) A	(110) C	(133) E
(88) E	(111) E	(134) D
(89) D	(112) D	(135) B
(90) A	(113) B	(136) A
		(137) C

(138) D	(161) A	(184) D
(139) D	(162) C	(185) C
(140) A	(163) E	(186) D
(141) C	(164) D	(187) B
(142) E	(165) A	(188) A
(143) B	(166) B	(189) B
(144) D	(167) D	(190) E
(145) B	(168) B	(191) E
(146) C	(169) D	(192) D
(147) C	(170) C	(193) C
(148) D	(171) E	(194) E
(149) B	(172) E	(195) C
(150) E	(173) A	(196) A
(151) A	(174) D	(197) C
(152) E	(175) E	(198) A
(153) B	(176) B	(199) C
(154) D	(177) C	(200) D
(155) E	(178) D	(201) A
(156) C	(179) B	(202) B
(157) A	(180) A	(203) A
(158) B	(181) C	(204) B
(159) C	(182) B	(205) A
(160) A	(183) A	(206) D
		(207) A

(208) E	(223) C	(238) C
(209) A	(224) C	(239) E
(210) D	(225) B	(240) A
(211) B	(226) D	(241) A
(212) E	(227) B	(242) C
(213) C	(228) C	(243) B
(214) E	(229) D	(244) A
(215) C	(230) C	(245) D
(216) A	(231) D	(246) B
(217) A	(232) B	(247) E
(218) D	(233) E	(248) B
(219) B	(234) A	(249) A
(220) D	(235) D	(250) B
(221) C	(236) A	
(222) E	(237) C	

9.2   Critical Reasoning

(1) A		(21) D		(41) B	
(2) D		(22) A		(42) D	
(3) E		(23) E		(43) E	
(4) E		(24) D		(44) D	
(5) B		(25) B		(45) C	
(6) D		(26) E		(46) C	
(7) C		(27) A		(47) E	
(8) E		(28) D		(48) B	
(9) D		(29) B		(49) A	
(10) B		(30) B		(50) C	
(11) B		(31) A		(51) D	
(12) E		(32) B		(52) E	
(13) B		(33) C		(53) B	
(14) A		(34) C		(54) D	
(15) C		(35) C		(55) E	
(16) E		(36) B		(56) D	
(17) C		(37) E		(57) A	
(18) D		(38) E		(58) A	
(19) B		(39) E			
(20) D		(40) B			

9.3   Reading Comprehension

9.3.1   Standard Reading

Passage 1

(1) D

(2) B

(3) C

(4) A

(5) E

(6) D

(7) C

(8) A

Passage 2

(1) E

(2) A

(3) D

(4) E

(5) A

(6) E

(7) B

(8) C

Passage 3

(1) C

(2) C

(3) B

(4) C

(5) E

(6) A

(7) C

(8) D

Passage 4

(1) D

(2) E

(3) E

(4) A

(5) C

(6) E

(7) A

(8) C

Passage 5

(1) B

(2) C

(3) A

(4) B

(5) C

(6) B

(7) C

(8) B

Passage 6

(1) B

(2) C

(3) C

(4) C

(5) B

(6) B

(7) C

(8) A

Passage 7

(1) A

(2) C

(3) C

(4) D

(5) A

(6) C

(7) E

(8) B

Passage 8

(1) E

(2) A

(3) B

(4) B

(5) B

(6) A

(7) D

(8) D

Passage 9

(1) A

(2) D

(3) E

(4) B

(5) C

(6) B

(7) B

(8) A

Passage 10

(1) A

(2) D

(3) E

(4) B

(5) B

(6) C

(7) A

(8) B

Passage 11

(1) D

(2) D

(3) C

(4) C

(5) B

(6) C

(7) E

(8) C

Passage 12

(1) C

(2) B

(3) C

(4) B

(5) B

(6) D

(7) D

(8) A

Passage 13

(1) C

(2) A

(3) D

(4) E

(5) C

(6) D

(7) D

(8) D

Passage 14

(1) A

(2) A

(3) C

(4) A

(5) C

(6) B

(7) D

(8) E

Passage 15

(1) D

(2) C

(3) D

(4) D

(5) B

(6) D

(7) C

(8) D

Passage 16

(1) D

(2) E

(3) E

(4) D

(5) C

(6) E

(7) E

(8) C

Passage 17

(1) C

(2) B

(3) A

(4) C

(5) D

(6) C

(7) E

(8) E

Passage 18

(1) D

(2) D

(3) C

(4) E

(5) E

(6) C

(7) B

(8) B

Passage 19

(1) C

(2) B

(3) E

(4) C

(5) D

(6) D

(7) C

(8) A

Passage 20

(1) D

(2) C

(3) D

(4) C

(5) A

(6) D

(7) D

(8) C

9.3.2 Supplementary Reading

Passage 21

(1) B

(2) E

(3) D

(4) C

(5) D

(6) A

(7) C

(8) D

Passage 22

(1) D

(2) A

(3) C

(4) D

(5) E

(6) E

(7) B

(8) A

Passage 23

(1) E

(2) D

(3) E

(4) C

(5) E

(6) D

(7) A

(8) A

Passage 24

(1) C

(2) D

(3) A

(4) D

(5) D

(6) B

(7) A

(8) E

Passage 25

(1) E

(2) A

(3) D

(4) A

(5) A

(6) D

(7) D

(8) B

Passage 26

(1) C

(2) D

(3) B

(4) C

(5) B

(6) C

(7) D

(8) C

Passage 27

(1) C

(2) E

(3) E

(4) B

(5) C

(6) A

(7) A

(8) E

Passage 28

(1) C

(2) B

(3) C

(4) A

(5) A

(6) B

(7) B

(8) A

Passage 29

(1) E

(2) D

(3) E

(4) D

(5) E

(6) D

(7) C

(8) C

Passage 30

(1) C

(2) D

(3) C

(4) D

(5) C

Passage 31

(1) E

(2) E

(3) E

(4) E

(5) D

(6) C

(7) B

(8) B

Passage 32

(1) E

(2) A

(3) E

(4) D

(5) D

(6) D

(7) A

(8) A

Passage 33

(1) B

(2) E

(3) C

(4) C

(5) E

(6) B

(7) E

(8) B

Passage 34

(1) C

(2) D

(3) E

(4) C

(5) E

(6) D

(7) C

(8) E

Passage 35

(1) E

(2) B

(3) B

(4) E

(5) A

(6) B

(7) E

(8) D

Passage 36

(1) A

(2) E

(3) B

(4) E

(5) D

(6) C

(7) C

(8) C

Passage 37

(1) D

(2) E

(3) D

(4) E

(5) C

(6) C

(7) D

(8) C

Passage 38

(1) D

(2) C

(3) D

(4) B

(5) C

(6) C

(7) D

(8) C

Passage 39

(1) C

(2) B

(3) E

(4) D

(5) D

(6) D

(7) D

(8) D

Passage 40

(1) C

(2) D

(3) B

(4) B

(5) C

(6) C

(7) D

(8) C

Chapter 10

Home Study Guide - Verbal Training Sets - Categorized

10.1   By Tested Concepts

All Verbal Questions – MR Verbal Training Sets

Note: CR – Critical Reasoning; RC – Reading Comprehension; SC – Sentence Correction; MR – Manhattan Review

Sorted by 1) Type - Main Category (SC, CR, RC); 2) Concepts – Main Category (Ascending)

Type - Main Category	Concepts - Main Category	Problem No.	Page No.	Notes (In-class / Homework
SC	Agreement	4	2	
SC	Agreement	44	11	
SC	Agreement	48	11	
SC	Agreement	70	16	
SC	Agreement	71	16	
SC	Agreement	74	17	
SC	Agreement	116	25	
SC	Agreement	120	26	
SC	Agreement	126	27	
SC	Agreement	132	28	
SC	Agreement	135	29	
SC	Agreement	138	29	
SC	Agreement	155	33	
SC	Agreement	168	36	
SC	Agreement	181	38	
SC	Agreement	205	43	
SC	Agreement	214	45	
SC	Agreement	220	46	
SC	Agreement/Idiom	88	19	
SC	Comparisons	11	4	
SC	Comparisons	23	6	
SC	Comparisons	24	6	
SC	Comparisons	47	11	
SC	Comparisons	57	13	
SC	Comparisons	68	15	
SC	Comparisons	83	18	
SC	Comparisons	90	20	
SC	Comparisons	97	21	
SC	Comparisons	105	23	
SC	Comparisons	129	27	
SC	Comparisons	150	32	
SC	Comparisons	164	35	
SC	Comparisons	170	36	
SC	Comparisons	184	39	
SC	Comparisons	217	46	
SC	Diction	51	12	
SC	Diction	60	14	
SC	Diction	61	14	
SC	Diction	154	33	
SC	Diction	160	34	
SC	Diction	187	39	
SC	Diction	202	43	
SC	Diction/Redundancy	22	6	

Type - Main Category	Concepts - Main Category	Problem No.	Page No.	Notes (In-class / Homework
SC	Diction/Redundancy	78	17	
SC	Diction/Redundancy	108	23	
SC	Diction/Redundancy	122	26	
SC	Diction/Redundancy	127	27	
SC	Diction/Redundancy	141	30	
SC	Diction/Redundancy	146	31	
SC	Diction/Redundancy	180	38	
SC	Diction/Redundancy	182	38	
SC	Diction/Redundancy	186	39	
SC	Diction/Redundancy	200	42	
SC	Diction/Redundancy	225	47	
SC	Diction/Redundancy	237	50	
SC	Idiom	13	4	
SC	Idiom	17	5	
SC	Idiom	29	8	
SC	Idiom	34	9	
SC	Idiom	49	12	
SC	Idiom	64	15	
SC	Idiom	66	15	
SC	Idiom	72	16	
SC	Idiom	75	17	
SC	Idiom	92	20	
SC	Idiom	99	21	
SC	Idiom	102	22	
SC	Idiom	115	25	
SC	Idiom	117	25	
SC	Idiom	124	26	
SC	Idiom	131	28	
SC	Idiom	136	29	
SC	Idiom	140	30	
SC	Idiom	144	31	
SC	Idiom	151	32	
SC	Idiom	153	32	
SC	Idiom	157	33	
SC	Idiom	159	34	
SC	Idiom	161	34	
SC	Idiom	169	36	
SC	Idiom	183	39	
SC	Idiom	185	39	
SC	Idiom	189	40	
SC	Idiom	190	40	
SC	Idiom	192	40	
SC	Idiom	198	42	
SC	Idiom	208	44	
SC	Idiom	213	45	
SC	Idiom	216	46	
SC	Idiom	219	46	
SC	Idiom	222	47	
SC	Idiom	230	48	
SC	Idiom	231	49	
SC	Idiom	241	51	
SC	Idiom	248	52	
SC	Logical Predication	1	2	
SC	Logical Predication	6	3	

Type - Main Category	Concepts - Main Category	Problem No.	Page No.	Notes (In-class / Homework
SC	Logical Predication	8	3	
SC	Logical Predication	9	3	
SC	Logical Predication	25	7	
SC	Logical Predication	32	8	
SC	Logical Predication	36	9	
SC	Logical Predication	50	12	
SC	Logical Predication	52	12	
SC	Logical Predication	58	13	
SC	Logical Predication	67	15	
SC	Logical Predication	69	16	
SC	Logical Predication	85	19	
SC	Logical Predication	110	24	
SC	Logical Predication	113	24	
SC	Logical Predication	121	26	
SC	Logical Predication	137	29	
SC	Logical Predication	172	36	
SC	Logical Predication	173	37	
SC	Logical Predication	175	37	
SC	Logical Predication	191	40	
SC	Logical Predication	203	43	
SC	Logical Predication	209	44	
SC	Logical Predication	212	45	
SC	Logical Predication	215	45	
SC	Logical Predication	218	46	
SC	Logical Predication	232	49	
SC	Logical Predication	234	49	
SC	Logical Predication	245	52	
SC	Logical Predication	247	52	
SC	Parallelism	2	2	
SC	Parallelism	3	2	
SC	Parallelism	5	3	
SC	Parallelism	10	4	
SC	Parallelism	19	5	
SC	Parallelism	20	6	
SC	Parallelism	28	7	
SC	Parallelism	42	10	
SC	Parallelism	45	11	
SC	Parallelism	81	18	
SC	Parallelism	89	19	
SC	Parallelism	104	22	
SC	Parallelism	111	24	
SC	Parallelism	118	25	
SC	Parallelism	119	25	
SC	Parallelism	123	26	
SC	Parallelism	128	27	
SC	Parallelism	139	30	
SC	Parallelism	145	31	
SC	Parallelism	152	32	
SC	Parallelism	163	35	
SC	Parallelism	165	35	
SC	Parallelism	166	35	
SC	Parallelism	167	35	
SC	Parallelism	178	38	
SC	Parallelism	197	42	

Type - Main Category	**Concepts - Main Category**	**Problem No.**	**Page No.**	**Notes (In-class / Homework**
SC	Parallelism	199	42	
SC	Parallelism	224	47	
SC	Parallelism	235	49	
SC	Parallelism	240	50	
SC	Parallelism	242	51	
SC	Parallelism	243	51	
SC	Parallelism	244	51	
SC	Parallelism	246	52	
SC	Parallelism/Idiom	38	9	
SC	Parallelism/Idiom	193	41	
SC	Parallelism/Idiom	221	47	
SC	Parallelism/Idiom	226	48	
SC	Passive Voice	84	18	
SC	Passive Voice	227	48	
SC	Passive Voice	229	48	
SC	Passive Voice	250	53	
SC	Pronoun/Idiom	59	14	
SC	Pronoun/Idiom	95	21	
SC	Pronoun/Idiom	196	41	
SC	Pronoun/Idiom	210	44	
SC	Pronoun/Idiom	228	48	
SC	Pronouns	7	3	
SC	Pronouns	18	5	
SC	Pronouns	39	10	
SC	Pronouns	40	10	
SC	Pronouns	55	13	
SC	Pronouns	56	13	
SC	Pronouns	77	17	
SC	Pronouns	82	18	
SC	Pronouns	91	20	
SC	Pronouns	106	23	
SC	Pronouns	114	24	
SC	Pronouns	125	27	
SC	Pronouns	130	28	
SC	Pronouns	142	30	
SC	Pronouns	158	34	
SC	Pronouns	162	34	
SC	Pronouns	171	36	
SC	Pronouns	177	37	
SC	Pronouns	206	43	
SC	Pronouns	236	50	
SC	Pronouns	238	50	
SC	Pronouns/Parallelism	26	7	
SC	Pronouns/Parallelism	73	16	
SC	Pronouns/Parallelism	93	20	
SC	Pronouns/Parallelism	179	38	
SC	Sentence Construction	27	7	
SC	Sentence Construction	43	10	
SC	Sentence Construction	87	19	
SC	Sentence Construction	134	28	
SC	Sentence Construction	149	32	
SC	Sentence Construction	223	47	
SC	Sentence Construction	239	50	
SC	Usage/Style	12	4	

Type - Main Category	Concepts - Main Category	Problem No.	Page No.	Notes (In-class / Homework
SC	Usage/Style	14	4	
SC	Usage/Style	37	9	
SC	Usage/Style	53	12	
SC	Usage/Style	65	15	
SC	Usage/Style	86	19	
SC	Usage/Style	101	22	
SC	Usage/Style	103	22	
SC	Verb Errors (Number)	16	5	
SC	Verb Errors (Number)	31	8	
SC	Verb Errors (Number)	35	9	
SC	Verb Errors (Number)	41	10	
SC	Verb Errors (Number)	62	14	
SC	Verb Errors (Number)	80	18	
SC	Verb Errors (Number)	194	41	
SC	Verb Errors (Number)	249	53	
SC	Verb Errors (Tense)	15	5	
SC	Verb Errors (Tense)	30	8	
SC	Verb Errors (Tense)	33	8	
SC	Verb Errors (Tense)	46	11	
SC	Verb Errors (Tense)	54	13	
SC	Verb Errors (Tense)	63	14	
SC	Verb Errors (Tense)	76	17	
SC	Verb Errors (Tense)	79	18	
SC	Verb Errors (Tense)	94	20	
SC	Verb Errors (Tense)	96	21	
SC	Verb Errors (Tense)	98	21	
SC	Verb Errors (Tense)	100	22	
SC	Verb Errors (Tense)	109	23	
SC	Verb Errors (Tense)	112	24	
SC	Verb Errors (Tense)	143	30	
SC	Verb Errors (Tense)	147	31	
SC	Verb Errors (Tense)	148	31	
SC	Verb Errors (Tense)	174	37	
SC	Verb Errors (Tense)	176	37	
SC	Verb Errors (Tense)	188	40	
SC	Verb Errors (Tense)	195	41	
SC	Verb Errors (Tense)	201	42	
SC	Verb Errors (Tense)	204	43	
SC	Verb Errors (Tense)	207	44	
SC	Verb Errors (Tense)	233	49	
SC	Verb Errors (Tense)/Idiom	21	6	
SC	Verb Errors (Tense)/Idiom	107	23	
SC	Verb Errors (Tense)/Idiom	133	28	
SC	Verb Errors (Tense)/Idiom	156	33	
SC	Verb Errors (Tense)/Idiom	211	45	
CR	Conclusion	22	61	
CR	Explanation	18	60	
CR	Explanation	40	67	
CR	Flaw	32	64	
CR	Flaw	38	66	
CR	Flaw	52	70	
CR	ID Assumption	13	58	
CR	ID Assumption	21	61	
CR	ID Assumption	23	61	

Type - Main Category	Concepts - Main Category	Problem No.	Page No.	Notes (In-class / Homework
CR	ID Assumption	26	62	
CR	ID Assumption	29	63	
CR	ID Assumption	48	69	
CR	ID Assumption	51	70	
CR	ID Assumption	57	71	
CR	ID Assumption	58	72	
CR	Inference	11	58	
CR	Inference	15	59	
CR	Inference	17	60	
CR	Inference	20	61	
CR	Inference	28	63	
CR	Inference	37	66	
CR	Inference	45	68	
CR	Inference	54	71	
CR	Inference	56	71	
CR	Least Weaken	53	70	
CR	Method of Reasoning	33	65	
CR	Paradox	16	59	
CR	Paradox	55	71	
CR	Plan/Proposal	5	56	
CR	Plan/Proposal	7	56	
CR	Plan/Proposal	10	57	
CR	Plan/Proposal	14	59	
CR	Plan/Proposal	44	68	
CR	Plan/Proposal	47	69	
CR	Strengthen	1	55	
CR	Strengthen	19	60	
CR	Strengthen	24	62	
CR	Strengthen	30	64	
CR	Strengthen	34	65	
CR	Strengthen	39	66	
CR	Weaken	2	55	
CR	Weaken	3	55	
CR	Weaken	4	55	
CR	Weaken	6	56	
CR	Weaken	8	57	
CR	Weaken	9	57	
CR	Weaken	12	58	
CR	Weaken	25	62	
CR	Weaken	27	63	
CR	Weaken	31	64	
CR	Weaken	35	65	
CR	Weaken	36	66	
CR	Weaken	41	67	
CR	Weaken	42	67	
CR	Weaken	43	67	
CR	Weaken	46	68	
CR	Weaken	49	69	
CR	Weaken	50	69	
RC	Detail	P1-3	75	
RC	Detail	P2-1	68	
RC	Detail	P2-3	69	
RC	Detail	P2-4	69	
RC	Detail	P2-8	69	

Type - Main Category	Concepts - Main Category	Problem No.	Page No.	Notes (In-class / Homework
RC	Detail	P3-3	78	
RC	Detail	P3-8	78	
RC	Detail	P4-7	78	
RC	Detail	P5-1	77	
RC	Detail	P5-6	77	
RC	Detail	P7-2	77	
RC	Detail	P7-5	77	
RC	Detail	P9-1	71	
RC	Detail	P9-5	71	
RC	Detail	P9-8	71	
RC	Detail	P10-1	80	
RC	Detail	P10-2	80	
RC	Detail	P10-3	92	
RC	Detail	P10-7	92	
RC	Detail	P11-1	79	
RC	Detail	P11-2	79	
RC	Detail	P11-3	94	
RC	Detail	P12-3	96	
RC	Detail	P12-7	96	
RC	Detail	P13-3	98	
RC	Detail	P13-7	98	
RC	Detail	P13-8	98	
RC	Detail	P14-1	81	
RC	Detail	P14-2	81	
RC	Detail	P14-6	81	
RC	Detail	P14-7	81	
RC	Detail	P15-1	98	
RC	Detail	P15-3	102	
RC	Detail	P16-3	104	
RC	Detail	P16-4	105	
RC	Detail	P16-5	105	
RC	Detail	P17-1	83	
RC	Detail	P17-2	83	
RC	Detail	P17-5	83	
RC	Detail	P18-1	100	
RC	Detail	P18-3	108	
RC	Detail	P18-6	108	
RC	Detail	P19-2	108	
RC	Detail	P20-1	107	
RC	Detail	P20-2	107	
RC	Detail	P20-3	112	
RC	Detail	P20-4	113	
RC	Detail	P20-5	113	
RC	Detail	P20-7	113	
RC	Detail	P21-3	114	
RC	Detail	P22-1	110	
RC	Detail	P22-7	110	
RC	Detail	P23-1	109	
RC	Detail	P23-2	109	
RC	Detail	P23-4	119	
RC	Detail	P23-5	119	
RC	Detail	P23-6	119	
RC	Detail	P24-2	119	
RC	Detail	P24-7	119	

Type - Main Category	Concepts - Main Category	Problem No.	Page No.	Notes (In-class / Homework
RC	Detail	P25-3	120	
RC	Detail	P26-3	121	
RC	Detail	P26-5	121	
RC	Detail	P26-7	121	
RC	Detail	P26-8	121	
RC	Detail	P27-6	121	
RC	Detail	P27-8	121	
RC	Detail	P28-1	121	
RC	Detail	P28-3	122	
RC	Detail	P28-6	122	
RC	Detail	P29-3	123	
RC	Detail	P29-4	123	
RC	Detail	P31-1	124	
RC	Detail	P31-4	124	
RC	Detail	P31-5	124	
RC	Detail	P32-1	125	
RC	Detail	P33-1	126	
RC	Detail	P33-3	127	
RC	Detail	P33-8	140	
RC	Detail	P34-6	140	
RC	Detail	P35-1	141	
RC	Detail	P35-3	142	
RC	Detail	P35-4	142	
RC	Detail	P36-1	143	
RC	Detail	P36-2	143	
RC	Detail	P36-6	143	
RC	Detail	P36-7	143	
RC	Detail	P38-1	144	
RC	Detail	P39-3	145	
RC	Detail	P39-7	145	
RC	Detail	P40-1	146	
RC	Detail	P40-5	146	
RC	Inference	P1-4	75	
RC	Inference	P1-8	75	
RC	Inference	P2-2	75	
RC	Inference	P2-5	75	
RC	Inference	P3-4	79	
RC	Inference	P3-5	79	
RC	Inference	P3-6	79	
RC	Inference	P4-2	79	
RC	Inference	P4-5	79	
RC	Inference	P4-6	79	
RC	Inference	P4-8	79	
RC	Inference	P5-2	79	
RC	Inference	P5-3	80	
RC	Inference	P5-4	80	
RC	Inference	P5-5	80	
RC	Inference	P5-7	80	
RC	Inference	P5-8	80	
RC	Inference	P6-3	84	
RC	Inference	P7-1	81	
RC	Inference	P7-3	86	
RC	Inference	P7-7	86	
RC	Inference	P7-8	86	

Type - Main Category	Concepts - Main Category	Problem No.	Page No.	Notes (In-class / Homework
RC	Inference	P8-1	82	
RC	Inference	P8-2	82	
RC	Inference	P8-5	82	
RC	Inference	P8-6	82	
RC	Inference	P8-8	82	
RC	Inference	P9-2	82	
RC	Inference	P9-4	91	
RC	Inference	P9-7	91	
RC	Inference	P11-4	95	
RC	Inference	P11-6	95	
RC	Inference	P11-7	95	
RC	Inference	P11-8	95	
RC	Inference	P12-1	84	
RC	Inference	P12-5	84	
RC	Inference	P12-6	84	
RC	Inference	P12-8	84	
RC	Inference	P13-1	97	
RC	Inference	P13-4	99	
RC	Inference	P14-3	100	
RC	Inference	P14-5	100	
RC	Inference	P14-8	100	
RC	Inference	P15-4	103	
RC	Inference	P15-5	103	
RC	Inference	P15-6	103	
RC	Inference	P17-3	106	
RC	Inference	P17-6	106	
RC	Inference	P17-7	106	
RC	Inference	P18-5	106	
RC	Inference	P18-7	106	
RC	Inference	P18-8	106	
RC	Inference	P19-1	105	
RC	Inference	P19-5	105	
RC	Inference	P19-7	105	
RC	Inference	P20-6	105	
RC	Inference	P21-2	105	
RC	Inference	P21-5	105	
RC	Inference	P21-6	105	
RC	Inference	P21-7	105	
RC	Inference	P22-4	105	
RC	Inference	P23-3	118	
RC	Inference	P23-7	118	
RC	Inference	P23-8	118	
RC	Inference	P24-3	119	
RC	Inference	P24-5	119	
RC	Inference	P24-6	119	
RC	Inference	P24-8	119	
RC	Inference	P25-4	119	
RC	Inference	P25-5	119	
RC	Inference	P25-6	119	
RC	Inference	P25-7	119	
RC	Inference	P25-8	119	
RC	Inference	P26-2	119	
RC	Inference	P27-1	121	
RC	Inference	P27-2	121	

Type - Main Category	Concepts - Main Category	Problem No.	Page No.	Notes (In-class / Homework
RC	Inference	P27-3	122	
RC	Inference	P28-2	122	
RC	Inference	P28-4	122	
RC	Inference	P28-5	122	
RC	Inference	P28-7	122	
RC	Inference	P29-7	122	
RC	Inference	P30-2	122	
RC	Inference	P30-3	123	
RC	Inference	P30-5	123	
RC	Inference	P31-8	123	
RC	Inference	P32-2	123	
RC	Inference	P32-7	123	
RC	Inference	P32-8	123	
RC	Inference	P33-2	123	
RC	Inference	P33-5	123	
RC	Inference	P33-6	123	
RC	Inference	P34-4	123	
RC	Inference	P35-2	123	
RC	Inference	P35-5	123	
RC	Inference	P35-6	123	
RC	Inference	P35-7	123	
RC	Inference	P35-8	123	
RC	Inference	P36-3	124	
RC	Inference	P36-4	124	
RC	Inference	P36-8	124	
RC	Inference	P37-2	124	
RC	Inference	P37-3	125	
RC	Inference	P38-2	125	
RC	Inference	P38-4	125	
RC	Inference	P38-5	125	
RC	Inference	P38-6	125	
RC	Inference	P38-8	125	
RC	Inference	P39-4	125	
RC	Inference	P39-6	125	
RC	Inference	P39-8	125	
RC	Inference	P40-3	126	
RC	Inference	P40-7	156	
RC	Inference	P40-8	156	
RC	Inference/Author Agreement	P1-5	75	
RC	Inference/Author Agreement	P2-7	75	
RC	Inference/Author Agreement	P3-7	75	
RC	Inference/Author Agreement	P4-3	76	
RC	Inference/Author Agreement	P4-4	76	
RC	Inference/Author Agreement	P6-6	76	
RC	Inference/Author Agreement	P6-8	76	
RC	Inference/Author Agreement	P10-5	76	
RC	Inference/Author Agreement	P12-4	97	
RC	Inference/Author Agreement	P13-2	97	
RC	Inference/Author Agreement	P13-5	97	
RC	Inference/Author Agreement	P15-2	97	
RC	Inference/Author Agreement	P16-7	97	
RC	Inference/Author Agreement	P18-4	109	
RC	Inference/Author Agreement	P19-6	109	
RC	Inference/Author Agreement	P20-8	109	

Type - Main Category	Concepts - Main Category	Problem No.	Page No.	Notes (In-class / Homework
RC	Inference/Author Agreement	P22-2	109	
RC	Inference/Author Agreement	P24-1	99	
RC	Inference/Author Agreement	P24-4	99	
RC	Inference/Author Agreement	P25-2	99	
RC	Inference/Author Agreement	P26-4	99	
RC	Inference/Author Agreement	P26-6	99	
RC	Inference/Author Agreement	P27-5	99	
RC	Inference/Author Agreement	P29-2	99	
RC	Inference/Author Agreement	P30-4	99	
RC	Inference/Author Agreement	P32-6	99	
RC	Inference/Author Agreement	P33-7	99	
RC	Inference/Author Agreement	P34-2	99	
RC	Inference/Author Agreement	P34-7	99	
RC	Inference/Author Agreement	P36-5	99	
RC	Inference/Author Agreement	P38-3	100	
RC	Inference/Author Agreement	P38-7	100	
RC	Inference/Author Agreement	P39-1	101	
RC	Inference/Author Agreement	P39-2	101	
RC	Logical Structure	P1-6	75	
RC	Logical Structure	P3-1	101	
RC	Logical Structure	P6-2	101	
RC	Logical Structure	P6-4	85	
RC	Logical Structure	P7-4	87	
RC	Logical Structure	P8-3	88	
RC	Logical Structure	P8-4	89	
RC	Logical Structure	P8-7	89	
RC	Logical Structure	P10-6	89	
RC	Logical Structure	P10-8	89	
RC	Logical Structure	P12-2	89	
RC	Logical Structure	P16-2	89	
RC	Logical Structure	P16-8	89	
RC	Logical Structure	P18-2	89	
RC	Logical Structure	P19-8	89	
RC	Logical Structure	P21-8	89	
RC	Logical Structure	P22-6	89	
RC	Logical Structure	P22-8	89	
RC	Logical Structure	P27-7	89	
RC	Logical Structure	P28-8	89	
RC	Logical Structure	P29-5	89	
RC	Logical Structure	P29-6	89	
RC	Logical Structure	P31-6	89	
RC	Logical Structure	P32-3	90	
RC	Logical Structure	P32-4	90	
RC	Logical Structure	P33-4	90	
RC	Logical Structure	P34-3	91	
RC	Logical Structure	P37-4	91	
RC	Logical Structure	P37-8	91	
RC	Logical Structure	P39-5	91	
RC	Logical Structure/Analogy	P2-6	91	
RC	Logical Structure/Analogy	P3-2	91	
RC	Logical Structure/Analogy	P9-3	90	
RC	Logical Structure/Analogy	P17-4	107	
RC	Logical Structure/Analogy	P21-4	107	
RC	Logical Structure/Analogy	P25-1	93	

Type - Main Category	Concepts - Main Category	Problem No.	Page No.	Notes (In-class / Homework
RC	Logical Structure/Analogy	P27-4	93	
RC	Logical Structure/Analogy	P31-7	93	
RC	Logical Structure/Analogy	P34-1	94	
RC	Logical Structure/Analogy	P40-2	94	
RC	Logical Structure/Assumption	P1-7	75	
RC	Logical Structure/Assumption	P7-6	75	
RC	Logical Structure/Assumption	P14-4	101	
RC	Logical Structure/Assumption	P19-3	110	
RC	Logical Structure/Assumption	P22-5	110	
RC	Logical Structure/Assumption	P32-5	110	
RC	Logical Structure/Assumption	P37-5	110	
RC	Logical Structure/Inference	P31-3	111	
RC	Logical Structure/Strengthen	P6-7	111	
RC	Logical Structure/Strengthen	P22-3	112	
RC	Logical Structure/Strengthen	P37-7	112	
RC	Logical Structure/Weaken	P17-8	112	
RC	Logical Structure/Weaken	P37-6	112	
RC	Main Idea	P1-1	74	
RC	Main Idea	P1-2	74	
RC	Main Idea	P4-1	113	
RC	Main Idea	P6-1	113	
RC	Main Idea	P6-5	113	
RC	Main Idea	P9-6	113	
RC	Main Idea	P10-4	93	
RC	Main Idea	P11-5	93	
RC	Main Idea	P13-6	93	
RC	Main Idea	P15-7	93	
RC	Main Idea	P15-8	93	
RC	Main Idea	P16-1	115	
RC	Main Idea	P16-6	115	
RC	Main Idea	P19-4	111	
RC	Main Idea	P21-1	95	
RC	Main Idea	P26-1	95	
RC	Main Idea	P29-1	95	
RC	Main Idea	P29-8	95	
RC	Main Idea	P30-1	95	
RC	Main Idea	P31-2	95	
RC	Main Idea	P34-5	95	
RC	Main Idea	P34-8	143	
RC	Main Idea	P37-1	144	
RC	Main Idea	P40-4	144	
RC	Main Idea	P40-6	144	

10.2 By Question Number Sequence

All Verbal Questions – MR Verbal Training Sets

Note: CR – Critical Reasoning; RC – Reading Comprehension; SC – Sentence Correction; MR – Manhattan Review

Type - Main Category	Concepts - Main Category	Problem No.	Page No.	Notes (In-class / Homework
SC	Logical Predication	1	2	
SC	Parallelism	2	2	
SC	Parallelism	3	2	
SC	Agreement	4	2	
SC	Parallelism	5	3	
SC	Logical Predication	6	3	
SC	Pronouns	7	3	
SC	Logical Predication	8	3	
SC	Logical Predication	9	3	
SC	Parallelism	10	4	
SC	Comparisons	11	4	
SC	Usage/Style	12	4	
SC	Idiom	13	4	
SC	Usage/Style	14	4	
SC	Verb Errors (Tense)	15	5	
SC	Verb Errors (Number)	16	5	
SC	Idiom	17	5	
SC	Pronouns	18	5	
SC	Parallelism	19	5	
SC	Parallelism	20	6	
SC	Verb Errors (Tense)/Idiom	21	6	
SC	Diction/Redundancy	22	6	
SC	Comparisons	23	6	
SC	Comparisons	24	6	
SC	Logical Predication	25	7	
SC	Pronouns/Parallelism	26	7	
SC	Sentence Construction	27	7	
SC	Parallelism	28	7	
SC	Idiom	29	8	
SC	Verb Errors (Tense)	30	8	
SC	Verb Errors (Number)	31	8	
SC	Logical Predication	32	8	
SC	Verb Errors (Tense)	33	8	
SC	Idiom	34	9	
SC	Verb Errors (Number)	35	9	
SC	Logical Predication	36	9	
SC	Usage/Style	37	9	
SC	Parallelism/Idiom	38	9	
SC	Pronouns	39	10	
SC	Pronouns	40	10	
SC	Verb Errors (Number)	41	10	
SC	Parallelism	42	10	
SC	Sentence Construction	43	10	
SC	Agreement	44	11	

Type - Main Category	Concepts - Main Category	Problem No.	Page No.	Notes (In-class / Homework
SC	Parallelism	45	11	
SC	Verb Errors (Tense)	46	11	
SC	Comparisons	47	11	
SC	Agreement	48	11	
SC	Idiom	49	12	
SC	Logical Predication	50	12	
SC	Diction	51	12	
SC	Logical Predication	52	12	
SC	Usage/Style	53	12	
SC	Verb Errors (Tense)	54	13	
SC	Pronouns	55	13	
SC	Pronouns	56	13	
SC	Comparisons	57	13	
SC	Logical Predication	58	13	
SC	Pronoun/Idiom	59	14	
SC	Diction	60	14	
SC	Diction	61	14	
SC	Verb Errors (Number)	62	14	
SC	Verb Errors (Tense)	63	14	
SC	Idiom	64	15	
SC	Usage/Style	65	15	
SC	Idiom	66	15	
SC	Logical Predication	67	15	
SC	Comparisons	68	15	
SC	Logical Predication	69	16	
SC	Agreement	70	16	
SC	Agreement	71	16	
SC	Idiom	72	16	
SC	Pronouns/Parallelism	73	16	
SC	Agreement	74	17	
SC	Idiom	75	17	
SC	Verb Errors (Tense)	76	17	
SC	Pronouns	77	17	
SC	Diction/Redundancy	78	17	
SC	Verb Errors (Tense)	79	18	
SC	Verb Errors (Number)	80	18	
SC	Parallelism	81	18	
SC	Pronouns	82	18	
SC	Comparisons	83	18	
SC	Passive Voice	84	18	
SC	Logical Predication	85	19	
SC	Usage/Style	86	19	
SC	Sentence Construction	87	19	
SC	Agreement/Idiom	88	19	
SC	Parallelism	89	19	
SC	Comparisons	90	20	
SC	Pronouns	91	20	
SC	Idiom	92	20	
SC	Pronouns/Parallelism	93	20	
SC	Verb Errors (Tense)	94	20	
SC	Pronoun/Idiom	95	21	
SC	Verb Errors (Tense)	96	21	
SC	Comparisons	97	21	
SC	Verb Errors (Tense)	98	21	

Type - Main Category	Concepts - Main Category	Problem No.	Page No.	Notes (In-class / Homework
SC	Idiom	99	21	
SC	Verb Errors (Tense)	100	22	
SC	Usage/Style	101	22	
SC	Idiom	102	22	
SC	Usage/Style	103	22	
SC	Parallelism	104	22	
SC	Comparisons	105	23	
SC	Pronouns	106	23	
SC	Verb Errors (Tense)/Idiom	107	23	
SC	Diction/Redundancy	108	23	
SC	Verb Errors (Tense)	109	23	
SC	Logical Predication	110	24	
SC	Parallelism	111	24	
SC	Verb Errors (Tense)	112	24	
SC	Logical Predication	113	24	
SC	Pronouns	114	24	
SC	Idiom	115	25	
SC	Agreement	116	25	
SC	Idiom	117	25	
SC	Parallelism	118	25	
SC	Parallelism	119	25	
SC	Agreement	120	26	
SC	Logical Predication	121	26	
SC	Diction/Redundancy	122	26	
SC	Parallelism	123	26	
SC	Idiom	124	26	
SC	Pronouns	125	27	
SC	Agreement	126	27	
SC	Diction/Redundancy	127	27	
SC	Parallelism	128	27	
SC	Comparisons	129	27	
SC	Pronouns	130	28	
SC	Idiom	131	28	
SC	Agreement	132	28	
SC	Verb Errors (Tense)/Idiom	133	28	
SC	Sentence Construction	134	28	
SC	Agreement	135	29	
SC	Idiom	136	29	
SC	Logical Predication	137	29	
SC	Agreement	138	29	
SC	Parallelism	139	30	
SC	Idiom	140	30	
SC	Diction/Redundancy	141	30	
SC	Pronouns	142	30	
SC	Verb Errors (Tense)	143	30	
SC	Idiom	144	31	
SC	Parallelism	145	31	
SC	Diction/Redundancy	146	31	
SC	Verb Errors (Tense)	147	31	
SC	Verb Errors (Tense)	148	31	
SC	Sentence Construction	149	32	
SC	Comparisons	150	32	
SC	Idiom	151	32	

Type - Main Category	Concepts - Main Category	Problem No.	Page No.	Notes (In-class / Homework
SC	Parallelism	152	32	
SC	Idiom	153	32	
SC	Diction	154	33	
SC	Agreement	155	33	
SC	Verb Errors (Tense)/Idiom	156	33	
SC	Idiom	157	33	
SC	Pronouns	158	34	
SC	Idiom	159	34	
SC	Diction	160	34	
SC	Idiom	161	34	
SC	Pronouns	162	34	
SC	Parallelism	163	35	
SC	Comparisons	164	35	
SC	Parallelism	165	35	
SC	Parallelism	166	35	
SC	Parallelism	167	35	
SC	Agreement	168	36	
SC	Idiom	169	36	
SC	Comparisons	170	36	
SC	Pronouns	171	36	
SC	Logical Predication	172	36	
SC	Logical Predication	173	37	
SC	Verb Errors (Tense)	174	37	
SC	Logical Predication	175	37	
SC	Verb Errors (Tense)	176	37	
SC	Pronouns	177	37	
SC	Parallelism	178	38	
SC	Pronouns/Parallelism	179	38	
SC	Diction/Redundancy	180	38	
SC	Agreement	181	38	
SC	Diction/Redundancy	182	38	
SC	Idiom	183	39	
SC	Comparisons	184	39	
SC	Idiom	185	39	
SC	Diction/Redundancy	186	39	
SC	Diction	187	39	
SC	Verb Errors (Tense)	188	40	
SC	Idiom	189	40	
SC	Idiom	190	40	
SC	Logical Predication	191	40	
SC	Idiom	192	40	
SC	Parallelism/Idiom	193	41	
SC	Verb Errors (Number)	194	41	
SC	Verb Errors (Tense)	195	41	
SC	Pronoun/Idiom	196	41	
SC	Parallelism	197	42	
SC	Idiom	198	42	
SC	Parallelism	199	42	
SC	Diction/Redundancy	200	42	
SC	Verb Errors (Tense)	201	42	
SC	Diction	202	43	
SC	Logical Predication	203	43	
SC	Verb Errors (Tense)	204	43	

Type - Main Category	Concepts - Main Category	Problem No.	Page No.	Notes (In-class / Homework
SC	Agreement	205	43	
SC	Pronouns	206	43	
SC	Verb Errors (Tense)	207	44	
SC	Idiom	208	44	
SC	Logical Predication	209	44	
SC	Pronoun/Idiom	210	44	
SC	Verb Errors (Tense)/Idiom	211	45	
SC	Logical Predication	212	45	
SC	Idiom	213	45	
SC	Agreement	214	45	
SC	Logical Predication	215	45	
SC	Idiom	216	46	
SC	Comparisons	217	46	
SC	Logical Predication	218	46	
SC	Idiom	219	46	
SC	Agreement	220	46	
SC	Parallelism/Idiom	221	47	
SC	Idiom	222	47	
SC	Sentence Construction	223	47	
SC	Parallelism	224	47	
SC	Diction/Redundancy	225	47	
SC	Parallelism/Idiom	226	48	
SC	Passive Voice	227	48	
SC	Pronoun/Idiom	228	48	
SC	Passive Voice	229	48	
SC	Idiom	230	48	
SC	Idiom	231	49	
SC	Logical Predication	232	49	
SC	Verb Errors (Tense)	233	49	
SC	Logical Predication	234	49	
SC	Parallelism	235	49	
SC	Pronouns	236	50	
SC	Diction/Redundancy	237	50	
SC	Pronouns	238	50	
SC	Sentence Construction	239	50	
SC	Parallelism	240	50	
SC	Idiom	241	51	
SC	Parallelism	242	51	
SC	Parallelism	243	51	
SC	Parallelism	244	51	
SC	Logical Predication	245	52	
SC	Parallelism	246	52	
SC	Logical Predication	247	52	
SC	Idiom	248	52	
SC	Verb Errors (Number)	249	53	
SC	Passive Voice	250	53	
CR	Strengthen	1	55	
CR	Weaken	2	55	
CR	Weaken	3	55	
CR	Weaken	4	55	
CR	Plan/Proposal	5	56	
CR	Weaken	6	56	
CR	Plan/Proposal	7	56	

Type - Main Category	Concepts - Main Category	Problem No.	Page No.	Notes (In-class / Homework
CR	Weaken	8	57	
CR	Weaken	9	57	
CR	Plan/Proposal	10	57	
CR	Inference	11	58	
CR	Weaken	12	58	
CR	ID Assumption	13	58	
CR	Plan/Proposal	14	59	
CR	Inference	15	59	
CR	Paradox	16	59	
CR	Inference	17	60	
CR	Explanation	18	60	
CR	Strengthen	19	60	
CR	Inference	20	61	
CR	ID Assumption	21	61	
CR	Conclusion	22	61	
CR	ID Assumption	23	61	
CR	Strengthen	24	62	
CR	Weaken	25	62	
CR	ID Assumption	26	62	
CR	Weaken	27	63	
CR	Inference	28	63	
CR	ID Assumption	29	63	
CR	Strengthen	30	64	
CR	Weaken	31	64	
CR	Flaw	32	64	
CR	Method of Reasoning	33	65	
CR	Strengthen	34	65	
CR	Weaken	35	65	
CR	Weaken	36	66	
CR	Inference	37	66	
CR	Flaw	38	66	
CR	Strengthen	39	66	
CR	Explanation	40	67	
CR	Weaken	41	67	
CR	Weaken	42	67	
CR	Weaken	43	67	
CR	Plan/Proposal	44	68	
CR	Inference	45	68	
CR	Weaken	46	68	
CR	Plan/Proposal	47	69	
CR	ID Assumption	48	69	
CR	Wcaken	49	69	
CR	Weaken	50	69	
CR	ID Assumption	51	70	
CR	Flaw	52	70	
CR	Least Weaken	53	70	
CR	Inference	54	71	
CR	Paradox	55	71	
CR	Inference	56	71	
CR	ID Assumption	57	71	
CR	ID Assumption	58	72	
RC	Main Idea	P1-1	74	
RC	Main Idea	P1-2	74	

Type - Main Category	Concepts - Main Category	Problem No.	Page No.	Notes (In-class / Homework
RC	Detail	P1-3	75	
RC	Inference	P1-4	75	
RC	Inference/Author Agreement	P1-5	75	
RC	Logical Structure	P1-6	75	
RC	Logical Structure/Assumption	P1-7	75	
RC	Inference	P1-8	75	
RC	Detail	P2-1	76	
RC	Inference	P2-2	76	
RC	Detail	P2-3	77	
RC	Detail	P2-4	77	
RC	Inference	P2-5	77	
RC	Logical Structure/Analogy	P2-6	77	
RC	Inference/Author Agreement	P2-7	77	
RC	Detail	P2-8	77	
RC	Logical Structure	P3-1	78	
RC	Logical Structure/Analogy	P3-2	78	
RC	Detail	P3-3	78	
RC	Inference	P3-4	79	
RC	Inference	P3-5	79	
RC	Inference	P3-6	79	
RC	Inference/Author Agreement	P3-7	79	
RC	Detail	P3-8	79	
RC	Main Idea	P4-1	80	
RC	Inference	P4-2	80	
RC	Inference/Author Agreement	P4-3	81	
RC	Inference/Author Agreement	P4-4	81	
RC	Inference	P4-5	81	
RC	Inference	P4-6	81	
RC	Detail	P4-7	81	
RC	Inference	P4-8	81	
RC	Detail	P5-1	82	
RC	Inference	P5-2	82	
RC	Inference	P5-3	83	
RC	Inference	P5-4	83	
RC	Inference	P5-5	83	
RC	Detail	P5-6	83	
RC	Inference	P5-7	83	
RC	Inference	P5-8	83	
RC	Main Idea	P6-1	84	
RC	Logical Structure	P6-2	84	
RC	Inference	P6-3	84	
RC	Logical Structure	P6-4	85	
RC	Main Idea	P6-5	85	
RC	Inference/Author Agreement	P6-6	85	
RC	Logical Structure/Strengthen	P6-7	85	
RC	Inference/Author Agreement	P6-8	85	
RC	Inference	P7-1	86	
RC	Detail	P7-2	86	
RC	Inference	P7-3	86	
RC	Logical Structure	P7-4	87	
RC	Detail	P7-5	87	
RC	Logical Structure/Assumption	P7-6	87	
RC	Inference	P7-7	87	
RC	Inference	P7-8	87	

Type - Main Category	Concepts - Main Category	Problem No.	Page No.	Notes (In-class / Homework
RC	Inference	P8-1	88	
RC	Inference	P8-2	88	
RC	Logical Structure	P8-3	88	
RC	Logical Structure	P8-4	89	
RC	Inference	P8-5	89	
RC	Inference	P8-6	89	
RC	Logical Structure	P8-7	89	
RC	Inference	P8-8	89	
RC	Detail	P9-1	90	
RC	Inference	P9-2	90	
RC	Logical Structure/Analogy	P9-3	90	
RC	Inference	P9-4	91	
RC	Detail	P9-5	91	
RC	Main Idea	P9-6	91	
RC	Inference	P9-7	91	
RC	Detail	P9-8	91	
RC	Detail	P10-1	92	
RC	Detail	P10-2	92	
RC	Detail	P10-3	92	
RC	Main Idea	P10-4	93	
RC	Inference/Author Agreement	P10-5	93	
RC	Logical Structure	P10-6	93	
RC	Detail	P10-7	93	
RC	Logical Structure	P10-8	93	
RC	Detail	P11-1	94	
RC	Detail	P11-2	94	
RC	Detail	P11-3	94	
RC	Inference	P11-4	95	
RC	Main Idea	P11-5	95	
RC	Inference	P11-6	95	
RC	Inference	P11-7	95	
RC	Inference	P11-8	95	
RC	Inference	P12-1	96	
RC	Logical Structure	P12-2	96	
RC	Detail	P12-3	96	
RC	Inference/Author Agreement	P12-4	97	
RC	Inference	P12-5	97	
RC	Inference	P12-6	97	
RC	Detail	P12-7	97	
RC	Inference	P12-8	97	
RC	Inference	P13-1	98	
RC	Inference/Author Agreement	P13-2	98	
RC	Detail	P13-3	98	
RC	Inference	P13-4	99	
RC	Inference/Author Agreement	P13-5	99	
RC	Main Idea	P13-6	99	
RC	Detail	P13-7	99	
RC	Detail	P13-8	99	
RC	Detail	P14-1	100	
RC	Detail	P14-2	100	
RC	Inference	P14-3	100	
RC	Logical Structure/Assumption	P14-4	101	
RC	Inference	P14-5	101	
RC	Detail	P14-6	101	

Type - Main Category	Concepts - Main Category	Problem No.	Page No.	Notes (In-class / Homework
RC	Detail	P14-7	101	
RC	Inference	P14-8	101	
RC	Detail	P15-1	102	
RC	Inference/Author Agreement	P15-2	102	
RC	Detail	P15-3	102	
RC	Inference	P15-4	103	
RC	Inference	P15-5	103	
RC	Inference	P15-6	103	
RC	Main Idea	P15-7	103	
RC	Main Idea	P15-8	103	
RC	Main Idea	P16-1	104	
RC	Logical Structure	P16-2	104	
RC	Detail	P16-3	104	
RC	Detail	P16-4	105	
RC	Detail	P16-5	105	
RC	Main Idea	P16-6	105	
RC	Inference/Author Agreement	P16-7	105	
RC	Logical Structure	P16-8	105	
RC	Detail	P17-1	106	
RC	Detail	P17-2	106	
RC	Inference	P17-3	106	
RC	Logical Structure/Analogy	P17-4	107	
RC	Detail	P17-5	107	
RC	Inference	P17-6	107	
RC	Inference	P17-7	107	
RC	Logical Structure/Weaken	P17-8	107	
RC	Detail	P18-1	108	
RC	Logical Structure	P18-2	108	
RC	Detail	P18-3	108	
RC	Inference/Author Agreement	P18-4	109	
RC	Inference	P18-5	109	
RC	Detail	P18-6	109	
RC	Inference	P18-7	109	
RC	Inference	P18-8	109	
RC	Inference	P19-1	110	
RC	Detail	P19-2	110	
RC	Logical Structure/Assumption	P19-3	110	
RC	Main Idea	P19-4	111	
RC	Inference	P19-5	111	
RC	Inference/Author Agreement	P19-6	111	
RC	Inference	P19-7	111	
RC	Logical Structure	P19-8	111	
RC	Detail	P20-1	112	
RC	Detail	P20-2	112	
RC	Detail	P20-3	112	
RC	Detail	P20-4	113	
RC	Detail	P20-5	113	
RC	Inference	P20-6	113	
RC	Detail	P20-7	113	
RC	Inference/Author Agreement	P20-8	113	
RC	Main Idea	P21-1	114	
RC	Inference	P21-2	114	
RC	Detail	P21-3	115	
RC	Logical Structure/Analogy	P21-4	115	

Type - Main Category	Concepts - Main Category	Problem No.	Page No.	Notes (In-class / Homework
RC	Inference	P21-5	115	
RC	Inference	P21-6	115	
RC	Inference	P21-7	115	
RC	Logical Structure	P21-8	115	
RC	Detail	P22-1	116	
RC	Inference/Author Agreement	P22-2	116	
RC	Logical Structure/Strengthen	P22-3	117	
RC	Inference	P22-4	117	
RC	Logical Structure/Assumption	P22-5	117	
RC	Logical Structure	P22-6	117	
RC	Detail	P22-7	117	
RC	Logical Structure	P22-8	117	
RC	Detail	P23-1	118	
RC	Detail	P23-2	118	
RC	Inference	P23-3	118	
RC	Detail	P23-4	119	
RC	Detail	P23-5	119	
RC	Detail	P23-6	119	
RC	Inference	P23-7	119	
RC	Inference	P23-8	119	
RC	Inference/Author Agreement	P24-1	120	
RC	Detail	P24-2	120	
RC	Inference	P24-3	121	
RC	Inference/Author Agreement	P24-4	121	
RC	Inference	P24-5	121	
RC	Inference	P24-6	121	
RC	Detail	P24-7	121	
RC	Inference	P24-8	121	
RC	Logical Structure/Analogy	P25-1	122	
RC	Inference/Author Agreement	P25-2	122	
RC	Detail	P25-3	123	
RC	Inference	P25-4	123	
RC	Inference	P25-5	123	
RC	Inference	P25-6	123	
RC	Inference	P25-7	123	
RC	Inference	P25-8	123	
RC	Main Idea	P26-1	124	
RC	Inference	P26-2	124	
RC	Detail	P26-3	125	
RC	Inference/Author Agreement	P26-4	125	
RC	Detail	P26-5	125	
RC	Inference/Author Agreement	P26-6	125	
RC	Detail	P26-7	125	
RC	Detail	P26-8	125	
RC	Inference	P27-1	126	
RC	Inference	P27-2	126	
RC	Inference	P27-3	127	
RC	Logical Structure/Analogy	P27-4	127	
RC	Inference/Author Agreement	P27-5	127	
RC	Detail	P27-6	127	
RC	Logical Structure	P27-7	127	
RC	Detail	P27-8	127	
RC	Detail	P28-1	128	
RC	Inference	P28-2	128	

Type - Main Category	Concepts - Main Category	Problem No.	Page No.	Notes (In-class / Homework
RC	Detail	P28-3	129	
RC	Inference	P28-4	129	
RC	Inference	P28-5	129	
RC	Detail	P28-6	129	
RC	Inference	P28-7	129	
RC	Logical Structure	P28-8	129	
RC	Main Idea	P29-1	130	
RC	Inference/Author Agreement	P29-2	130	
RC	Detail	P29-3	131	
RC	Detail	P29-4	131	
RC	Logical Structure	P29-5	131	
RC	Logical Structure	P29-6	131	
RC	Inference	P29-7	131	
RC	Main Idea	P29-8	131	
RC	Main Idea	P30-1	132	
RC	Inference	P30-2	132	
RC	Inference	P30-3	133	
RC	Inference/Author Agreement	P30-4	133	
RC	Inference	P30-5	133	
RC	Detail	P31-1	134	
RC	Main Idea	P31-2	134	
RC	Logical Structure/Inference	P31-3	135	
RC	Detail	P31-4	135	
RC	Detail	P31-5	135	
RC	Logical Structure	P31-6	135	
RC	Logical Structure/Analogy	P31-7	135	
RC	Inference	P31-8	135	
RC	Detail	P32-1	136	
RC	Inference	P32-2	136	
RC	Logical Structure	P32-3	137	
RC	Logical Structure	P32-4	137	
RC	Logical Structure/Assumption	P32-5	137	
RC	Inference/Author Agreement	P32-6	137	
RC	Inference	P32-7	137	
RC	Inference	P32-8	137	
RC	Detail	P33-1	138	
RC	Inference	P33-2	138	
RC	Detail	P33-3	139	
RC	Logical Structure	P33-4	139	
RC	Inference	P33-5	139	
RC	Inference	P33-6	139	
RC	Inference/Author Agreement	P33-7	139	
RC	Detail	P33-8	140	
RC	Logical Structure/Analogy	P34-1	141	
RC	Inference/Author Agreement	P34-2	141	
RC	Logical Structure	P34-3	142	
RC	Inference	P34-4	142	
RC	Main Idea	P34-5	142	
RC	Detail	P34-6	142	
RC	Inference/Author Agreement	P34-7	142	
RC	Main Idea	P34-8	143	
RC	Detail	P35-1	144	
RC	Inference	P35-2	144	
RC	Detail	P35-3	145	

Type - Main Category	Concepts - Main Category	Problem No.	Page No.	Notes (In-class / Homework
RC	Detail	P35-4	145	
RC	Inference	P35-5	145	
RC	Inference	P35-6	145	
RC	Inference	P35-7	145	
RC	Inference	P35-8	145	
RC	Detail	P36-1	146	
RC	Detail	P36-2	146	
RC	Inference	P36-3	147	
RC	Inference	P36-4	147	
RC	Inference/Author Agreement	P36-5	147	
RC	Detail	P36-6	147	
RC	Detail	P36-7	147	
RC	Inference	P36-8	147	
RC	Main Idea	P37-1	148	
RC	Inference	P37-2	148	
RC	Inference	P37-3	149	
RC	Logical Structure	P37-4	149	
RC	Logical Structure/Assumption	P37-5	149	
RC	Logical Structure/Weaken	P37-6	149	
RC	Logical Structure/Strengthen	P37-7	149	
RC	Logical Structure	P37-8	149	
RC	Detail	P38-1	150	
RC	Inference	P38-2	150	
RC	Inference/Author Agreement	P38-3	151	
RC	Inference	P38-4	151	
RC	Inference	P38-5	151	
RC	Inference	P38-6	151	
RC	Inference/Author Agreement	P38-7	151	
RC	Inference	P38-8	151	
RC	Inference/Author Agreement	P39-1	152	
RC	Inference/Author Agreement	P39-2	152	
RC	Detail	P39-3	153	
RC	Inference	P39-4	153	
RC	Logical Structure	P39-5	153	
RC	Inference	P39-6	153	
RC	Detail	P39-7	153	
RC	Inference	P39-8	153	
RC	Detail	P40-1	154	
RC	Logical Structure/Analogy	P40-2	154	
RC	Inference	P40-3	155	
RC	Main Idea	P40-4	155	
RC	Detail	P40-5	155	
RC	Main Idea	P40-6	155	
RC	Inference	P40-7	156	
RC	Inference	P40-8	156	

Chapter 11

Evaluation Form

Student Course Feedback Form

(Instructor: Please ask a student volunteer to collect all feedback forms and place them in the envelope provided.)
(Students: For additional compliments or concerns, please feel free to email us directly.)

Salutation: Mr.   Ms.   Mrs.   Dr.   First Name _____   Last Name _____

Company Name: _____   Your Email Address: _____

School Name: _____   Degree: _____

Major(s): _____   Graduation Date: _____

Country of Origin: _____   Native Language: _____

Other Languages (by Descending Order of Fluency Level): _____

Did you travel from a different country to this course?   Yes (Name of Country _____)   No

Please circle your method of transportation: Flight   Train   Car   Local Transit   (Departure City: _____)

Course Information

Course Date(s): _____   Course Location: _____   Name of Instructor: _____

General Feedback

1. What are your major likes about the course and the instructor?

2. Do you have any suggestions for the instructor and on the course? (We value your comments greatly and will do our best to incorporate your comments into our future course.)

3. Do you think this course is helpful for your academic and professional development? Please be specific.

4. Why did you choose to take this course? Were your goals accomplished?

Course Feedback

How would you rate this course overall? (Please circle)
(Poor)   1   2   3   4   5   (Excellent)

Did you feel the course/service adequately covered all the topics/material?
Yes   No

How would you rate the quality of course material?
(Poor)   1   2   3   4   5   (Excellent)
Additional Comments:

Did you feel adequate time was allocated to each topic?
(Poor)   1   2   3   4   5   (Excellent)
Additional Comments:

Did anything in the course stand out as particularly helpful?

How would you rate our administrative support?
(Poor)   1   2   3   4   5   (Excellent)
Additional Comments:

Have you previously taken a similar course? If so, which one and when and where?

How likely will you recommend this course to others?
(Unlikely)   1   2   3   4   5   (Highly recommend)

About Instructor

How would you rate your instructor overall?
(Poor)   1   2   3   4   5   (Excellent)
Additional Comments:

How would you rate your instructor in the following particular areas?

Clarity:	(Poor) 1 2 3 4 5	(Excellent)
Speaking Volume:	(Poor) 1 2 3 4 5	(Excellent)
Teaching Ability:	(Poor) 1 2 3 4 5	(Excellent)
Preparedness:	(Poor) 1 2 3 4 5	(Excellent)
Knowledge of Subjects:	(Poor) 1 2 3 4 5	(Excellent)
Responsiveness to Questions:	(Poor) 1 2 3 4 5	(Excellent)
Accuracy:	(Poor) 1 2 3 4 5	(Excellent)
Facilitation of Discussion:	(Poor) 1 2 3 4 5	(Excellent)

Reference Matters

Please circle all the sources from which you heard about us.

Direct Emails	Friends & Colleagues	Magazine & Newspaper Ad
MBA Fairs	Online Search (Please Specify Search Engine) _____	
Online Ad (Websites) _____	Other (Please Specify) _____	

Please list specific private tutoring subject(s) if you need any additional one-on-one training.

Please circle all other Career Training Course(s) you are or might be interested in.

Basic & Business Chinese	Business English	Capital Markets & Trading Essentials
Computer/MS Office Skills	Corporate Finance	Corporate Governance
Corporate Law	Cultural Sensitivity & Etiquette	Decision Models
Effective Leadership	Effective Sales	Entrepreneurship
Excel for Productivity	Financial Statement Analysis	Investment Banking Essentials
Managerial Accounting	Managerial Auditing	Marketing
Micro & Macro Economics	Negotiation & Decision Making	Operations Management
Presentational Skills	Project Management	Supply Chain Management